Arnold Thomas Fanning was born in London and raised in Dublin. His stage plays include the acclaimed *McKenna's Fort*. *Mind on Fire* is his first book.

Mind on Fire

A Memoir of Madness and Recovery

ARNOLD THOMAS FANNING

PENGUIN

IRELAND

PENGUIN IRELAND

UK | USA | Canada | Ireland | Australia
India | New Zealand | South Africa

Penguin Ireland is part of the Penguin Random House group of companies
whose addresses can be found at global.penguinrandomhouse.com.

First published 2018

001

Copyright © Arnold Thomas Fanning, 2018

The moral right of the author has been asserted

Part of this book was previously published in a different form in *The Dublin Review*, no. 65,
Winter 2016/17. Grateful acknowledgement is given for the quote taken from *Into Extra Time*
by Michael Paul Gallagher SJ, published and copyright © 2016 by Darton Longman and
Todd Ltd, London, and used by permission of the publishers.

Arnold Thomas Fanning received financial assistance from the Arts Council.

Set in 13.5/16 pt Garamond MT Std
Typeset by Jouve (UK), Milton Keynes
Printed in Great Britain by Clays Ltd, St Ives plc

A CIP catalogue record for this book is available from the British Library

ISBN: 978–1–844–88429–2

www.greenpenguin.co.uk

for Tessa

O the mind, mind has mountains; cliffs of fall
Frightful, sheer, no-man-fathomed.

– Gerard Manley Hopkins, 'No Worst There is None.
Pitched Past Pitch of Grief'

Contents

Author's Note

In writing about my decade of madness, I drew upon my own memories as deeply as I could. But while my recollections were often vivid and detailed, they could not tell me everything I needed to know about the period, so I undertook detailed research. I consulted medical records; police records; emails; and my own diaries and notebooks. I also interviewed several people who knew or encountered me while I was seriously ill: acquaintances, professionals, friends, and my sister. What follows does not purport to be definitive, but is as true and accurate an account as my memories and this research have allowed. Writing in the present tense, I have attempted to capture as precisely as possible the state of a mind that was often subject to the distortions of mania, depression and delusions.

. . . you charge through Heathrow two days after Christmas, it is imperative you get on a flight now, the tsunami has struck in Sumatra and you need to go and volunteer there, join a relief agency, only you can help all those people in need of succour, but first you require equipment, tools, an outfit, something that will indicate the seriousness of your intent, and on the wall you see the perfect thing, an emergency kit in a glass case, containing a defibrillator and a hazard jacket, so you pull open the door of the case, ignoring the alarm that goes off when you do so, and you put on the jacket, and put the defibrillator pack over your shoulder, and now you are ready for your mission, now you must go and find a flight that will take you to the disaster zone, there must be dozens of relief agencies flying out today, you can join one, they will be glad of another volunteer, so you go up a level to the departure lounge, eager and hopeful, but first there is the security guard to deal with, and now he angrily wrenches the emergency kit from you, too furious to understand your explanations, he takes your details, calls the police, you are arrested, charged with theft of a defibrillator, the police take you then, but after they have finished with you all they have said is forgotten and you go back to Heathrow, into the crowd of travellers thronging the airport, push, then run through the lines of people waiting to check in to flights all over the world, and another idea comes to you, as urgently as the last, an obvious idea, so obvious you wonder why it didn't occur to you before, you can join the British

Army as a chaplain, so you go down the lift again two levels where you saw the squaddies hanging out earlier, join them, tell them your idea, and they are all enthusiasm, all chums, it is a lark, they are just young lads, and you run with them through the lower levels of the airport, they are your new friends, and you will travel with them to Cyprus and be their spiritual counsellor, but one by one they break away, drift off, disappear until you are left alone to wonder what to do next, and then of course another obvious idea strikes you as suddenly as the other ideas, another vital thing you can do, you can fly to Israel and convert to Judaism and join the Israeli Defence Forces, defend the Promised Land, it is your destiny, you have always had an affinity with the Jewish people after all, and now you will demonstrate this by being with them and fighting to secure their homeland for them, it all makes sense to you, you have some feeling of guilt and responsibility towards them, there are historical injustices only you can put right, and so you find the check-in counter for a flight to Tel Aviv, and join the queue of Orthodox Jews dressed all in black, with their bewigged wives and neat children, as well as secular passengers dressed casually, and you start to chatter about your plans to convert, to enlist, to fight, to defend, and they watch you as you edge closer to the check-in counter, you are positive they will let you fly when you tell them that you are a Jew, the conversion is a mere formality, it is the covenant of faith you've made between yourself and God that really matters, so they will believe you when you declare you are a Jew and then they will have to let you go to Israel to enlist, and they will pay for the flight themselves, it is well known, it is the Law of Return, but you have no identification whatsoever, it is all lost, and you have an Irish accent, and are pale, very pale and thin, and the people around you are finding it hard to keep up with all your ideas, to understand you at all, and you are not allowed to go any further in the queue by the ticketing agent, who has come down the line to check what the fuss is about, to do a check on your documents, which you do not have, and you begin to explain it all again to the ticketing agent, who does not understand, only blocks your progress towards the check-in counter, and so you start to argue, then object loudly, because you must be allowed on the flight, it is imperative, pressing, it is your destiny, and so you physically resist, until there is a struggle between you and the ticketing agent, and you lie down on the floor and wrap yourself around a bollard and grip tightly on to it, and refuse to leave unless you are given a ticket and access to the plane, and so the police are called now, and they come rapidly, black-clad, in body armour, bearing machine guns cocked and at the ready, and they loom over you, in their helmets and sunglasses, pointing their guns at you warily, unsure what exactly they are dealing with here, and don't reduce their hostility when you grin, and begin to laugh, and concede defeat in the face of overwhelming force, no, they just grab you by the arms and pull you off the ground and frogmarch you to the nearest exit on to the road outside the airport, and shove you roughly into the back of a police van, drive you several miles down the motorway, then open the van door, push you out, and tell you not to return to the airport anytime soon, and then they speed away, and you turn and walk the lay-by past light-industrial centres, Traveller encampments with horses that you momentarily think could bear you back to the city quicker, then continue walking towards London, no end to the highway, the night dark and cold, nowhere to shelter from the wind, but still you don't feel tired, your energy does not abate, so it is not hard to keep walking, but then finally you get a lift from a kind man who listens as you talk rapidly about what you've been doing, how you've been living, and he drops you in Camden Town, tells you there is a centre giving away free dinners to those in need like you, so you go, but it is too late, when you arrive at the community centre the food is gone, the tables deserted, the centre empty apart from the few tired volunteers who move from table to table clearing up, so you go on walking deeper into the night, and you arrive in Regent's Park and lie on a bench exposed to the cold still and try and sleep, listening to the lions roaring in the nearby zoo, and this sound strangely arouses you so you slip your hand down the front of your trousers and rub yourself, and then take your cock out in your hand and jerk it off furiously, coming with the sound of the lion's roar, and wipe the ejaculate on to your trousers, and now you no longer feel in any way tired, you feel energized once more, so you get up off the bench and go on walking, the streets are deserted, you are all alone in this city, momentarily standing lost in a colonnaded square wondering where to go now, because you have nowhere to go, save a doorway off the street, there is nothing to eat now but the pickings from a bin, and it is winter, harsh, it is night, cold, and you feel suddenly bereft, adrift, alone, but then you feel the energy surge through you once again so you continue walking, walking miles to another part of the city, until you can walk no further, it is impossible, you must rest, must stop, so you find some cardboard, and then a sheltering doorway, and you attempt to settle for the night at last, and manage some form of sleep despite the freezing cold and the hard steps you lie against, despite your seething mind, full of thoughts and fleeting ideas, and almost as soon as sleep descends you wake to another day, dull morning, to face a man in an overcoat and a suit standing over you carrying a briefcase who looks down at you as you are blocking the way to his office door, so you stumble to

4

your feet as quickly as you can, afraid he will hit you, pleading with him that you didn't do anything wrong, but he assures you he is not angry, but rather he holds out a ten-pound note and urges you to go and get some food, and you walk away with the money he gives you and you go to a shop and buy a pack of cigarettes, and smoke some quickly, momentarily joyous at this good fortune, then go on walking, walking, through the city, thinking all the time of who you are and what you need and what you will do next, because you are actually a private detective following up on a complicated case, one that only you can understand and solve, but no one knows that about you, they don't understand why you suddenly fall to the ground and roll there, shouting, then run and hide yourself, and no one knows either that you are the star of a movie being made about your life, so they cannot comprehend why at one moment you laugh and the next you cry, and they don't understand that you are the survivor of a slaughter that has taken place, and the only witness to a genocide that is occurring outside the city, which is why you stand in train stations and weep as the trains pull out on their way to the concentration camps, taking the people in them to their deaths, and all these ideas are swirling around inside your head at once, hurling through your mind, it is on fire, so when you speak it all comes out muddled and confused and no one can understand you, so when you go into a pub and demand food and drink for nothing off the landlord expecting to be granted it because you are entitled to it, you are an important person after all, he just refuses and tells you to leave, and you have annoyed him so he follows you out, a big heavy man, follows you out on to the street, and though you smile at him before you turn to go, he lashes out and slaps you, hard, across the side of your head to send you on your way, removing that smile and driving you off with your ear ringing, and you stumble then, on through the city, sometimes hopping on buses, sometimes on trains, but now you need to shit, you are unsure where you are, where you can shit, and you can't hold it in much longer, and there's no way any premises will let you in to use their toilet, you are dirty and your clothes are torn, so you grab some newspaper out of the drain and go into a phone booth, so as to be relatively unseen as you squat and expel an enormous turd, and wipe yourself with the newspaper, and go, leaving your stinking mess behind, go with nowhere to go still, through this city, this endless city, into shops where you are followed around by security guards, and sometimes evade them, so you are able to pocket things unobserved, and sometimes observed, so you are caught, and so end up in a police van hurtling at speed through the streets of London to yet another police cell for the night before another appearance in court to be arraigned for a trial you will never turn up for, but these police who now ferry you in the back of their van have not searched your pockets, which was a mistake, because you have a box of matches, and so now you take them out and pull off your suede jacket that was given to you in a shelter, and you set fire to your jacket with the matches, until the back of the police van fills with thick smoke, and the police have to brake suddenly, stop in the middle of the street, get out of their van, and come and open the doors at the back to get you out, pull you out in a plume of smoke, wrench you out, see you laughing, dismiss you as a waste of time and effort and go and attend to the fire in their van, and so off you go, you continue to walk through the city, to a train station, and on to a train, you don't even know the destination, and get out and are lost, and yet you feel all is well, there is nothing wrong, and your mind is racing full of rushing thoughts, each more beautiful and fascinating than the last,

6

and you have nowhere to go today or tomorrow, and still the energy surges through you, so you get back on a train that brings you back to the city, and you just decide you will keep on walking, endless walking, and even though you have nowhere to go and nothing to do you feel that there is something pressing that must be attended to, and it must be attended to now, immediately, which gives a sense of urgency to everything you do, so you don't stop, and the thoughts don't stop, and you are so alone, so far from home, and friends, and family, and you don't think of any of that, of them, you have too many other things to think about, you are full of energy, and plans, and things to do, to get done, and it all makes sense to you, you actually feel so happy, despite being hungry and alone and cold, yes, euphorically happy, as you walk on, walk on through the city, full of rushing thoughts, and your mind is burning, burning, burning . . .

PART I

1. As It Was

By day the suited office workers stroll along the canal-bank path or sit on benches near the water to eat their lunch. By night the prostitutes walk the same canal banks and service their clients in the empty office car-parks. Late into the night I can hear them while I try to get to sleep three floors above. My bed is a futon mattress without a frame, pushed into one corner of this extremely cheap bedsit. One wall is a wooden partition that opens to reveal the kitchenette; the fridge hums and judders and clatters all day and night. Between the noise of the prostitutes and the noise of the fridge I don't sleep well, and feel constantly sleep-deprived, which makes me edgy and irritable.

Against one wall is a desk with a computer, bought for what was for me a huge sum, an extravagant gesture meant to symbolize the seriousness of my intent in pursuing my ambition to be a writer. I have quit my full-time, pensionable job in stage management to give myself more time to write. Now, in the summer of 1997, aged twenty-eight, I have found myself a routine, a mode of living. Working three days a week in the literary department of the National Theatre, claiming social welfare assistance for the days I don't work, I get up on my days off and write, write, write. Short stories mainly, but also film scripts and the beginnings of a novel. My short stories have recently begun to get published, in Ireland, in America, and broadcast on British radio. I have written a film adaptation of one of my short stories and this script has just received funding from the Arts Council and is in pre-production. Another one-hour TV drama script that I co-wrote is in development, funded by the Irish Film Board for RTÉ. A literary agent has been in touch, expressing an interest in representing me.

My girlfriend and I spend a lot of our time together discussing jobs, careers, sources of income. My decision to pursue a vocation as a writer comes under a lot of scrutiny, especially as I am barely scraping by financially. Debbie tells me that I could be, should be, making more money. I have a full Equity stage-management union ticket and a trainee card with the film union in design.

'I suppose I could get a job in a bar on Friday nights,' I tell her. 'Just to make some extra money. I only need a little more. A friend of mine does that.' I'm thinking of night-time work because I don't want anything cutting into my days: I write in the mornings and afternoons.

But she doesn't want to go out with a lounge boy. She is significantly older than me, separated from her husband, bringing up her two children alone in Dublin's embassy belt.

She persuades a friend of hers who works in advertising to meet me to discuss the possibility of being a copywriter. 'I know the kind of people who become good copywriters,' the friend tells me in her office after I have shown her my 'portfolio' of published stories and reviews. 'They're all a bit wacky, they have something. And I can see that you don't have it.'

After that, Debbie doesn't introduce me to any more of her friends to get work.

Being around Debbie produces in me a constant tension, a pressure to be what I am not, who I am not. She likes my youth and energy, but she doesn't seem to like me as a person very much. If I weren't so needy and afraid of being alone, I would leave her.

Occasionally, in the past, I have tried to talk about my mental health with girlfriends. One encouraged me to see a therapist about it, a therapist I left after a few sessions as he summarized my case with a brutal candour that left me in tears: 'So, your mother's dead and your father doesn't give a shit. So what are you going to do about it?'

Depression has become something I endure several times a year, at its worst in the summer, when all my energy dissipates and my thinking becomes blackened by pessimistic ideas and self-hatred. These spells of black mood have been afflicting me since my mother's death from cancer in the summer of my twentieth year. If, during these periods, I have to go to work, then I force myself to do so with great effort, working through a miasma of actual physical pain in my head and torso and deep in my stomach. When I don't have to work, I just stay in bed or crawl out of it to lie on the floor, the hardness a comfort, feeling the waves of pain washing over me, feeling there is no future, that my past is all mistakes and lost opportunities, that it is simply too late for me to achieve anything or be happy, to have a fulfilling life. Then, when the depression lifts, I am infused with enthusiasm and energy. At these times I feel all is well, all is wonderful in fact, and always will be. Autumn and winter energize me: I make plans, I write more, apply for funding opportunities, feel I will be a success.

An application to fund a film has been shortlisted and I am full of optimism about the project. On impulse, I decide to go and meet my father to tell him about it, walking the short distance from my bedsit in Percy Place to a pub on Leeson Street. My father, long retired from his job in an advertising agency that was located near the pub, still meets his former colleagues for pints and conversation there.

As a general rule, he and I do not have much to say to one another, and if we do attempt a conversation it often ends in bickering. Now, however, feeling buoyed up, suddenly benevolent and well disposed towards him, and indeed towards the whole world, I will find him in the pub and tell him my good news. Good news, because I have decided that the funding application will be successful.

When I arrive, my father is at one end of the bar, surrounded by his friends and drinking Guinness. He gets me a pint while I jabber at high speed about my plans for the film, the application process, the production company, the funders. There is talk of development, pre-production, casting, shooting.

'So what does that actually all mean?' my father asks. His ex-colleagues have been listening too, trying to keep up.

'It means I'm going to direct a fucking film!' I exclaim in exasperation, frustrated by his obtuseness, leaning over the bar to attract the barman's attention and order another pint. Behind me, I hear one of my father's friends whisper to him through the din of the bar: 'Is he all right?'

Then I hear my father's reply: 'He's just excited.'

My enthusiasm is being put down, my plans not appreciated; of course there is nothing wrong with being excited. Irritated now, I finish my pint and go.

As the summer progresses, my mood dips, the depression returns. My job at the theatre, which until so recently I loved so much, has become a source of unhappiness. I am not getting on well with the person who is covering my boss's maternity leave. Moreover, when I am in a low mood, I can be cranky or even aggressive. One of my colleagues, a pleasant young stage manager, who is gay, likes to talk theatre with me, a former stage manager myself. Sitting at a late-night bar after a performance in the theatre, he half jokingly, half flirtatiously puts his hand on my thigh and rubs it. Aggression boils up in me and I pick up my pint: 'You see this glass? If you don't take your hand off my knee, I'll shove this glass down your fucking throat.'

It has been my role as literary assistant to send out scripts for assessment to our panel of readers. One member of the panel is frequently late returning his reports. Abruptly, I pull him off the panel, thus depriving him of a source of income in this underpaid sector.

There are few friends in my life at this time. One friend I do see regularly is Seamus, whom I met in college when we studied English. He and I meet for a pint or two most weeks in city-centre pubs, and we often attend openings at his brother's contemporary-art gallery just off Fitzwilliam Square. My best friend from college, Elliot, has moved to Limerick with his girlfriend in pursuit of regular teaching hours, and we seldom manage to see each other. Another friend, Pritch, a friend of an ex-girlfriend, spends much of the year travelling since his marriage broke down.

My most fulfilling friendship is with someone I get to see only once or twice a year, as he lives in Rome and is back only occasionally in Dublin. This is my former lecturer at university, the Jesuit writer and intellectual Michael Paul Gallagher. When I meet him, he lights me up from within, makes me see the gift of life and beauty in myself. Taking me by the shoulder, he guides me to a mirror and makes me look at my reflection.

'Look,' he says gently. 'You're going to be okay.'

Looking up, I see what he sees, light shining from me, see there is hope after all, goodness in me after all, and I smile.

There is a job going on a film production: props buyer on a low-budget featurette, working directly with the designer.

My union ticket is still valid, and the job would pay well, and also represent a step up in grade from the role I had on the last movie I worked on. The tension is building in me and I feel I desperately need a change in my life. I'm unhappy at the National Theatre, unhappy with Debbie. In the heat of summer, the bedsit is becoming oppressively small, I still can't sleep properly, and an attempted burglary sets me on edge, making me jump at every sound. Also I'm under financial pressure: I have not been able to live off my part-time wage and social welfare supplements and have taken out loans and maxed out my credit card to get by.

A car and a mobile phone are required for the film job, so I cajole my father into lending me his Ford Sierra for the duration of the production and buy a pay-as-you-go phone. The job is mine.

I hand in my notice to the National Theatre, thus leaving the job that has sustained my writing career for almost two years, and which I have, until so recently, loved. The artistic director of the theatre, a kind and thoughtful man, sits me down in his office to talk about my move before I go.

'Are you sure you want to leave?' he asks me.

'Yes,' I nod. 'Quite sure.'

'Is there something wrong? Something I should be aware of?'

It is an opportunity to talk, perhaps to reverse everything. But I consider all the other things that I have set in motion now. I've handed in notice to my landlady, too, decided to move back into my father's house for a few months while I work on the movie. The plan is to save money for a while to clear my debts, and then to buy my own car so I can become a freelance props buyer. And I can't back out of the job I've accepted: it would ruin my reputation in the film industry.

'No,' I tell the artistic director firmly. 'Nothing wrong.'

He is looking at me with concern, so I continue: 'I just got offered a really good post on a film and I really want to do it, to get back into production while I still have my union ticket.'

He considers this for a moment, and seems to find it convincing.

'Okay, then,' he says. 'I'm sorry to see you go, but as long as you are happy with your decision, that is fine.'

And so I go.

Home now is the box room at the top of the stairs in my father's small house in a suburb by the sea in the south of County Dublin.

I break up with Debbie, with minimal discussion. It is as if I have lost track of her, or of her place in my life. When she comes to my father's house with a box of my belongings a few weeks later, we stand awkwardly at the door and I don't ask her in.

I've miscalculated financially. I had thought the job would bring in enough income to allow me to pay off my debts, buy a car and have the deposit for a new flat. But the pay for the film is quite modest after tax. By the end of the production, I am completely dependent on social welfare payments and a free roof over my head.

The reality of all I have done in the course of the summer strikes me like a blow:

I have left the job I loved.

I have ended a serious relationship.

And I'm living in my father's house, outside the city.

My father and I spend little time together. We are incapable of being open with one another about our lives. When we do occasionally sit down opposite each other at meals, he noisily angles his chair with a sudden jerk, so that he is facing away from me and can gaze out the window as he eats.

I find I am quickly into the black, low mood again, the one of immobility and aching, that mood that has dogged me at intervals through my twenties, since my mother's death. The symptoms are so familiar to me now, I know exactly what is coming, and I dread it.

Finally, the fear of the impending fall becomes too great and I concede to myself that I need professional help.

During my third year at university, grieving over my mother's death, I had a few sessions with a kindly psychiatrist in the student health services, a Dr Malvey. She worked, I recall, in St Vincent's Hospital. A plan is formed: as I can't afford private therapy, I will seek a referral from my GP and ask Dr Malvey to get me counselling through the public health system.

The GP is not at all convinced.

'You're a young man,' he tells me. 'Well, youngish. You don't seem depressed.'

I'm having a slight upswing this day, a day of a little more energy, energy that has got me out of my father's house and as far as this doctor's office. I recognize that this does not mean I am well, and I refuse to leave until the GP agrees to give me a referral to Dr Malvey.

There is almost a month to wait until the date of the appointment. Christmas intervenes, and in my depressed state I cannot do more than endure it. During this period of waiting, a letter arrives from the Tyrone Guthrie Centre, the artists' retreat in Annaghmakerrig in County Monaghan. My application has been successful; a month-long residency will begin in February.

Early in the new year, there is further positive news; the production manager of a theatre where I once worked as a stage manager phones me and offers me a job as assistant to the stage designer for a festival there. The job starts in March, which is perfect timing: just after my residency at Annagh-makerrig. Despite my low mood, I feel the stirrings of optimism.

When the date of my appointment arrives, I go to St Vincent's, fully expecting to be seen by Dr Malvey. The waiting room is crowded and it is a considerable time before my name is called. I am directed to one of several curtained-off booths. The booth contains a table and two chairs. It is not the kindly Dr Malvey from my college days that comes to assess me, however, but rather a young, distracted, harried male consultant. He takes fifteen minutes to question me, noting my loss of appetite and motivation and my inability to sleep well. Although I've been hoping to be referred to a psychotherapist, it is agreed hurriedly between us that the best course of action in the short term is for me to begin taking antidepressants, and I leave with a prescription.

In the following weeks, I take the pills and prepare myself for Annaghmakerrig. My plan is to write a novel there, and I organize my notes and materials on it. Feeling an upswing in energy and alertness, I finish my first full-length stage play, a three-hander I call *Those Powerful Machines*. Taking it out, tweaking and revising it, in a sudden burst of optimism and energy I submit it to the very literary department I have just quit.

The low energy and black thinking of just two weeks before seem gone for ever.

2. The Breakdown

The Tyrone Guthrie Centre in Annaghmakerrig is situated by a small lake and surrounded by forest. Scattered around the main house are a series of cottages and artist's studios. A fine communal dinner is offered every evening in the main house.

My room is on the first floor. Quickly, I settle into a routine.

In the mornings I work on the novel for several hours, sitting at a large mahogany desk. Then I go and make myself a lunch from the leftovers of the previous night's dinner. After lunch I go for long, aimless walks along the tracks that run through the dark, damp forest. Then I nap a while in my room, or read, waiting for the dinner gong to ring downstairs. When it does, I join my fellow residents for the communal dinner at the long wooden table.

After dinner, I might take a walk in the darkness along the road that runs by the lake and out of the centre's grounds, then on to the main road that cuts through the forest, over a hill to the nearest pub. Or I might stay in, chatting with the other residents in the large, bright living room. There's an old record player there and a battered LP of Neil Young's *Decade*. Sometimes when on my own I try to play 'Helpless' on the piano, although I never learned to play the instrument, by transposing what I know of guitar chords to the keyboard and singing along quietly to myself.

But usually the room is occupied by other residents. There's John, an artist, who talks of driving around the border counties when younger and getting into scrapes with the British Army when he found it hard to explain what he was up to, scrabbling around fields looking for things to inspire his work. Sometimes I go with him in his battered 2CV while he seeks out subjects and landscapes to sketch, and he points out the features we pass: drumlins, lakes, barns with their doors painted red. 'There's always a red door,' he'll say when we pass one. On these drives we pass a joint back and forth. In the pub at night we observe the locals, including the teenage girl who works there; she seems out of place in this rough place, faintly angelic in her delicate beauty, vulnerable in the bar full of older men.

But mainly I want to spend time with Rebecca, a young painter with a piping voice that affects me strangely. I find any excuse to drop by her studio and engage her in conversation. After dinner, I linger and try to talk to her, and later in the evening I sometimes even knock on her bedroom door. In the throes of my crush, it is not apparent to me that my feelings are not reciprocated and I am getting on her nerves.

The walls of her studio in the grounds of the centre are newly painted in white, and she tells me they intimidate her with their starkness, their blankness; they goad her to cover them with artworks. Facing the large expanse, she takes up a stick of charcoal and makes a small mark with it on the wall.

'Just so I can make a start,' she tells me. 'Just so it's not all white.'

This action makes a deep impression on me, intimidated as I often am by the sight of the blank page, and I determine to follow the same practice: make a mark, make a start, to overcome the blockage.

Also resident is Tom Murphy, a famous playwright whose intensity and seriousness I find intimidating, who seems so at ease in these surroundings, so confident, and whom I

Leabharlann
7035901
Contae na Mídhe

cannot bring myself to talk to. He has been a presence in my mind for almost a decade, and a deep influence on my playwriting. At the end of my final college exams, my friends from class and I went to see *A Whistle in the Dark*, a play about emigration, in the Abbey. We were all on the verge of emigrating ourselves, and the power of the play left us speechless. I desperately want Tom to like me, and my writing, but I do not know how to make that happen. There is the play I've just written, a copy of which is in my room; I wonder if I could persuade him to read it, to validate it, validate me as a writer. But it seems impossible.

My course of antidepressants has come with me to Annaghmakerrig, and it seems that the pills are working; I am almost startled to realize one day that I no longer feel in any way depressed. Now I wonder if I am, in fact, completely cured of whatever had previously ailed me. But I keep taking the pills.

There's a dog that belongs to the man who lives in the gatehouse, a fine rust-coloured mastiff called Axle, and I find him outside the front door of the big house in the courtyard nearly every time I go outside for my walk. Invariably, he joins me. The days are mild for the time of year, and often I just borrow a sky-blue hoodie from the mud room to wear on my walks in place of a jacket, then set off through the forest, Axle following. A feeling of contentment and peace fills me on these walks. The forest is beautiful and silent, dense, damp and dripping, a place of calm and solitude. I walk, mulch crunching underfoot, dog at my heels.

Coming out of the trees and into a forest clearing, sky suddenly above me and lighting me, it occurs to me that I am actually happy, really happy, for the first time in many years; for the first time, it feels, since my mother died. This brings another feeling: one of bereft sadness that my mother is not here to witness my happiness, to share in my joy with me, to know that I am well. My happiness is instantly replaced by a feeling of yearning, of desperate aloneness and grief. Standing in the centre of the forest clearing, I begin to sob uncontrollably. There is no one to hear me, and I sob and sob, huge, heaving, lung-wrenching cries that leave me gasping, my face red and hot and wet with tears. I have never cried for my mother before now. It seems it has been dammed up in me, waiting to burst, and now I can't stop crying. The forest absorbs it all.

Eventually, I calm down and head back to the big house. The feeling of sadness fades as I retrace my route through the forest and is replaced by the buoyancy I'd felt before. Everything, after all, is going well in my life. I am in a prestigious artists' residency; I have written two short films that will shortly be in production; I have completed my first play; and I have an exciting job lined up which will set me back on track with my career and allow me to move out of my father's house.

Yes, I conclude, pushing thoughts of my mother's absence to the back of my mind: I am happy, this is what happiness feels like; that feeling of despair I experienced in the forest was just temporary, the happiness is what is permanent and enduring.

The next morning, when I take out the blister pack of antidepressants, I pause: if I am happy, not depressed, why go on taking them? Putting the pack back into my suitcase, I decide not to take one, and then get on with the day.

I continue with my routine: writing, walking, conversing, going to the pub, smoking hash on drives with John and finding ways to bump into Rebecca; likewise, I continue my awestruck silent homage to Tom, the playwright, from a distance.

After a few days I notice a change. It is just a faint tremor at first, but it is unmistakeable: depression, returning to afflict me once again. It terrifies me that it could come back in this place that makes me happy. This seems intolerable. Immediately then, upon feeling the shadow pass over me, I go to my room, open my case, take out the blister pack and swallow an antidepressant.

That evening, I feel my heart pounding in my body, a furious thumping in my chest. It occurs as I walk across a field on my way to the tiny parish church on an urgent mission to go to Mass, my first Mass in years. Earlier, in the big house, I found a copy of the Bible. On the first page of Revelations I read:

> Behold, he cometh with clouds; and every eye shall see him, and they also which pierced him: and all kindreds of the earth shall wail because of him. Even so, Amen.
>
> I am Alpha and Omega, the beginning and the ending, saith the Lord, which is, which was, and which is to come, the Almighty.

Yes: I understand it fully; the words could have been written especially for me. I feel close to John the Apostle, who I believe to be the author of the Book of Revelation; author also of my favourite Gospel. This is why I am crossing the field of high grass between stone walls and crossing the stile to go to the little church and attend evening Mass, heart pounding in my chest: because the words speak to me.

In my head I feel a strange, breathless joy. The happiness I felt before as a mood or emotion is now a solid thing that surges and pulses through me, through my entire body, from stomach to chest to brain, and it lights and brightens my very limbs as I walk. God feels alive to me now, a presence, right beside me, in me.

I go into the church, energy coursing through me, and it is virtually impossible to sit still through the service that follows. I am smiling at the other congregants, trying to make eye contact, connect with them somehow; because I do feel connected to them, love them, indeed. I recognize the parish priest from the pub I've been going to and I feel him to be a good man, sincere, his sermon full of meaning to me, making me nod and exclaim at its key points. But I am restless, so restless, moving my legs constantly as I sit, it is so hard to concentrate on all the words, and I feel a constant urge to leap out of my seat and stand, and shout out loud: 'Yes! Yes! God is here, I believe, and He is great!' I want to explain that I understand so much now, that much has been revealed to me suddenly, about John, the author of the Book of Revelation, John of the Cross, St John the Divine, the one whom Christ loved; it is unclear to me whether they are one and the same person or different people, but it does not matter really, because I understand and empathize and connect with them all in any case, in a unique way I understand about the one Christ loved the most, feel indeed an affinity with him; yes, perhaps, I, too, am the one Christ loves the most.

The priest stands outside the church doors after Mass, bidding goodnight to the parishioners. Giddily, I join the line to meet him and, when it comes to my turn, I cannot contain my excitement any longer.

'I believe, Father!' I shout at him with vigorous enthusiasm. 'I believe in God again, and it is great, He is great! I feel so good to believe again!'

I jump up and down in great excitement, the priest still clutching my hand to shake, and now I jerk his arm up and down as I jump.

He lays a hand on my bouncing shoulder to settle me.

'Easy, son. Easy now,' he says, startled.

*

Back at the big house, seething with thoughts and notions, I do not even attempt to sleep. Rather, I continue to read the Bible, furiously writing notes; then, in the early hours, the house silent around me, I begin to write, and illustrate lavishly, a children's book I call 'Titanic', an ambitious and rambling melange that will, I intend, contain all I know about God and the world.

Ideas and notions enter my head. One is to go to Dublin and bring my father up to Annaghmakerrig and get him to meet the other artists residing there; perhaps this will reignite his interest in his own painting, so long neglected, which in turn will help him deal with his grief at my mother's death, which I feel must have afflicted him over the years, and which, I now decide, he is unable to overcome without my intervention. It is startlingly clear to me now that my father is profoundly depressed and needs my help; indeed, only I can help him.

So I ask the director of the Tyrone Guthrie Centre if it is permissible to bring a guest here. He baulks at the idea, but after considerable haranguing and insisting and pleading on my part he agrees to allow my father to attend one of the communal dinners.

My father, too, needs some convincing to come, when I phone him and tell him of my plans, but I tell him I'll come to Dublin and then drive back with him the next day, and he, too, eventually agrees.

After dinner that night, there is a residents' reading from work in progress. Tom will be there, so I decide to participate.

It is difficult for me to sit still and to concentrate while one of the other residents reads from his play. I feel mine to be the superior work and find his full of clichés, flaws and inanities. Unable or disinclined to restrain myself, I begin to chuckle, then snigger.

'Is anything wrong?' the director hisses at me.

'No, nothing,' I reply, thinking fast. 'Irritable bowel syndrome, that's all.'

Thinking this reply is hilarious, I let out another snigger.

Then it is my turn to read, and my enthusiasm for the play grips me and I bound out of my seat and begin to pace the room back and forth, reading ever more loudly, gesticulating wildly, acting out all the parts with as much vigour as I can. After this performance, there is a stunned silence, and I notice Tom is grinning. I take this as a good sign; he must like the play, must like me.

Then he speaks: 'You have to ask yourself what your characters want, what is at stake, and what is stopping them from getting that.'

This is not the response I have been hoping for; this is feedback, but I want unadorned praise, immediate recognition of my talent and, yes, further, recognition of me as a kindred spirit, and, further still, Tom's friendship. Now I feel crushed and humiliated. The reading ends, and I retreat to my room; again, I do not sleep.

The next morning, before departing for Dublin, I decide to visit Rebecca in her studio. Walking through the forest, I find a small twig that I decide is very pretty, prettier than a flower, so I pick it up and resolve to give it to her.

When she comes to the door of her studio to answer my knock, I hold out the little stick.

'This is for you,' I tell her ponderously. 'It's a special stick.'

If she is puzzled or thrown by this, or by my interrupting her work, she does not allow it to show.

'Thanks,' she says, taking the twig. 'I needed a special stick.'

There is a significance to the stick that I understand and I believe she, too, now understands; I linger a moment longer outside her studio, expectantly. But she does not ask me in, does not offer to show me what she is painting. She is eager to return to her work and so, reluctantly, I leave her and go on my way.

It is important now, I realize, to make Tom like me and accept me as a playwright. With this idea in mind comes a notion for a ceremony, a rite, that will demonstrate to him all that I feel for him: the Zen Orange Juice Ritual.

Gleefully, I rush to the kitchen to execute it: I squeeze a glass of fresh orange juice, wrap the glass in a white table napkin, and slowly, reverentially, bring it to his cottage and lay it gently on the step at the front door. Retreating, I walk some steps backward then go into a laundry room opposite, place myself at a window and peer out, waiting to catch the moment he will see my offering. By following this ritual, I reason, I will make him see that I am a true servant to him, a genuine supplicant, ready to abase myself, to acknowledge his superiority to me in every way, and he will further recognize that I should be taken under his wing as an acolyte.

Then I notice that he is standing inside his cottage, gazing out at me where I stand behind the laundry-room window, that he has seen all my antics and is now observing me observing him; I am in full view. Slowly, I edge backwards until I think he can no longer see me; then, after a while, too restless to remain any longer, I leave the laundry room and move on.

Next is getting to Dublin, an urgency in that desire now.

Arriving in the city centre by bus, I immediately go to meet with the acting literary manager of my former employer, the National Theatre, to discuss my play, which she has by now read. It is the best play ever written, I am convinced; it will be acknowledged as such, and it will be produced on the main stage before touring the world, bringing me the fame and fortune that are mine by right. This meeting, then, is just a formality.

We sit in a café opposite the theatre on tall stools as the acting literary manager goes through her feedback point by point. As I sip my coffee, it dawns on me that, far from being offered a contract, dates, a guarantee of production, I am merely being offered notes, a critique of my play. What works in it, what doesn't, how it can be improved.

Growing irritable and impatient, unwilling to listen any longer, I quite suddenly go on the attack; she is taken aback by my belligerence. 'Why are you being so aggressive?' she asks, bewildered and hurt. She has known me for years – I once worked as an assistant stage manager on a play she directed – and is stunned by this change in my character.

'Why are you being so passive-aggressive?' I shoot back, delighted by my witty response.

The meeting ends there.

When I finally turn up at my father's house, he is sceptical about the proposed trip to Annaghmakerrig but I will not be denied.

Although I haven't gone fishing since I was a teenager, now I feel a sudden urge to do so; into the car goes my folding rod, my best fixed-spool reel and my green ex-army tackle knapsack. This contains, packed into pockets and boxes, my lines, lures and a small wooden-handled, folding hunting knife with an extremely sharp blade that I will use to gut and scale the many fish I know I am going to catch when I go fishing in the lakes of Cavan and Monaghan while my father goes sketching, just as we did in my youth on jaunts to the canal banks of Kildare and the rivers of Kerry. Now, on this trip, I am determined to catch a pike for the first time in my life, and just know it will happen.

A notion occurs suddenly to me, to apply to the Arts Council for funding for an ambitious project that will combine film and theatre and drawing. Phoning the Arts Council impulsively, I grow frustrated when the person I speak to does not comprehend me or my notions. Growing more and more exasperated with her, I become confrontational until she gets equally exasperated with me and tells me my idea is not eligible for funding.

'Why not?' I demand to know.

'We have to draw the line somewhere,' she replies.

Enraged at this, I end up verbally abusing her over the phone.

I decide it is important to buy flowers, and I set off to find a florist. The idea I have is to give the flowers to someone I have insulted; I know I have caused offence to someone, but now I am no longer sure who it is. Was it the person in the Arts Council, or was it the acting literary manager of the National Theatre? But I am confused. I don't manage to buy flowers, and I return to my father's house for a sleepless night before we set off for Monaghan in the morning.

During the drive up North I am full of ideas and plans for the future.

'I'm going to buy a house in Monaghan or Cavan and convert it into a bed and breakfast and artists' retreat that writers can come to and I'll make meals but then write and go fishing in my spare time,' I gush, full of excitement at my new career plan.

'I don't know how you're going to do any of that when, as far as I can see, you don't have any money,' my father says. I bristle; he won't take me, my plans, my dreams, seriously.

My father is booked to stay in a local B&B, but as it is getting late we head straight to the big house for dinner. Despite being convinced I knew the quickest route, I have managed to get us lost quite frequently. This I have compensated for, in my mind, by pointing out all the beautiful examples of drumlins and other notable features of the landscape we pass as we drive, great places for my father to sketch, I suggest; he is unimpressed, unenthusiastic.

We arrive just in time for dinner. The other residents are uncomfortable to have an outsider in their midst, and they appear increasingly wary of me also. I talk to my father about a painting I once saw in the Prado in Madrid, *The Garden of Earthly Delights* by Hieronymus Bosch. It is a triptych painted on three hinged panels. On each panel is a different stage in the progress of mankind from Earth to damnation or salvation; I explain to my father how, if you look at only one panel, you will see nothing but Bosch's vision of Hell, but if you merely turn your head, alter your perception, view a different panel, you will see a glimpse of Paradise.

Eagerly, I tell him his own life could be like this.

'It's up to you,' I whisper to him ever more urgently, convinced that my understanding of this painting has given me a unique perspective on the world. 'You don't have to be depressed, always looking at the dark side of life. You can simply choose to turn and look at a better side of the world. It's easy.'

My father's eyes widen in shock and embarrassment that I am broaching such personal issues, and he replies through gritted teeth.

'Not for me,' he asserts firmly. 'Not for me.'

We leave the house, intending to check my father in to his B&B nearby. But my irritation has turned to anger at him quite suddenly and, while driving, we get lost again, frustrating me further. Pulling over to consult the map, I take the opportunity to unleash all the resentment I have felt towards him ever since my mother's death, which I have held in check until now.

He is silent, but his silence only goads me further. I have by now worked myself up into a state, begin to sob and cry, and, as he is ignoring me, poke and paw at him to get his attention.

'Ach, stop it,' he says, with what I perceive as a sneer. 'This is getting boring now.'

Between sobs, I try and tell him how I feel, but he doesn't appear to be interested.

'It's all an act,' he declares firmly, as if I am merely seeking attention and sympathy. 'It's like a bad play.'

'It's not an act,' I scream back at him. 'This is me.'

He jerks his head away, avoiding eye contact. Furious now, and energized, I continue to paw and push at him, and then begin to pound and pummel my father with flailing blows; he sits frozen, but still I go on punching him as best I can, sobbing, increasingly desperate, increasingly vicious, wanting him to acknowledge me.

When he can take no more of this, he releases his seat belt and stumbles out of the car, my blows glancing off his head and back as he does so. He turns and walks up the road towards the nearby village. Further up the road is a turn with a few houses and a corner shop, still open at this late hour. My father goes inside, and I pursue him.

'Is there a phone?' my father wants to know, asking the youth standing behind the counter. 'I need to phone the Guards.'

'What is it, man?' drawls the youth, coming out from behind the counter, excited by this turn of events in his otherwise dull evening. No public phone is apparent.

'I just need a telephone,' my father repeats, irritated by the youth's insolent curiosity. Then he sees that I have followed him in, that I am standing watching all this, and that I am gleeful at his shock, fear and apparent helplessness; gleeful because all the resentment and pent-up anger I have carried in me since adolescence and as a young man have been released and expressed, and I feel good about this. Moreover, I have expressed it physically: I have hit my father at last, something I have always wanted but been too afraid to do, and he is helpless in the face of my physical superiority, has no power over me now, must simply take it, take his beating. This has made me jubilant, all tears forgotten, and I show it, my father staring at me in horror.

Under the scrutiny of both the youth and my grinning self, my father gives up on the phone and retreats back to the car.

This time, I drive, and we give up now on the idea of going to the bed and breakfast, instead drive back through the night to Dublin. I talk the whole time, hunched over the steering wheel, pouring out all my grievances once more, all the resentments I have built up over the years, all the accusations against my father, all my complaints.

'Ah, would you ever stop?' he pleads frequently. 'This is getting boring now.'

We drive and drive, and we arrive at his house hours later. When he gets his suitcase and goes inside I inform him that I am borrowing his car for a few days so I can return to Annaghmakerrig. And then I drive off, despite the fact it is the early hours of the morning, that I need sleep, should sleep, haven't slept. I am full of bright, sparkling energy. I pass a twenty-four-hour amusement arcade, the one I went to as a schoolboy, a bright beacon on the side of the road. Pumped up, restless, easily distracted, I pull in and go inside, and under the glaring lights play video games, shoot pool, bowl a few rounds. Then, still feeling wide awake, I get back in the car.

Much countryside is crossed; I spend time in Clones and Monaghan town, parking the car and going to get photographs developed, photographs of drumlins and red doors on barns; I go to the cinema to fill time while I wait for the photographs to be ready, getting into an urgent conversation with a nun when the film is over.

Everything seems so clear to me now, and everything is very beautiful indeed; the sky seems to be a deeper blue than before, the air is fresher, my body is fitter and more itself and alive and vibrant and fecund, its motion more perfect, its senses more attuned to the wonder of the world, more sensitive, more alive than it has ever been. Even the buildings in the dull towns I pass through stand out as paragons of architectural splendour.

I drive on.

Back in the vicinity of Annaghmakerrig, I stop at the pub I have so recently been frequenting with the others, go in, thinking the locals will be glad to see me, and now on my own, too, so they can give me their full attention. But I am over-energized for the early-evening drinks and card games that are going on, I am intrusive and annoying and just can't stop talking. The local men fall silent, sit around staring at their cards or into their pints. They ignore me completely. The pub seems suddenly still, like the air has been sucked out of it, like everyone is waiting, motionless, for something to happen.

Retreating into the toilet, I wonder what I have done wrong, what has been done to offend them; I thought they liked me. Then I try to recall what it is I have been saying since I arrived in the pub. This, after all, is border country, and it is easy to speak out of turn, cause offence. Was I rattling on about my new-found faith in Catholicism? Is that an issue? Was I talking about the IRA? My unease grows, my heart chilling: what did I just say?

When I return, the room is as still and silent as it was when I left, nothing moving but faint dust motes in the lamplight. Not one of the men looks at me, yet I have an unnerving sense that they have been waiting for me to return.

Then it hits me: they know I am a dead man walking, a ghost already in their midst. What are they going to do to me? What have they done? What have they set in motion? How am I to die?

And it is so blindingly obvious then: the car, it is the car; while I was in the bathroom they placed a booby-trap bomb under my car and it will explode and kill me when I turn the key to the ignition. It is their guilt at my impending execution that causes them to avert their gaze: they feel remnants of guilt already that they have killed me.

A sudden sob escapes me. I momentarily break down in front of them, in fear of what is about to happen, and in self-pity. Defeated, deflated, totally abject and bereft now, I accept my fate.

Cold and alone, I leave the pub. Outside, the car sits in the car-park; I go to it heavily, weary, go to my death.

Sitting in the driving seat, I pause, take a few deep breaths, then slide the key into the ignition. Bracing myself for the blast, the fireball to come, I feel a profound sadness, a sense of loss over all that was going to be. My plans, my hopes and ambitions, all rendered null and void, all dashed.

Then I turn the key.

The engine growls into life and the car does not explode. There is no flash of light, no boom, no fireball.

I am alive.

At the awareness of this, I feel a rush of pure pleasure coursing from head to toe such as I have never felt before. This is what it feels like to be alive. Alive and shimmering, I grin wildly and pound the steering wheel in excitement and gratitude. Life surges through me; I can feel it like a solid thing in my very veins, my pulsating mind, in my tingling skin and in every cell of my body.

Pushing down on the accelerator, I pull out of the car-park

with a screech and a clatter of gravel and speed away; I start driving into yet another night, joyous, excited, grinning and thankful to be alive. Driving fast through the dark country lanes as snow is falling, I do not know where I am going. The road is icy and the car skids, then spins, but somehow remains on the road. I am invincible, indestructible.

The night air is crisp, cold, fresh, and I step out of the car to breathe it in and calm my heart, still pounding furiously in my chest. I gaze up at the sky, as the scudding clouds, dropping snowflakes, briefly part. The stars have never seemed so bright and the plump moon has never seemed so dazzling and luscious.

I get back in the car and go on driving.

It is long past midnight now – these country lanes have taken me into the next day – but still I do not feel like sleeping, still there are too many things to think about, thoughts that come to me in a rush and which I must write urgently into my notebook, stopping the car and pulling into the verge to do so.

Another motorway then, that takes me further north, then off again into the lanes to look at the countryside, backtracking over my route, criss-crossing the border, in and out of Tyrone, Fermanagh, Cavan, Sligo, Armagh, Donegal, hundreds of miles through the night, hours and hours, driving endlessly, still energized, fresh, not wanting or needing sleep. The landscape of the north-west and border counties seems almost familiar now, even in darkness: the drumlins looming out of the black as I rush down country lanes, the black surfaces of the lakes reflecting the occasional flash of moon.

It is euphoria that I feel, mostly, but every so often it is punctuated, punctured, by sadness, a sense of what I have lost. Then there is sudden sobbing, but still I go on driving, swinging now violently between euphoria and despair, between joyous excitement and grief.

Still unable to sleep as dawn breaks, my mind a burning thing, I do not stop. Pleasure shoots through me as the light builds upon yet another beautiful day, a beautiful world.

Finding myself back in Monaghan with the new day, on a dusty back road not far from Annaghmakerrig, I pass near the house of the family of the teenage girl who serves bar in the pub I had frequented, and I pull over. The girl's mother is standing in the driveway and I get out of the car and talk to her, an urgent conversation. There is a mission I have to pursue, to protect her daughter from the dangers of this world, the brutality of this dark, brooding locality where who knows what threat is lurking. The mother, I decide, is ostracized from this community, needs my help, too; only I can offer salvation, only I can deliver them both from all that threatens them.

But I am unable to articulate my concern for her, for her daughter; faltering, I get back in the car and drive on, puzzled by myself, perturbed.

In my mind, I see all the problems facing the world line up like dominoes: if I choose, I can simply push one and all the problems will topple. Only I can do this: I am Alpha and Omega, the beginning and the end, I have all the answers, I can see through the muddle of the world, see the patterns there, I can cure the world of its ills. Only me.

Driving on, putting petrol on my credit card until it is maxed, the day passes, another day of driving and sitting in the car, writing furiously in my notebook, or standing staring at the drumlins, in awe of their simple, calm beauty, and so another night comes, another night without sleep. Dawn again, coming up over the border counties, haze on the ground shimmering, a mist now over the lakes and fields and drumlins spreading out far before me, gentle green hillocks and black water shining, all dotted across the landscape, the most beautiful vista I have ever seen.

Driving through a small town, I pass a telephone booth in the diamond and stop the car and make a collect call to the US, to a friend who has not heard from me in quite a while. She is surprised to hear who is calling her after all this time and is taken aback by the urgency with which I talk to her, almost shouting now, overwhelmed by fear and sadness and guilt all of a sudden, desperately exclaiming:

'It's happening, it's happening! No matter what you hear, I didn't do anything wrong!'

Back in the car then, driving on until, late at night, the journey brings me to a destination: Annaghmakerrig.

The big house is in darkness and silent, all the residents asleep, and the doors are locked for the night, so I enter through a window in the kitchen. In my room I sit and brood, pick through my belongings. Out of the fishing-tackle bag I take the hunting knife, open its blade and fiddle with it idly. Rebecca is on my mind; I feel an overwhelming need to talk to her.

Standing at her bedroom door, I whisper through it: 'Rebecca, it's me. Are you up?'

Then I start to scratch at the door with the knife, which, I am surprised to see, I am still clutching in my hand. I'm a trickster, a court jester, an evil clown. Bearing truths, revealing secrets, acting out gestures that no one wants to hear or see but that need to be made known to the world. I am the messenger, and I shall deliver my message.

'Rebecca! I'm going to cut you!'

The knife in my hand, I continue to scratch at the door.

The door is abruptly wrenched open. Rebecca is here. She is in her pyjamas and dressing gown, and when she sees it is me who is disturbing her sleep she seethes and reddens, eyes widening in mute rage. Then she sees the knife in my hand, my crazed expression, and she pales in terror. Before I can speak or act, she rushes past me and down the stairs.

Momentarily confounded by her reaction to me, I return to my room, bewildered. The director of the centre arrives, finds me sitting, still dazed.

'Right, you,' he snaps. 'You're out.'

There is no point in even trying to reason with him: I see that he is livid at me for disturbing another resident, for my behaviour in general up to this point. I pack my suitcase quickly, and he impatiently picks it up and storms out of the room. Gathering everything else, I follow him on to the landing and down the stairs, out of the house into the night.

'Have you come off some sort of medication?' the director barks at me as he lugs my suitcase across the gravel-covered yard on the way to my car.

'No,' I reply, and I am now grinning inexplicably, euphoric again, as if the trickster in me is having its existence justified and verified by my actions. 'I've *gone on* some sort of medication.'

We cross the courtyard, and I notice him struggling with my overloaded suitcase, which is weighed down with my books and manuscripts.

'Hup! Hup! Hup!' I yell, to make him go faster. He glances over his shoulder at me at this, his face contemptuous, then walks on to the car.

A vague idea strikes me, that I could stay with relatives in County Donegal.

Close to dawn, somewhere on the main road between Omagh and Derry, the car runs out of petrol and rolls to a halt on the lay-by. Raging, I punch the steering wheel over and over again until my fists pulse and smart, then stumble out of the car on to the dual carriageway and begin to roar at all the passing traffic, my voice drowned out by the thunder of the articulated lorries. When I can scream no more I get back into the car, and I cannot stop myself from sobbing. It takes me over completely: an overwhelming sadness, a pain in my chest and stomach, a feeling of devastating loss.

My hands shaking, I take out my mobile phone and dial 999. The operator comes on the line and asks me what emergency service I require. It is too much to articulate, to explain. I don't even know myself.

'I need help,' is all I can manage.

My head is resting against the steering wheel when there is a knock on the window. It is unclear to me how much time has passed since I made the call.

Glancing out, I see a holstered pistol at eye level: it is an RUC officer, peering at me, taking in my tear-stained red and blotchy face, my trembling hands.

I roll down the window, and he asks: 'Is this some sort of breakdown?'

3. Admission

There are two RUC men, and they put me in the back of their car and drive me to the police station nearby. Watching the back of their heads, how they glance at each other now and then, and then at me in the rear-view mirror, I begin to calm, and want to chat with these two saviours of mine.

'Do you have families?' I ask them.

'Oh, aye, we have families,' says one of the officers after a moment, looking over at his companion; he's conscious of my southern accent, my Dublin-registered car.

'Families are important,' I pronounce solemnly. 'You have to take care of your families.'

Again the glances go back and forth. One of them smiles. 'Aye,' he says. 'We'll look after our families.' We drive on.

In the RUC station a blanket is thrown over my shivering shoulders while the officers make phone calls, trying to figure me out and what to do with me. Eventually, they confer and bring me back out to their car. They drive me a short distance to the Tyrone and Fermanagh Hospital. Huddled in the back of the car, I get just an impression of its low-rise campus, several one-storey concrete structures, a central two-storey brick building – quiet, neat, ordered, innocuous. We drive up to one of the single-storey units, where two people wait for me, dressed in white. The RUC allow me out of the car, hand me over to the pair, who are introduced as nurses. The officers explain to them: 'Found him in a D-reg car. Nothing else on him, really.'

The nurses bring me inside. I feel nothing but exhaustion now. I picture beds inside.

'Can I sleep a while?' I ask the nurses.

'First you see the registrar,' one of them says.

Waiting for the registrar in a small, plain office, I struggle to stay awake. The door opens and a middle-aged woman enters.

'I just need to sleep,' I tell her. 'If you could just let me sleep tonight. I haven't slept in so long.'

'This first,' she says, tapping her clipboard. 'Sleep later.' I sink back in my chair. 'Now,' she goes on, 'how did you get here?'

'Night. Driving. The road, just driving at night. No sleep.' I am slurring.

'Pardon?' she says. I sit up.

'I was at the Tyrone Guthrie Centre,' I sigh. 'The artists' residency, you know? I got kicked out at 3 a.m. today.'

'Why?'

'I was knocking at the door of the bedroom of a girl there, an artist.' I don't mention that I was brandishing a hunting knife at the time, how frightened Rebecca was to see me, how she fled in terror. 'Please – I haven't slept in four weeks.'

'First I will see are you to be admitted,' she says, scribbling her notes.

I talk about feeling strange at Annaghmakerrig, without going into the details. But it's all a jumble in my mind and the drowsiness returns as the rage subsides.

'How do you feel now?' she asks.

'Depressed,' I admit.

'Any thoughts of suicide?'

'No.'

'What date is it?' she asks now.

'About – about the tenth of March, 1998. I just saw a newspaper yesterday, at least I think it was yesterday, so –'

'The place?'

'In a hospital, apparently, somewhere up North.'

'What country, please?'

'That's a moot point.'

Definitely on fire with the comebacks. But she is not impressed. More note-taking.

'Does anyone know where you are?'

'No one knows where I am. Except you, me and the police.'

My leg is now out of control under the table, it is so hard to keep it still, so hard to keep myself still, I try to continue, but I want to jump up now and go. But go where? To sleep? To the car?

'Now, remember three things I tell you. Pen, table, head.'

'Easy. Pen, table, head.'

'Not for now. Later.'

'Okay.'

'Count the numbers backwards from one hundred, like this: a hundred, ninety-three, eighty-six, seventy-nine. Yes?'

'I can do that. A hundred. Ninety-three. Eighty-six. Seventy-nine. Uh – Seventy. No. Uh –'

My agitation increases. The numbers seem within reach but impossible to grasp.

'Now –' she says.

'No, wait. Seventy-two! Seventy-two, sixty-five, sixty-five, uh –' Suddenly I need to leave, to get moving. 'Look,' I tell the doctor, leaning forward. 'If you just give me some money, I'll get petrol for my car and I'll go, I'll just go.'

'First you want in, then you want out.'

'I don't need any treatment,' I tell her, afraid of incarceration, of what could be done to me here. 'I just need to rest a bit and then I'll be fine to go on my way.'

'We will decide what treatment you need.'

'I don't want ECT. Do you have ECT here?'

'We will decide,' she repeats. 'The day the patient gets to decide their own treatment –' She doesn't finish the thought.

'Am I a patient?'

'That is what I am trying to decide,' she tells me. 'So, back to this.'

Sagging back into my seat, I wait as she returns to the questionnaire.

'Now,' she says, 'what are the three things I asked you to remember?'

I stare at her blankly. 'Fuck it,' I say. 'You got me at last.'

The nurses take charge of me for the rest of my processing. Two male nurses in white uniforms: bluff, blunt men. They offer me tea and biscuits, but now I suddenly just want to sleep again, as soon as possible, exhaustion flooding over me, so they bring me to my bed. It is in a row of metal-framed cots in a shared ward.

They pull a curtain around the bed, get me to empty my pockets and undress, to hand over everything to them. They give me flimsy hospital pyjamas. They take my temperature and pulse, listen to my breathing, check my blood pressure. All of this agitates me, even while I long for sleep. My impatience is growing, making me jittery again, invigorating me strangely.

Medication is brought, green liquid in a small plastic beaker.

'I don't need that,' I tell them.

'It will help you sleep,' says one of the nurses.

'It's funny, I don't feel like sleeping now,' I tell them. 'I feel wide awake.' And it is true, now I feel alert and energized again, my mind racing.

The nurses glance at one another, then they move as one,

pin me down on the bed. One of them pushes my head back and opens my mouth while the other forces the green liquid down my throat. The plastic bites my nose and lip. I splutter and swallow.

'Fuck it,' I say, coughing. 'That hurt.'

They stand back and watch me as the drowsiness hits.

Beside the bed on a cabinet are a toothbrush, a tube of paste, a wooden hairbrush. Each item is stamped with 'Property of hospital'. The pyjamas I wear bear the same legend as the other items: 'Property of hospital'. This saddens me, strangely.

I lie back on the bed, rapidly sinking into sleep. The nurses watch me a moment longer, seem satisfied, leave me alone. Sleep now overcomes me, darkness dropping like blackest night.

Then I awake, and I am in a new white world, hot and airless.

I am restless, unable to stay still. Pacing the corridors all day, up and down, despite the attempts of nurses to get me to settle. The duty medical officer is called and I am given pills to take; I do not know what the pills are, just take them dutifully, hopefully. But still I can't settle, and when I talk, it is in urgent bursts of speech.

'What's the matter, Arnold?' asks one of the nurses.

'I'm scared of the other patients.'

'There's nothing to be scared of.'

'They want to take my notebook off me, and it's important. It has all my notes, my theories about language. That stuff is important, vital.'

'No one is going to take your notebook.'

'How the fuck do you know?'

'Calm down, now.'

'They could attack me or anything and you wouldn't be able to do a thing about it.'

'They won't attack you. Why don't you go have your lunch now?'

Being told to calm down, not having my fears addressed, causes me to snap. Turning away from the nurse, I prance down the corridor, shouting as loudly as I can as I do so: 'Give me the ECT!'

The nurses just observe all this and wait for me to burn out. When I've stopped shouting they reassure me that there will be no ECT and that I am safe.

The circulating incumbents of the ward, who walk aimlessly around all day when they are not sitting staring at nothing very much, regularly rouse themselves and form an orderly line at a doorway in the corridor. No signal has been made, but somehow the patients know it is time. The top half of the door opens. The lower half acts as a counter over which medication is dispensed. A forearm dressed in white, a hand holding out a plastic vial, followed by a longed-for drink of water to down the required dose of medication, under observation.

The newest arrivals to the hospital refer to the drugs being dispensed as 'medicine'. Those incumbent a little longer use the more formal term, 'medication'. Those who have been in the system quite a while, the old hands, refer to them as 'meds'.

'You got to take your meds.'

'Did you take your meds?'

'They're giving out meds.'

The heat in the ward is unbearable, my hands sweat constantly, so I frequently ask to go to the toilet to wash my hands and complain to the nurse about the temperature.

'You're just making us hot in here so as to keep us all

drowsy and compliant,' I accuse them. Water is coveted. I am always thirsty, dry-mouthed, asking constantly for glasses of water, to alleviate the dryness, but it is difficult to get the nurses to bring me any water; there is no font or source of water available, and they seem to resent the bother of having to go and get me some.

It is an all-male ward. My theory is that all the other patients are ex-Loyalist terrorists who have been spirited away to this hospital, interned without trial as it were, and drugged up to forget their fate, their histories, their very identities. If they do remember who they are, and realize I am from the South, then I could become a target for sectarian violence.

As I go around the ward I feel their eyes on me. In an empty room while I practise my t'ai chi I become aware of them staring in at me through the small meshed window in the door and become scared and self-conscious; now they will think of me as a martial arts expert, even more of a threat. So I take to carrying an improvised weapon at all times to defend myself: a toothbrush I hold in my fist, around which I wrap a towel: my sword and shield.

One patient called Ed, a huge, lumbering man, gets to catching my eye then fixing me in a stare. He scares me: what is he looking for in my eyes, and what will he do when he finds it? Afraid, I manage to rush out of the ward, out past the reception desk and into the car-park, still in my pyjamas, and there I shout at the nurses through an open window. They stand in the ward inside and watch me, wait patiently for me to return, listen as I voice my fears, accuse them of not helping me. Finally, they persuade me to abandon my protest and come inside, and then I explain to them what is wrong.

'There's one guy keeps looking at me,' I tell them, 'I'm scared of him.'

The nurses glance at each other when I identify who it is and immediately decide to take me to a different ward in a different wing of the hospital.

'Where are you taking me?' I ask as we walk down the corridor to the new ward, having expected them to do something to get the other patient under control, not me.

'That guy Ed you were talking about, who you said was looking at you?' says the nurse.

'Yeah?'

'It's better you don't share the same space as him any more.'

When we reach the intensive care unit, they bring me to a small, square room that is lined and floored with blue plastic foam: a genuine padded cell. The sight of it, its confined dimensions, makes me baulk, and I refuse to go in. The two nurses force themselves against me and I push back harder, making them shove and then punch me until I am propelled inside and they shut the door behind me.

They watch me through the window in the door as I lie on the plastic floor and cry: debased, humiliated, powerless and afraid.

A urine sample is requested later in the day. A large cardboard receptacle is handed to me and I go into a corner and urinate into it; I piss and piss, it never stops, and I fill the container, which must hold a litre of fluid, right to the brim. Then I hand it back to the nurse, who looks at it in disgust, taking it gingerly so as to not spill a drop, and I slink back into the cell, feeling slightly delirious.

When they come to me in the padded cell I repeat to the nurses over and over that I am a voluntary patient, that I should be allowed into the ward, that they have no control over me. When I see the registrar I tell her that all that is happening to me is that I am getting in touch with my feelings with regards to my mother's death. I start pushing for discharge. The registrar does not agree I am ready for discharge.

With time, the medications begin to take effect. I am allowed back to the ward, allowed to wear my own clothes again instead of the hospital-issued pyjamas.

In the heat of the ward I grow sleepy and lethargic like all the others. There is little to do. The other patients all seem so otherworldly to me, so unwell compared to how I think I am, and so while I am mixing with them I remain aloof. It is not always possible to avoid conversation, however.

One man speaks to me in a slow drawl. I mention to him that I am writing a novel.

He replies: 'I'm writing a novel,' drawing out and slurring the words with a nasal whine. It makes me wonder: am I like him, clearly delusional in my belief that I am writing a novel, too? The exchange unnerves me, makes me doubt who I am.

At meal times, we wait half an hour, sitting idle in the dining area, to be brought food. The food is cooked in another wing, then ferried to our wing in foil containers before being reheated on small catering stoves in our eating area. The nurses stand around waiting while the caterers heat up the food and watch us waiting for it. The caterers show us laminated menus with the same food choices written on them every day, and we study them before ordering the same things. The caterers take the tinfoil containers and open them, stick meat thermometers into the food and show the temperature to the nurses for approval, and then we are served.

The young man sitting opposite me has crossed eyes and on both arms there are long scars: eight-inch-long gashes criss-crossed many times with the shorter white lines of stitching, a train-track effect. If he can do that much damage to himself, I think, looking at his mutilated arms, what could he do to me?

Another patient takes food out of his mouth and leaves it half-chewed on the side of his plate; another smothers all his food in tomato ketchup and every other condiment on the table to make it more palatable, not caring whether the condiments are sweet or savoury, just pouring them all on over his chops and bangers and eating them. He does not seem to be relishing the food in any way. No one is.

Jack is young and desperately thin. His skin is shiny, his eyes are red sores drilled into his skull. He moves with an unstoppable energy, and he is exhausting to watch, to be near to, to have to listen to. His thoughts go everywhere, his speech is nearly impossible to follow; impossible, too, is the speed of his delivery, the speed with which he changes subject. He notices me, starts to pay attention to me. He begs the staff to be allowed to come and talk to me, and when he finally does so he asks me would I kneel and pray with him.

It is the first time in a week that I have had to consider my relationship with God, with faith, and I realize, quite calmly and rationally, that the religious fervour I felt just a week ago has dissipated completely.

I need to explain to the over-zealous Jack standing before me why I won't pray with him in terms that he will understand. 'No,' I tell him, gently, 'I can't pray with you. I feel so far from God, there's no God in this place, I've been abandoned by Him.'

Jack seems to understand this, to accept it as sincere, and he leaves me alone.

Later that night I hear him thrashing in his bed and the nurses come and take him away. When I ask the next day what was wrong with him, the nurse merely says: 'He's a very sick lad.'

When next I see Jack he is heavily tranquillized. He sees me, looks as if he vaguely recognizes me, but he does not ask to pray with me.

In the outside world, Lou was a fitter. Now he stands with his mouth open, staring into space, or else walking in endless circles. He never has much to say for himself but is a good listener. When some men come to fit new carpets in the recreation room Lou stands stock still for hours and silently watches them work. Just before the men leave, Lou speaks at last: 'That's a nice piece of carpet you've got there, lads.'

The thought goes through my mind that maybe goes through Lou's: the fitters don't know how lucky they are to be able to come into this place, fit carpets, and then leave.

We are always being watched and assessed and listened to, and this makes us modify our behaviour slightly, alter our actions and reactions, our responses to others. The staff are very visible as they observe: they sit at the end of the hallway, or in the centre of the recreation room, in their flimsy white uniforms, clipboards in their hands or on their laps, constantly making notes: they observe us, and we observe them observing.

'The RUC just phoned,' a nurse tells me. 'Your father is at the station and wants to see you. Do you want him to come and visit you?'

He's probably gone there to pick up the car, I reason; they have tracked him from the registration. I don't feel ready to see him.

'No,' I tell the nurse adamantly, feeling panic. 'That would send me berserk.'

'We'll tell that to the RUC.'

I'm left shaking at the thought of my father coming, and go and talk to the nurse again.

'I want to leave.'

'It's best if you stay here a while, Arnold, so we can continue to observe you.'

'But I'm a voluntary admission. I want to leave and go to a hostel.'

'Calm down now.'

'See that window over there?' I point to a nearby window. 'I'll smash that fucking window if you don't let me go.'

The doctor on call attends to me; reassurances are given that it is better for me to wait until my official discharge, and gradually I calm down.

My sister visits. She is distressed at the state of me, at everything that has happened. We have not been close in recent years and there is little common ground upon which to build a conversation. Nonetheless she sits on the arm of the armchair I am sitting on and hugs me around the shoulder; I begin to sob, in shame, fear and confusion, and at her gesture of kindness.

The registrar assesses me again; I tell her I feel isolated and threatened by the others in the oppressive atmosphere of the hospital.

'I'm an artist, a creative, I'm not mentally ill,' I declare. 'I can handle the world.'

The registrar points out to me that my speech is still 'pressured', that my thoughts jump around, that I can't concentrate and am visibly restless. Considering all this evidence for a moment, I concede: 'Well, maybe I'm a little mentally ill.'

There's a piano in the day room. Slowly regaining my equilibrium and interest in things, I manage to form some basic chords, and over the course of a few days start playing and singing Neil Young's 'Helpless' once more; the song calms me and saddens me at the same time.

Finally, the talk from the registrar and the nurses is of my discharge. I speak on the phone with my uncle, my father's brother, and recount to him all that has happened. Close to tears, I beg him to contact my father on my behalf and ask him to come and get me. After everything I have done it is uncertain to me will he let me home, but there appears to be no alternative.

The registrar sees me one final time for assessment before discharge, and when she hears my plans she asks: 'What do you really want to do?'

I have a fantasy in my mind of what I'd like to do, and so I answer her, smiling:

'I'd like to go to Peru and play music in a piano shop.'

It is the first time I have smiled since admission.

That night I chat at ease with the other patients on the ward, then go to bed at ten fifteen and sleep very well after taking my medication. The following day, my sister and father arrive. The doctors give me three days' supply of meds, along with a letter for my consultant in Dublin.

Shaky and withdrawn, I get in the car, clutching the clear plastic bag of meds, hoping that they will make everything go right for me now, will make me well.

I have been hospitalized for ten days.

4. Fury

Back home now to my father's house in the small estate in the suburbs not far from the sea in south County Dublin. I am not able to concentrate on anything for more than a few moments. Reading is virtually impossible.

The job in the theatre working as a design assistant is still pending, but I realize I am in no fit state to do it. I go to the kitchen and phone the production manager who made the offer and tell him I have been unwell.

'They told me I have bipolar disorder,' I say, still not used to the words, still not fully believing that I could have such an illness. 'I don't think I'm going to be able to work for you next week.'

After only a moment's hesitation, the production manager says, 'I know someone who had that. Don't you worry yourself at all.'

Something seems wrong with my legs. They tingle, and feel over-energized, like they contain dynamos or engines, and they want, seemingly of their own volition, to squirm and shift and jerk, and be in motion constantly.

To satisfy this need, I pace the landing upstairs in my father's small house. To extend my pacing I open the bathroom door at one end of the landing and the box-room door at the other and I pace from one extremity of the house's length to the other, back and forth, endlessly, until I am utterly exhausted; but still my legs refuse to allow me to rest, they want to keep moving when I sit or lie down, so I am forced to get up and pace again.

Pace and pace and pace.

The whole day passes thus, from the moment I wake until the moment I go to bed. Then I take my sleeping tablets and attempt to sleep. When I wake, it feels as though I have slept only briefly. After a quick breakfast of toast I feel the agitation building in my legs once more, and so it is back upstairs to start pacing again, pace the landing all day long, to the point of exhaustion again, and beyond.

Although I am taking all the medications the doctors have prescribed for me, a variety of pills of different shapes and colours and sizes whose purpose I only dimly comprehend, my body is agitated and my mind seethes and boils with rushing thoughts, endless brooding, self-recrimination. I am ashamed of my breakdown, embarrassed by all the things I have said and done, unable to face anyone. The diagnosis feels like a shameful, fearful label. I do not know how to explain any of it, what kind of language to use. I assume my friends would be embarrassed to hear me attempt to do so, and so I don't contact them. The only people who ask after me are relatives, and I grow increasingly embarrassed talking to them, feeling a burden on everyone, a source of shame to the family.

Fear grips me: the thought that I will never be able-minded again, never be able to concentrate on anything, to work, to live by myself, to get back to writing; that I will always be mad. It occurs to me also that no woman will ever want me now, someone with a mental illness, and I will never experience a loving relationship again.

I go to an out-patient appointment at St Vincent's Hospital. When the registrar asks me what I think are the causes of what happened, I say that it was probably the combination of the antidepressant, cannabis and alcohol in the over-stimulating environment of the Tyrone Guthrie Centre that caused me to become first insomniac, then agitated. I am putting as positive a spin on everything as I can, determined to avoid being hospitalized again.

Then I go back home to my pacing.

The next time I see the doctor I feel less positive and tell her I need more tranquillizers; the agitation is exhausting me, stringing me out, pushing me close to an edge I am afraid to fall from. The doctor prescribes me an increased dose of one of the medications and agrees that I am not fit for employment.

Then, after the appointment, back to the house for more pacing.

Then, finally, I crash.

It is impossible to take it any more: this inability to stay still, this feeling of crawling and scraping in my legs, the sensation that my body is a puppet whose strings are being jerked and pulled violently and brutally by forces I cannot identify. Is my mind doing this to me? Or is it the medications I take, the ones I depend on to make me well? All I know is that I am not myself; my self is lost, gone, in abeyance.

Up to now my father has mostly just left me to my own devices. Now I go downstairs and sit on the arm of his armchair, where he sits by the fire in the living room.

'I need a hug,' is the first thing I say.

If he still feels anger and fear over my treatment of him, he does not show it; rather, he puts his arm around me and hugs me.

'I don't feel well,' I go on, and I begin to cry.

'Ah, fella,' he says kindly.

My outbursts, my accusations and condemnations, my violence during the breakdown are all set aside for now; I cry because it feels nice to be close to my father again, feeling his kindness, as I did during my childhood.

'I think I need to go back to hospital,' I tell him.

Still restless in my legs, I pack a bag and we get in the car, drive to St Vincent's. Now, I no longer feel anxious at the idea of hospitalization but rather an intense relief that I will be going to a place where I will be cared for.

A registrar-on-call sees me: Dr Doran. She is young, slim, blonde and very pretty. Despite my anxiety and agitation, I feel a little shy and abashed with her, and wonder if she is aware that I find her attractive; at the same time, I find myself wanting to tell her everything about myself so as to endear myself to her.

'Can you tell me how you feel right now?' she asks me.

'I just can't stop moving,' I say.

'But how do you feel?'

'I feel like my spinal cord is whipping my legs to move.'

It is true: some force is now torqueing through my body and making me twist and squirm and twitch and turn; it is the first time in a while I've been forced to sit for any length of time, and it is unbearable.

'What about your mood? Are you depressed?'

'No.'

'How's your appetite?'

'I'm not really eating much these days.'

'What about sleep?'

'My doctor gave me sleeping tablets, so I take those. I guess I sleep about five hours a night on them.'

'Your records show you were hospitalized in Omagh recently. For a manic episode.'

'Yeah.'

Dr Doran takes notes, watches me closely.

She asks me about my past relationships with women, and this embarrasses me: I find it hard to talk to this attractive female doctor about sex and love. I try to convince her that, normally, I am cheerful, intellectual, analytic, creative, active and hard-working. That I am a writer and – for some reason I am keen to emphasize – a good listener.

She tells me she is going to admit me for observation; I am relieved. She will stop the antipsychotic medication so as to relieve the agitation I am feeling; this sounds good, too. Admission proceeds.

But suddenly I am afraid to be back in a hospital ward. The fear is that someone will come into my room during the night and sexually assault me. The nurses reassure me I will be safe, that they will be nearby all the time, that no one will come into my room. But I am on edge now.

Then it is time to go to bed, and medications are dispensed once more, medications I swallow down without a thought, trusting, giving myself over to the people in white, hoping they will help me.

Settling, growing drowsy from the meds, I lie on the hard, crisp hospital bed and soon fall asleep.

The routine here is familiar: woken early with all the other patients to go to breakfast; meds; sit around in the day room; go to another meal; more meds; more waiting aimlessly for nothing at all to occur; another meal; evening meds; then waiting until bedtime and the dispensation of sleeping tablets, and so to sleep.

In this hospital there is a more concerted effort to find medications that suit me, and to observe me closely. Clearly, the combination of medications I have been taking since leaving the Tyrone and Fermanagh Hospital was not having the desired effect. Trying out different medications will take weeks of observation and questioning and blood tests, weeks of waiting, weeks of the hospital routine.

Sleep is difficult. It takes time to settle in this alien place, and even after I do fall asleep I wake several times during the night, disturbed by the noises of the ward: the nurses chatting at their station just outside in the corridor; their occasional arrival into the room as they check am I asleep; the sounds of the other patients moving around and talking.

One morning, I confront the nurses. 'I'm going to make a formal complaint about the noise on the ward,' I tell them. 'All the other patients are trying to sabotage my sleep.'

The nurses have to calm me, and reassure me this is not the case. But I am growing cranky and cantankerous now.

Once more I phone my friend in America, reversing the charges from the payphone in the corridor not far from the nurses' station, and try to convince her that I am being held against my will, that there is in fact nothing wrong with me, that I don't need to be hospitalized. Her husband is connected to the legal profession, and, I reason, my friend should thus be in a good position to help me.

'You have to get me out of here!' I roar into the phone. 'Get me a fucking lawyer!'

She is unable to comprehend me. In frustration I slam the receiver down in its cradle, breathless, fuming, hot and red-faced. The nurses scold me for my bad language and for abusing the payphone. They try to persuade me to take my medications early, to calm me down, but I refuse. Dr Doran is informed. Still fuming, I tell them I'm going to go for a walk in the grounds of the hospital and turn around and leave the ward.

On my return I spend time alone in my room. Dr Doran comes in for a consultation and finds me writing in my diary.

'What are you writing?' she asks as she sits down, clipboard at the ready to take notes. Quickly, I hide my diary: I don't want anyone reading my innermost thoughts.

'Nothing, nothing,' I snap.

'How are you feeling today?'

'I can't sleep at night. There's too much noise. I'm bloody exhausted by it.'

'You haven't been socializing with the other patients,' she notes.

'The day room is too fucking smoky. Anyway, I don't want to, I want to stay in my room.'

'Why?'

'I need to sleep during the day because I can't sleep at night.'

'Maybe if you were to stay awake during the day and socialized, you'd be able to sleep at night.'

'You understand nothing of my difficulties,' I reply. 'You're not even listening to me. You don't even care.'

She writes some notes, giving me time to vent, to calm down; eventually continues: 'If you were on the ward, talking to people –'

'Nah.'

'Why not?'

'I'm a bit of a loner. Always have been.'

Admitting this makes me feel sad suddenly. She notices the change in mood, grows more solicitous.

'How's your appetite? You're very thin.'

'Can't eat the food here, it's shite.'

'How do you feel today, apart from the tiredness?'

'Low. I feel low.'

'What does that feel like?'

'I feel like an empty stump. Like all of my feelings have been amputated.'

'Is it always like this?' she asks.

'No. Every so often I have more energy, I'll be in great form.'

'Like you were in Northern Ireland?'

60

'Similar. But milder. But then I get bouts of depression. Then a bit of, I don't know, elation, I suppose. And in between I just get by. It's a bit of a struggle but I'm not overly depressed. Most of the time.'

It is easy to talk to Dr Doran; I like her and want her to like me.

'How long has this been going on?' she asks.

'Since my mother died I guess. Ten years ago now. She had cancer. I tried talking to my father about it all recently, but I don't know – I don't think he got over it himself, really.'

I'm lost in thought a while.

'How's your concentration?' she asks, bringing me back to the present.

'Better,' I tell her.

The meeting is over; she gets up to go. But something is bothering me.

'Am I bipolar?' I ask her, just before she leaves. She stands at the doorway, pauses, considers my question.

'It might just be irritable depression,' she replies.

Then she leaves, and I take out my diary and go on writing, wondering what it is that afflicts me, what I am, and what will become of me.

In the TV lounge, I ignore the other patients when they ask can they switch channels; I just want to watch what I want to watch. The nurses don't confront me about this, wary of my unpredictable temper. But the other patients are annoyed with me: I am isolated on the ward, isolating myself, not engaging with the others.

As I walk towards the exit, a nurse asks me where I'm going. I tell her I'm going for a walk on the grounds. She wants to know where exactly, what are my plans, when I'll be back. Irritated, I snap back at her that she has my mobile phone number and she can call me if she wants to talk to me any time I leave the ward. She isn't happy with this, and tells me forthrightly that it is not an appropriate response. Getting enraged, I turn on her.

'You know, I'm going to leave here soon, but you're going to be stuck coming in here the rest of your life,' I spit at her. 'And I'm going to get a job in film production, I'm going to make five hundred quid a week, and I just hope they pay you enough to clean the shit off old women's arses.'

Then I turn and go out for my walk, leaving the nurse staring at me, aghast.

Dr Doran visits me on her rounds and tells me they are going to try me on lithium. This has positive, promising, associations, for me. I wrote part of my MA thesis on Robert Lowell, the American poet who suffered from what was then called manic depression, and lithium helped him. Dr Doran explains the side-effects, including tremors of the hands, weight gain, dry mouth, acne and feeling dizzy or drowsy. These seem worth enduring if the lithium can help with my depression and prevent mania.

There's a book I've brought with me to the hospital about depression. The book explores how childhood trauma and family dysfunction can lead to psychological problems later in life. In my copy of the book I have underlined many passages that I think are relevant to my case. On one of his mostly silent visits to me, I give the book to my father.

'Read this,' I tell him. 'It will help you understand me.'

He takes the book without a word.

A few days later I see the book behind the counter of the nurses' station. On his next visit I confront my father about this.

'Why did you give my book to the nurses?' I want to know.

'I wanted them to see the kind of rubbish you were reading,' he replies.

'It's not rubbish. Family history can lead to depression. Look what happened to me.'

'You just have a salt missing from your brain,' he tells me, referring to lithium. He doesn't seem to be aware that this salt, while it does occur naturally in nature, does not occur naturally in the brain. He is convinced my illness is the result of a simple physical deficit. His obtuseness on this point enrages and frustrates me.

All through this conversation he gazes at a point slightly above and behind me, as if it is impossible to look at me.

My condition improves as I begin to respond to treatment and rest, and I am allowed occasional sorties outside the hospital, always accompanied by friends or family. On a visit home I receive an acceptance letter from an artists' residency in the state of Virginia: I have been offered a six-week residency there. Now I need to fund the trip, so I decide to apply to the Arts Council for a Travel Award.

Back in the hospital, I fill in the required forms. I need to get money to pay for a stamp, but my wallet is locked up for safe-keeping. A nurse tells me that it will take some time for my wallet to be retrieved. I grow belligerent.

'I can't wait for my wallet. I have to go to the post office to post this letter, it's urgent.'

The nurse is in no rush, talks to me slowly and calmly. 'Arnold, when you are a bit elated, everything gains a sense of urgency.'

'I'm not elated, this is important. It's an Arts Council application I have to get in quickly.'

The nurse finally hands me a five-pound note out of his own wallet. I hurry to the post office and send off the application.

Later, my wallet is handed to me and the nurse who gave

me the fiver asks for his money back. But I don't give it to him, even after he repeats his request. 'That will teach you to lend money to a manic depressive,' I tell him, laughing. Something of the trickster possesses me still.

Debbie comes to visit. She sits by my bed as I lie back on it, feeling strangely subdued for a change. We talk, at ease with each other, and I tell her about what I've been through, the breakdowns and medications I've been prescribed. She is sympathetic; says one of her daughters was put on anti-depressants and didn't respond well to them, was not herself afterwards.

'I'm sorry you're broken,' she tells me. 'I hope they fix you.'

A package arrives for me at the hospital one day. It contains the blue Levi's hoodie I used to wear while out walking in Annaghmakerrig. The wife of the director of the Tyrone Guthrie Centre has followed up on me, managed to find out about what happened to me, where I am. Now she writes me a letter, full of kindness and concern, and enclosing the hoodie. She knows how much I liked to wear it and she hopes it will comfort me now.

I wear it every day: comforter, armour, talisman.

During bursts of energy I reapply myself by phone or by post to the business of the world outside. My two film scripts are moving closer to production; I hear from the producer that full funding is now in place for both. There was a literary agent who was interested in my work and wanted to talk about the possibility of signing me up; but when I get back in touch with her and try and arrange for her to come to the hospital to conduct the meeting during visiting hours, she loses interest quickly.

My back erupts with acne, a side-effect of lithium. The huge red sores burn and itch, agitated by the clothes I wear, or when I lie on my back; they erupt and bleed, and the blood stains my clothes.

Some days, when I am calm and compliant, I am allowed to walk the grounds, or even cross the road for a quiet pint or a cup of tea in the local pub, or even, as long as I get permission and state when I will return, go further afield, into town or back to my father's house for a proper home-cooked meal. Always then the sadness at the end of such outings to be returning to the hospital.

A cousin phones and tells me he will visit. I get permission to go out for the day in his company. I wash, and dress, and at the appointed time I am ready and waiting, sitting on the edge of my bed in anticipation of his arrival. Still sitting, still waiting, I remain there for hours, hoping he will come. Eventually, it grows too late to go out. I assume my cousin was too ashamed to meet me, a mentally ill relative confined to a psychiatric ward. Ashamed, or afraid.

A home visit.

My father drives me to his house from St Vincent's and we don't talk much on the way. Once we get there, I go to my room. During the afternoon my sister arrives. From my room I hear her and my father talking downstairs animatedly; I feel strangely left out, but can think of no pretext upon which to go and join the conversation. Instead I get up off the bed and go to the beach for a walk.

It is a fine sunny day, but the exercise and the weather fail to cheer me. A small dog breaks free from its owner, an old woman wrapped in a large wool coat, and approaches me and starts growling. I jerk my arm at it to drive it away, but this only aggravates it, and it begins to bark and snap at my feet. In a fury I stoop to the ground and pick up a pile of stones and hurl them at the dog. The owner shouts at me to stop, as the dog is driven back, but I shout back and keep throwing the stones, closer to the dog, closer to where the owner stands, still shouting at me. In my rage I don't even care where the stones land.

Then a stone hits the old woman on her hip. This stops me, and I stand still a moment, waiting for her to react. But she just stares at me blankly, in shock, so I turn away and go home, furious that my walk has been spoiled by the snapping dog, the angry owner, and now the trouble I may be in over hitting her with a stone.

My sister is in the kitchen when I get back and my father is in the living room. In a brief exchange with my father my anger suddenly overwhelms me, or rather, I unleash it. My father stands before me, drinking from a cup of tea by the fireplace. I scream at him and kick the cup out of his hand. Tea splatters across the walls and bookcases on the other side of the room. Still shouting with rage, I bend and pick up the small wickerwork table by my father's armchair and hurl it as forcefully as I can at the wall, breaking it. My father retreats, goes to my sister for help, and eventually they manage to persuade me to return to the hospital.

When I arrive on the ward my shoulders are hunched with tension, I am coiled now into myself, a dark ball of fury. My father and sister trail behind me, shaken.

'Tell my visitors to leave,' I command the nurses. My father and sister go.

When I am left alone with the nurses I grow contrite and explain what happened and begin to cry over it: such a waste of a visit out of the hospital. The nurses settle me, give me a tranquillizer to help calm me down, and I swallow it greedily, sick of this burning agitation I am experiencing.

Finally, I sleep.

*

There's a piano in the day room, and I wake early and go in to play the one tune I know how to play, Neil Young's 'Helpless'.

I'm pounding away on the keys and singing at full throttle when the nurses come and tell me it is inappropriate to be playing the piano so loudly at eight thirty in the morning.

'How are you going to stop me?' I say to them.

Feeling trapped and confined in the hospital system, I write a letter to my doctors, venting all my frustrations:

Dr Doran, Dr Malvey 20 April 1998.

I am a unique creative free spirited individual human being with my own special personality which I have a God given right to retain in its natural state.

I do not fit into the public health psychiatric care system. I feel my hospitalisation as institutionalisation and my treatment both by staff and medication has now fulfilled its role of restoring my balance of mind. I further feel that any more treatment would be both oppressive of my personality and damaging to me as an individual. Therefore as a voluntarily admitted patient I am requesting the stabilising of my Lithium dosage at its current level of 800mg p.d., and my prompt discharge from hospital as soon as can be arranged. In the short term I would appreciate freedom to leave the grounds within meal hours or hours set by mutual agreement.

Thank you for your kind consideration.

Arnold Fanning

They receive the letter; they do not comment or act upon it.

My friend Michael Paul, on a visit to Dublin from Rome, comes to St Vincent's and takes me walking in the grounds.

As always when in his company, I feel at peace, accepted and loved for who I am.

'You're fine,' he tells me gently when I recount my worries and concerns, and I believe him, believe that I will be well, that indeed I am well. His smile of kindness, love and acceptance make me feel it is true.

My frustration at being hospitalized grows, and I take this out on Dr Doran at our next consultation.

'The treatment here is inadequate,' I inform her haughtily, 'and the food is intolerable, and the other patients are beneath my level. I never get to see the doctor, and the nurses have too many rules for me to keep. They shouldn't apply to me. Do you understand?'

She lets me vent, takes her notes, and leaves.

The next time I see her I feel calmer and, chastened, I apologize to her. 'I was a bit high yesterday,' I admit. 'But it's all my father's fault. He was so fucking mean to me, he's to blame for how I feel.'

I bombard her with questions about my treatment and medications. She answers them patiently, then suggests I try occupational therapy. On a couple of occasions previously, when less volatile, I have briefly attended some sessions.

'I don't want to,' I tell her.

'Why not?'

'My stuff, what I do, is over the heads of everyone else doing it. The therapists aren't very good either. I'm never given enough attention.'

She stoically listens to all my complaints, then tells me that my lithium is to be increased further.

On a visit home I find a letter from the Arts Council. They have granted me a Travel Award to go to the artists' residency in Virginia. It seems an impossibility, however: how can I travel, the way I am now? What would I do there, when I can't even write? Will having bipolar disorder bar me from entering the US? It all seems out of reach, even while it is in my grasp; everything will have to be postponed, perhaps for ever.

Lithium: after a while you don't feel anything. You feel the same all day long, day after day. You don't feel sad, you don't feel happy. You don't feel interested, you don't feel bored. You don't feel excited and you don't feel indifferent. You just feel nothing, a total absence of feeling. After several weeks of lithium, watching its levels rise then stabilize in my bloodstream, my mood flattening in response, I tell Dr Doran about this feeling it induces in me, or rather, this complete absence of feeling. Within a quarter of an hour, after she has consulted with another doctor, I am told to cease taking the lithium. ✗

Walking down the corridor of the ward, I glance into a room. A young woman is sitting on the edge of a bed, the window bright behind her, picking out her form in silhouette. Dark-haired, slim, she sits with her head bowed forward and down, and her shoulders slightly hunched, tense. Her hands sit motionless in her lap. She barely seems to breathe.

It is a posture I recognize, the posture of one in the throes of deep depression. It moves me to see this stranger in this state, and I long to comfort her. But I don't feel I can go into her room without her permission, and she has not noticed me watching her, so I move on.

Her name, I discover, is Eimear. At meal times, and in the smoking lounge, once she does appear, I attempt to talk to her, drawn to her pale beauty and wanting to help in her sadness; but to do so is difficult, she is sunk so far into herself.

69

I go to her room, stand at the door. Again she is hunched on the bed, lost to everything except the drumming torment of her existence. Finally, she appears to notice my presence.

'Can I come in?' I ask her.

She acquiesces, allows me in. She does not move as I sit down beside her. Gently, I place the headphones of my Walkman on her head and press 'Play'. The song I have lined up on the cassette is 'Everybody Hurts' by R.E.M.

As soon as she hears the opening bars of the song she looks at me. She suddenly comes to life, her body uncoils and she leans forward and hugs me. Smiling, I hug her back; the song plays to the end. She looks at me, as if for the first time.

'Thank you,' she says, and we are friends.

Now, we spend most of our time together on the ward. I do most of the talking, because of a mood upswing, but I also hear her story, too, about her history of self-harm, her fractious relationship with her mother, her chronic, seemingly intractable depression. I ask her why she is currently in hospital.

'I swallowed all my pills and a bottle of vodka,' she says.

'That would do it,' I reply, and we both smile, knowingly, because we understand each other in a way the doctors do not, she can tell me things she won't tell them, and vice versa. With glee I tell her that I can control my hypomania: this current, pleasant high can be maintained at will. 'The more liquids I drink, the higher I become,' I tell her. 'It dilutes the meds, so I can ride the high any time I like.'

She tells me about the time her mother grabbed her by the throat and tried to strangle her; I expound my theory that this is why Eimear now wants to choke herself on pills and vodka. I feel I know everything, have answers to everything.

The nurses and the doctors have noticed the bond we have formed, have noticed our attachment to one another. So it is that I walk down the corridor to go to Eimear's room and find it empty. When I enquire, one of the nurses informs me that Eimear has been transferred to another hospital to continue her treatment. This information hits me like a blow and I let out a cry.

'You seem upset that Eimear has been transferred,' the nurse says, unnecessarily and, I think, with a smug air of satisfaction.

Late that night the payphone in the ward corridor rings and I am summoned to it. Eimear is on the line, calling from the hospital she has been transferred to. It is difficult to have a phone conversation with her, as she is not capable of speaking much; to compensate, I babble at her.

'When I can go out unaccompanied next time, I'll come and visit you,' I assure her. The silence grows between us again. 'I promise.'

We say goodnight, and make promises to phone each other frequently. But it is not the same as being in one another's company.

With the stabilization of my mood comes privileges, and I am once more allowed out of the hospital by myself; the only restriction is that I must return for meal times. At the first opportunity, I leave the hospital early and walk the few miles to the hospital that Eimear has been transferred to.

It is a gloomy place, a mixture of Victorian-era edifices and flimsy prefabs. The ward Eimear is in is a large one, open plan, the beds in two rows facing each other down each side; no private room here, no chance of even a modicum of privacy.

The nurses' station is at the top of the ward. I tell the nurse who I am visiting and I'm brought to Eimear's bed.

71

We are completely exposed to the ward, so I stand up and draw the curtains around the bed. We sit then, holding hands in our curtained-off cocoon, just looking at each other.

Almost immediately the curtains are pulled back and a nurse glares down at us. We let go of each other's hands abruptly.

'You can leave these open, thank you very much,' says the nurse, then turns and walks away at a neat clip.

'This is hard,' says Eimear.

'It won't always be like this,' I reassure her. 'We'll both be out someday, and then . . .'

After talking to the social worker in St Vincent's about what I can do after I am discharged from hospital, I apply for, and am accepted on, a publicly funded catering course. I have always had an interest in cooking, and to be a professional chef seems a natural progression of that interest. There'll be a payment for doing the course, to replace the disability benefit I am currently claiming.

The future seems a little brighter now. I tell Dr Doran that I have a plan: to live independently, down the country, and work in a hotel as a chef. My idea is to work split shifts so I have lots of time to write in between them. I picture being offered accommodation with the job, so I won't have to pay rent and I'll be truly independent at last. It seems a wonderful prospect, and for the first time in months I feel hopeful and optimistic, at times even cheerful.

Eimear also improves. Now when I visit her she is sometimes allowed out with me; it is unclear to me whether the nurses realize that I am a patient in another hospital. We go to the nearby campus of University College Dublin. Sometimes we lie in the long grass behind the playing fields and hold each other and kiss. Then always, always, as the light fades on the early-summer evenings, there is the return, for both of us, to our respective hospitals.

Eimear and I go to the Irish Film Centre to see a movie. As usual, we discuss our illnesses, our meds and hospital matters. In the bar after the movie I keep my sunglasses on, feeling sensitive to the presence of people around me, wanting to distance myself from them, their scrutiny. Eimear understands and does not mind; she knows she is included in the world I have retreated to.

But then a film producer I know spots me and comes to our table. This catches me off guard: I hadn't anticipated meeting anyone from my former professional life. I stare up at him blankly through my sunglasses, acutely ashamed. He watches me, unsure what is wrong; then he leans forward and very gently lifts the sunglasses up and looks into my eyes in concern, as if to see how I am really doing. The gesture moves me.

Eimear is allowed out for an overnight visit to her family home, and I am allowed out until the final dispensation of medications on the ward at the end of the night: we will have an entire afternoon and evening together. We walk around the suburbs for a while, then go to her house, and Eimear brings me to her room. It is the first time we have ever been together in a completely private interior space.

With infinite care and shyness we undress each other and go to bed; we have a few hours alone before I have to go back to the ward, and intend to enjoy our bodies, naked, together. But it becomes rapidly apparent as we make love that something is wrong. It is like we are in a fog of numbness; all the sensations of our bodies have been blunted. We are making love, for sure, there are the actions and movements, I am deep inside her, moving, but we are not feeling anything close to sexual satisfaction and neither of us can get anywhere near to orgasm.

'It's the meds,' says Eimear after a while.

The spell, the intimacy, is broken and I pull out, lie back. We are both frustrated; worse, we are both now acutely embarrassed, almost ashamed of our condition, of lying together naked in this way when there is no sexual energy between us, no desire left, despite our best efforts and intentions, despite our feelings for each other.

We get dressed in silence and say goodnight. I walk back to the hospital, go on the ward, take my meds and go to bed, seething.

Eimear and I continue to see each other. We go for drinks and coffees and walks. But somehow the intensity of feeling that we experienced before cannot be rekindled.

We don't attempt to sleep together again. As my mood stabilizes, then flattens and deadens, I find myself less capable of keeping a conversation going with Eimear. More and more often we find ourselves in long silences. We can't seem to overcome the shame over the failure of our bodies. What should have been the consummation of our relationship and the beginning of its next chapter instead marked the beginning of its end.

Dr Malvey tells me it is very difficult to have a relationship with a depressed person; I wonder how much she knows about Eimear and me.

Eventually, Eimear and I stop seeing each other completely, lose touch. While I feel sad at losing her, I also feel guiltily relieved that I no longer have to see her: the long, silent encounters were beginning to wear me down.

The night before my catering course begins, I ask the nurses to wake me at seven thirty in the morning so I am not late for it. I'm nervous about starting the course, but think it will be a good step, the start of a new career, a new life.

In the morning I take the commuter train into the city and walk the short distance from Connolly station to the training college. Each member of the incoming group is issued with aprons, whites, caps, a textbook and a large, extremely sharp chef's knife. I feel out of place and extremely awkward. I am the oldest in the group; the others are teenagers, early school-leavers it would appear, or just out of school.

Back in the hospital it is explained I am to be discharged, and promptly. There is no reason for me to stay, after all; I am no longer unwell, and I have returned to a normal level of functioning in the world, pursuing a training course. Hospitalization is now unnecessary, and my bed is needed for other patients.

The nurses give me some black plastic bin bags to put my belongings into and I pack everything I have up. My father arrives to collect me. We leave the hospital and he drives me to his house in the small estate near the sea in south County Dublin, and I settle myself into my own room at last, back to being by myself, and in privacy.

I have been away in hospital for five and a half weeks.

5. The Institution

Every weekday for the remainder of the summer, I attend the catering course. We are taught how to make industrial quantities of food using industrial methods. There is no joy in it, no relish for the ingredients or in producing something enjoyable to eat; rather, it is all about units and cost efficacy and speed.

I realize that I am nervous around some of the equipment: afraid of burning myself on one of the huge stoves or ovens, or of cutting myself with my chef's knife, whose sharpness we are constantly warned about. My main fear relates to the waste grinder that is at the bottom of the sink. Into the sinks we pour all the day's leftovers and waste after cleaning out the pots and pans and roasting dishes, creating a glutinous mass of floating solids. We watch as the grinder sucks it all down into a vortex and reduces it to a pulp that can then be washed away. Inevitably, some solid matter gets stuck in the grinder and needs to be pushed through and I become terrified that in doing this my hand will get caught and be ground to a pulp.

In appointments with a psychiatrist in the out-patients' department of St Vincent's Hospital, I complain of feeling low, with little motivation to do the course. Lithium is prescribed again, along with an antipsychotic and a different sleeping tablet. As the summer goes on, I feel worse and worse, and experience panic attacks; I end up missing some days of the course due to these. Dr Malvey writes a letter to my supervisor explaining my 'psychological difficulties' and expressing the hope that I may be allowed to continue with the course. For the panic attacks she suggests I try breathing exercises and listen to relaxation tapes. The antipsychotic is replaced with another, to see will it work better. At times I find myself fantasizing about suicide and think about how I would carry it out. The psychiatrists I see consider that my mood is caused by my circumstances, and I agree about the importance of finding meaningful work, and of moving out of my father's house.

One of our tutor chefs demonstrates how to make one chicken serve eight people. The chicken is roasted, along with dozens more, in a huge oven, until the flesh and bone ooze and loosen and fall apart, and then is left to cool. The carcass is then ripped apart by hand into eight pieces. These pieces are reheated and covered in a thick brown sauce made from a powder kept in a four-gallon keg. The resulting mess is considered suitable for serving in hotels and other large-scale catering environments.

The whole demonstration makes me realize I am totally sick of the whole thing, and I decide there and then to drop the course. The next day I manage to motivate myself to write up a new CV and go to bookstores around the city centre. Within a few days I'm offered work as a clerk in the academic department of Fred Hanna's, in Nassau Street.

It is autumn now, and the new-term rush of students from nearby Trinity College is over, so the academic department is quiet. I spend most of each day trying to look busy: tidying and cleaning, lining up books neatly on the shelves and wiping the dust off them. The other staff member in the academic department, a young stand-up comedian, frequently grabs the railing of the counter and rocks back and forth in agitation, complaining loudly: 'I need sex!'

I become fascinated by some of the books in my department. One, from the medical section, is a lavishly illustrated medical encyclopaedia of sexually transmitted diseases, full of the most disgusting, appalling images I have ever seen: photographs of deformed and diseased bodies and genitals, bloated and bulging with disease, or, conversely, withered away with infection. This book is loathsome and terrifying, but I cannot stop myself from taking it from the shelf as I clean around it, delving ever deeper into its horrors.

In the same section is a book aimed at pathology students depicting in graphic detail the effect on the body of hanging, shooting and other acts of self-destruction. This saddens as well as horrifies, but I cannot stop looking into its grotesque galleries.

But, generally, I've lost interest in many things I used to enjoy, including my interest in food and cooking. I'm now eating one or two slices of toast a day, just the bare minimum of food, to stave off hunger pangs. Once a week or so I'll have a proper meal, one that my father has prepared, but little else. I can no longer write.

'I feel as though I don't belong in this world,' I tell my doctor at my next appointment. 'I feel I don't fit in.'

The doctor is concerned, suggests I be admitted to hospital again for observation, but I'm adamant I don't want or need to come in. After discussion, it is agreed to stop the lithium.

At the next out-patients' appointment I inform the doctor that I don't feel any different off the lithium. 'I don't feel I will ever enjoy life again,' I tell her. I'm on an antidepressant and a sleeping tablet now, both supposedly to help stabilize my mood, but nothing is helping me with the depression.

One day I simply can't get out of bed, and so I don't go to work; I stay in bed all that day.

Then the next day I do the same.

Then the next.

Eventually, the phone rings, and my father answers it in the kitchen. He calls up the stairwell, letting me know that it is the bookstore manager demanding to know when I'll be back in work.

'I don't know,' is all I can manage to call out in reply.

A few days later I receive a notice of termination of employment in the post.

Sometimes I simply don't have the energy to get to an out-patients' appointment. When I finally do so, Dr Malvey expresses concern for me. 'You need to come in to us at times like that,' she tells me. She prescribes a trial of yet another antidepressant.

By November, I am spending most of my time dozing in bed, often daydreaming an elaborate fantasy of an alternative, fulfilling life. Hours, days, pass in this alternative world, which is clean, ordered, suburban. In this world I have a job, a relationship. I participate in this world's offerings and activities, doing all the normal things I cannot do now: going to work; taking a drive to the city, or to the country for a hike; being with someone. I can even see the woman I am with: she drives me, we talk, I am with her. It is a vivid world, and I sink into it. But it is not real; only the bed is real.

As winter descends, my sleep becomes ever more erratic and my energy levels begin to fluctuate. Finding myself irritable, I feel alarmingly full of energy while at the same time overwhelmed by an inner tiredness; the agitation is in my body while the enervation is in my mind.

After Christmas dinner, at the house of relatives, I leave the dining room and go by myself and lie down for a while in a bedroom upstairs. My aunt is concerned and sits with me for a while, but I just want to be by myself. Depression has overcome me again and it feels like it will never end.

On St Stephen's Day I feel palpitations in my chest, my heart begins to pound erratically and I feel faint at times, with blood rushing to my head. Feeling overcome by the physical sensations I am experiencing, I go to the A&E of Loughlinstown hospital, which is not far from my father's house, and get a physical check-up; they find nothing wrong with me.

The following day, I go to the A&E of St Vincent's to be assessed by the psychiatrist on call, a visit outside my normal out-patient appointment schedule. I tell her that my mood has improved; it is the physical sensations alone that are bothering me. The doctor listens as I tell her all the plans I have recently formulated: plans to buy a car, to drive to Monaghan and visit that teenage girl who worked in the bar I used to go to, to help her, rescue her; and to exercise more, to participate in more employment schemes and to get back to work.

'There's a million things going around my head,' I tell her.

There's that breathless head-rushing feeling also, and during the assessment I tell the doctor that I feel faint. She watches, startled, as I lie down on the floor and wait until the swimming sensation in my head subsides.

When the doctor offers to admit me to the hospital as an in-patient for observation, I decline.

'I don't want to worry my father,' I explain.

She prescribes me medication to counter the growing mania I am experiencing: yet another antipsychotic.

There's an improvement: sleeping settles, and one of the employment schemes I have applied for offers me a placement. Now I'm making plans to swim, to socialize once more, and to start this new placement.

Suddenly, I feel a new energy, a motivation to do things, to do lots of things. Waking at 4 a.m., I find myself tidying my room, then putting together my fishing equipment and driving in my father's car out to Wicklow, to go fishing, alone, at Blessington Lake. As dawn breaks over the chill grey waters I wonder what has brought me there, what I am doing.

Friends are contacted again, and I dig out my old tennis gear and play long, over-energized games of tennis with them on the grounds of UCD. At a party I'm brought to by one friend I become overwhelmed by all the people there, feel claustrophobic and agoraphobic, so I go and sit in a room by myself; after a while my friend comes and tells me I have to leave as I am making the hosts and the other guests feel uncomfortable. It is unclear to me what I have done wrong, but I feel ashamed and self-conscious. Sleep is elusive.

Convinced I am becoming manic, and remembering with shame and terror how I behaved during my previous episode, I decide to go to the A&E of St Vincent's and request to be admitted for care as an in-patient. It's 10 p.m. and the Accident and Emergency room at St Vincent's Hospital is packed. Pacing, agitated, jumpy, unable to speak slowly or coherently, I grow increasingly impatient with the idea of waiting to see the psychiatrist on call to be assessed for admission; instead I take it on myself to go straight to the psychiatric ward I was in before.

On the way down the corridor I begin to crave a cigarette, thinking that it would help me to settle; but I don't have any, haven't bought any in a long time, so I'll have to ask a patient for one.

Approaching the ward, I decide I'll go into the day room and see is there anyone there I can bum a cigarette from, have a smoke, and then just wait for the registrar to come to the ward and see me.

'Just going to get a cigarette,' I announce to the nurses after marching into their office. Then I head towards the day room.

'He's not allowed in there until he's been admitted,' I hear one of the nurses tell her male colleague. The male nurse persuades me to leave the day room and go back into the corridor. But soon I storm back into the nurses' office, demanding to be allowed to smoke.

'You have to wait for the psychiatrist to review you in A&E,' they tell me.

The office is small, and with me standing in it, fuming, facing down the three nurses there, it is suddenly very crowded. The need I have to smoke a cigarette is strong; I have to have my way, they have to let me, they will let me.

There's a scissors on a bureau near me, and I reach out and grab it, open it up and hold one of the blade edges to my wrist.

'You don't let me smoke, I'm going to slash my wrist,' I tell the nurses.

This is histrionics on my part; I have no intention of harming myself over a cigarette, but I hope it will force them to comply with my wishes.

Instead, a nurse triggers an emergency alarm, and when I lower the hand holding the scissors and just stand there with it limply, they become even more alarmed, because now it looks like the blade is pointing towards them and they think I am threatening them all directly.

No security guard turns up; so a nurse bolts past me out the door of the office and down the corridor towards the A&E. I just stand and watch him go, and the other nurses just stand and wait, watching also.

Now, finally, Security does turn up, and after a bit of nego-tiation I agree to surrender the scissors. One of the security guards, an older man, is particularly kind to me during this, and I grow tearful as he stands with me.

'All I wanted was a cigarette,' I tell him. He puts his arm around my shoulder.

'What brand do you normally smoke, son?' he asks gently.

'Camel Light,' I tell him.

'Camel Light?' he replies. 'Sure, that's shite.' He pulls out a pack of his own cigarettes from his pocket and offers one to me. 'How would you like a Major?'

I look at the pack, then up at him, stop crying, and smile.

'I'd kill for a fucking Major,' I tell him.

The security guard now brings me back to the A&E and then to a fire exit, where we stand outside and smoke for a while together. When I'm finished, placated and settled at last, he brings me to the registrar for my assessment.

We sit in a small office as she interviews me. I babble on and on about how I am feeling, the words pushing out of me: 'I can't sleep, I don't think I can manage, I've been driving around a lot in my father's car. I think I proposed to three women today. There's a friend of mine, an ex-girlfriend, and she has two daughters. One is seventeen. I'd like to go out with her. The other one is twenty-one. I'd like to go out with her, too. I want to be lean, fit and healthy. I want to eat properly. I need to be mellow, need to drink some booze and take a tranquillizer with it. That would do it. I was brushing my teeth today, and I was fucking agitated, I broke the edge of my fucking tooth. I had a dream about Dr Doran as well. It was an erotic dream. I think I'm in love with her. Do you think I should tell her? Do you think she feels the same way about me?'

The registrar, taking notes, struggles to keep up; I am talking too fast, jumping from one idea to the next.

'I need help,' I admit to him. 'I want to come into hospital. I can't manage my present condition on my own.'

He dispenses more medications to me there and then, and

slowly I calm down. It is decided that I will be admitted for observation; further, at the request of the staff, I'm to be allocated a Special Nurse to manage me.

There's the usual change into hospital pyjamas and registration of my property and clothes. As they take each item I make sure the nurses write down the exact monetary value of it; I'm pedantic and obsessive about this. Taking off my coat and handing it to the admitting nurse, I say: 'This is a Sisley coat. It's worth £130.' He writes this down. I continue, as I undress: 'Levi's trousers, £55. Reebok runners, £50. Socks, £12. My top is worth £55. My jumper cost £25. My Walkman was £15. My bumbag is worth £50. This is my hat, it's unique, it's a corduroy trilby, it can't be replaced, I'd say it's worth £1,000. My wallet is worth £250. Uh, my watch is a Seiko, about £125, I guess. And there's these three biros.' I pause, considering the disposable plastic pens I've brought with me. 'They're not worth much, really.'

In hospital I am restless and obsessive; I pace constantly around my room and move what few items of property I have with me from bed to locker to bed again, get out of my pyjamas and get dressed, then get out of my clothes and back into my pyjamas, dressing and undressing constantly.

I tell the nurses: 'I think there's some lady hiding in my wardrobe and under the bed.' I am prescribed a sedative to calm me.

The St Vincent's team want to get a second opinion on me, and are seeking a transfer to St John of God's, a dedicated psychiatric hospital nearby, as soon as a bed becomes free.

Eventually, a bed becomes available in St John of God's. My property is returned and the doctor explains that the other hospital has better facilities, that the treatment will be better. Quickly, by taxi, I am transferred.

By now I have become hopeful that St John of God's will indeed be better for me, might actually make me well at last. During my assessment interview I tell the doctor: 'I'm here for a second opinion.' When asked why, I reply: 'Because I'm elated.'

St John of God's carries associations for me. I attended primary school not far from here, and used to see denizens of the hospital on their day outings, conspicuous in the way they walked: hunched over, balled up, constricted, eyes down to the ground, visibly disturbed. We cruelly referred to these people as 'mentallers', though never to their faces or within earshot, as we were frightened of them.

Now I, too, am a mentaller.

On the ward, there is a jitteriness in my head, almost like a light bulb is too bright, making reading or watching TV for any length of time impossible. Mostly I just pace up and down the corridor. Sometimes I turn up music on the stereo in the TV lounge and dance, wildly, and the nurses try to calm me down.

When not pacing, I spend much time smoking in the room designated for this; and in the small box room in the far corner of the ward, the one with the high-up window, where, with several other patients, most of whom are younger than I am, we sit and listen to the Beatles' *White Album*, over and over again.

The dining area is huge, with long, communal tables. The patients are observed closely as we eat. One table is designated for those with eating disorders. These patients receive extra-large portions of food. Late at night they can be seen pacing fast up and down the corridors, trying to burn calories, the calories they have been forced to consume during the day. They are weighed regularly, and if they don't make their target weight they are kicked off the programme.

The nurse doesn't appear to believe me when I tell her I've got films in pre-production and I've written a play; she thinks this is all a fantasy in my head. When asked how I am feeling, I say: 'I'm manic. My thoughts are racing, I can't concentrate. I'm distracted and feel irritated by everything.'

The food in the hospital is a problem for me: I find I can't eat it, and I'm worried that I've lost lots of weight and will lose more if I'm not able to eat properly. So I write a list of dietary demands, which I give to the nurse to pass on to the catering staff:

17.02.99

Arnold Fanning: Requested Specialist Diet

1. Breakfast: Okay as is.
2. 'Midday' meal: Brown bread (as is) + cheese.
   Real not processed cheese,
   e.g. cheddar
   Old Dubliner
   Cracker Barrel
   Philadelphia
   Cheshire
   Leicester
   Etc
3. '6pm meal' – pasta and spinach.
   + parmesan and olive oil.
   Boil-cook spaghetti no longer than 5 mins
   Or
   Rice with parsley and pulses mixed
   E.g. red Kidney beans
   Chickpeas
   (Both cook as recommended.)

This missive has no effect; the hospital food continues as normal.

I ask my father to bring me things to make me feel more at home: my stereo and CDs, books, my guitar. The room I'm in begins to resemble my bedroom in my father's house.

Cathy is another guitar player, and we become friends. We talk a lot about our problems, our treatments. She tells me about the programme she is on for her anorexia; she wants to get well and frets about not meeting her target. Her guitar-playing is very fine, and she sings very beautifully. We spend many hours on the corridors and in annexes, singing and playing guitar together, and she teaches me some new songs.

On impulse, using a safety razor, I manage to shave the hair off my head. When the doctor sees me, she is shocked by my appearance: tufts of hair still remain here and there, while other parts are shaved close to the skull. It's a mess; I look frightful. She directs me to the hospital hairdresser, where I am given a neat shave by the barber.

When Cathy next sees me, she likes the style a lot, and the next day she goes to the hairdresser and gets her own head shaved, making her look even more tiny than before. No hips or breasts are visible, and with the cropped haircut she has become totally androgynous. Now we look like twins.

Cathy has her own room in one of the endless corridors, and when I am allowed off-ward by myself I spend time there alone with her. We seem to be able to wander through the hospital together at our whim: the nurses leave us alone and do not mind where we go, as long as we are back on the ward for meals and meds. We go to the public café; we go to the chapel and pray or meditate; we go to the other wards, where there are other guitar players, and play guitar and sing; and then we invariably end up alone, talking in her room.

There we strip down to our underwear and give each other massages. Sitting astride her, I gently stroke her naked back. She really is a tiny thing, barely there at all. These massages are not erotic; we truly are twins, we feel no desire towards each other whatsoever.

My father visits and we sit in the ground-floor café. He tells me he has traded in his old car for a new one. This makes me a little sad and nostalgic; I realize I miss the old Ford Sierra already, the one I drove through the North. Now he has a red Ford Fiesta, which doesn't appeal to me at all.

I get a visit from an old family friend, Donal. He has known me since I was born. When I am well enough to get day leave from the hospital, he brings me out to a nearby hotel for pints or tea. During these excursions I smoke heavily, nervous, fidgety. He does not approve, remembers me as a fit and healthy teenager who he brought hiking in Wicklow.

'I understand why you do it, though,' he tells me, referring to the chain smoking; to me it is simply an essential, something to help me with the endless anxiety I feel, the jitteriness, the unease. It seems unfathomable that I will ever return to hiking, as we did before, walking for long hours across the mountains.

When Donal leaves me back at the hospital, he always tells me exactly when he will be back for his next visit, and he is always true to his word. I come to rely on these excursions in the company of this gentle, supportive, non-judgemental person. I look forward to them and appreciate knowing when the next one will be.

The social workers and occupational therapists organize social outings for the patients. Beforehand in the day room there is a desultory routine whereby – at the prompting of the stern, humourless social worker – we decide as a group what the activity is to be. None of us really feels very social; most of us would rather just be left to our own devices. But the social worker will not let us be and demands we offer a suggestion. It has the vague air of the punitive about it, and of forced jollity.

So we make the same suggestions that no doubt countless previous groups have made before: go to the cinema, go for coffee, go bowling. We are encouraged to debate these options, so as to demonstrate we are interacting: this is what the social worker wants. But none of us really cares; we will say and do anything to get the social worker to stop haranguing us.

We walk in a tightly formed group, shuffling, hunched, over-medicated: mentallers. Thrust out into public view with this group that broadcasts its status for all to see, I burn with shame. When the social is over I am glad to return to the hospital, feeling safe, secure, not noticeable.

Relaxation sessions in the day hospital: we lie in a large room on mats on the floor and a cassette is played, usually a spoken-word meditation. Invariably, I fall asleep during these sessions; it is as if I am catching up on the rest I need. At the end of the session the OT gently rocks my shoulder to wake me. Groggy, I get up and return to my ward.

At night, though, I find it hard to sleep. Often I lie in bed, propped up on my pillows, my mind full of thoughts, feeling fresh and alert at four in the morning. The nurses, doing their rounds, come into the darkened room with torches which they shine on the faces of the patients to see if they are asleep. When they get to me, they see me sitting up awake, eyes shining back at them.

'Go to sleep,' they admonish; eventually I do.

*

I decide I need a good wash. Seeking out a nurse, I tell her of my intention to have a bath.

'Aqua-therapy!' she beams. In the bathroom, lying in the water, I am alone. It is the only period of solitude I have had, apart from being on the toilet, since being admitted to hospital; everything else takes place with the others, and under the observation of the nurses.

When my mood swings for the worse and the nurses want to observe me more closely, I get transferred to different wards, different rooms. Every time I move, all my belongings get shoved into black bin bags and lugged down corridors to yet another ward or section of the hospital. Then comes the unpacking and resettling of all my things in the new room. The moves agitate and disturb me.

I tell the nurses about my mother's death and how that still upsets me all these years later. The nurses listen as I admit to fantasizing about suicide; but when they press me on this I deny I will actually act on these fantasies. Sitting in the main corridor on the ground floor of the hospital, I tell the other patients when they pass me by that I am in need of help, that I feel confused. A nurse approaches me after a while of this and asks me what is wrong. Sheepishly, I change tack: 'I just need attention,' I tell her.

There's a patient on the ward, a thin, balding man who has an eight-year-old son. This boy is left to wander the ward alone when the patient's family come and visit him. The boy irritates me, intrudes upon me, and I reprimand him for this.

He turns to me in the corridor and says solemnly: 'Fuck off.'

Rage surges through me; I want to punish the boy, but I can do nothing, not even shout at him, because the nurses are nearby and I am under observation. Seething with frustration, I turn away and go back to my room.

*

After six weeks of medications, observation, occupational therapy, day leave and even some overnight leave, it is decided I am in good enough form to be discharged. The intention now is that I continue to attend the day hospital for OT and observation as an out-patient. All my belongings are packed into black plastic bin bags. I bring them down to my father's red Ford Fiesta in the car-park, and then he drives me home.

Two days later, after finishing a session of relaxation during OT at the day hospital, walking back through the visitors' café, I see the eight-year-old boy who told me to fuck off just a few days before. The rage and frustration I felt when he insulted me suddenly resurfaces. Quickly crossing the café to where he stands – as usual, unsupervised – I confront him, full of pent-up fury, and strike him once across the ear.

As soon as the blow lands I regret it; and just as immediately there is a flurry of activity. His parents now appear; the patient, his father, is angry. There is talk of calling the Guards and pressing charges against me. A moment before, I had been just a few yards from the exit, about to go home. Now I am put in an office, where a psychiatrist will decide if I am to be readmitted to hospital or, conversely, left to my own devices to deal with the child's furious parents and a possible arrest.

Pacing back and forth in the office as the doctor tries to assess me, I acknowledge the wrong I've done. 'I'm sorry for what I did,' I assure him. 'I'm just feeling on edge and I haven't really been sleeping well.'

The doctor decides it is best for me to return to the hospital as an in-patient. Two days after being discharged from a six-week-long hospitalization, I am admitted to hospital once again.

*

I slip into the hospital routine once more, and my father is eventually allowed to take me on an accompanied outing to the city centre. Leaving him to browse in a bookstore, I wander off for a while by myself, enjoying the normality of being in town alone at last, and on a whim go and consult with a psychic in a basement room, have my Tarot read. The psychic tells me I will remain in hospital for a long period of time.

On the way out, ascending to the street, I see that above the psychic's room is a body-piercing parlour. On impulse I go in and, excruciatingly, have my right nipple pierced. Afterwards I drink a whiskey straight in a nearby pub to recover, put on my Walkman headphones and return to the bookstore. Drowning out the sound of the world with music, brooding on what the psychic has told me, I don't notice my father's anger at being kept waiting so long.

'Take those stupid things off,' he snaps at me, indicating the headphones; I ignore him, and we return, without speaking, to the hospital once more.

In the dining hall I cause difficulties, argue with a caterer over my food. The next meal time, I am prohibited from going to the food hall.

'You have to eat your meals in your room for a while,' I am told. Now my meals are brought to me, and I eat in bed.

With more time in this room alone I find the opportunity and peace to start writing again; I start to write a screenplay, a fictionalized version of my breakdown the previous year.

The doctor comes to assess me, asks how I am feeling:
  'I'm feeling high.'
  'How high?'
  'How high is a piece of string?'

'What do you do when you get high?'

'I like to listen to music, to talk to people, I like to go shopping, I like to go swimming, I like to wear nice clothes, I like to have sex with beautiful women.'

He is unfazed by all of this; then I pull up my top and show him the nipple piercing I got in the city and say, 'A psychic told me I'd be here for six more weeks.' Then: 'The PA system in here irritates me.' This jumble of disconnected thoughts and associations makes sense to me; to the doctor it means I need further stabilization with antipsychotics.

One youth hangs around with me frequently. He tells me it is easy to get hash and other drugs in the hospital, or nearby in Stillorgan. We talk about keeping fit, about the best way to build muscle quickly, and I demonstrate some exercises to him. He immediately gets down on the floor and does a few dozen vigorous reps. He is full of energy, hyperactive. Later I come into the room where we sleep; he has a girl with him. They have drawn the curtains around the bed and are fucking with the same vigour he applied to his press-ups. The nurses don't notice; it's over quickly enough, the curtains are drawn back, and when nurses finally do appear everything is back to normal.

My doctor checks in with me during her rounds and I tell her that I like it in the hospital and that I don't want to leave.

'I know,' she replies, regarding me, apparently, with regret. 'You're becoming institutionalized.' In response, I smile, thinking nothing of this; to me there is nothing wrong with staying on in the hospital.

One patient meets me every day in the corridor of the ward we sleep in. He tells me, every day, that he was raped the previous night, that he is raped every night. It is unclear is he being raped by staff or patients or outsiders; his speech is rambling, fragmented, sometimes incoherent. Nonetheless, I listen to him, and he seems to get something from these encounters.

My ex-girlfriend Serena, who works in a bookshop in Stillorgan, brings me a beautiful large-format illustrated history of art. But when I go to look for it later in my room I can't find it; then I see that another patient in my room, a man my own age, is holding the book. He is using it as a hard surface upon which to write a letter as he sits up in bed. Angrily I pull the book off him and examine it: the cover is scored with marks where the pen has pressed through the paper he was writing on.

'Don't take my stuff again,' I tell him.

Lithe and agile and energized, he jumps off the bed and shoves me hard in the chest, causing me to stumble back, shocked: he is seething with fury.

My agitation over this roommate lingers, and so I am moved to another room. There I write a short letter and give it to the nurses, to be passed on to the Guards:

Dear Garda:

I am a patient also. I was *assaulted* by thrust of two hands by a patient of a —
  He also threatened me, saying, 'I will — you.'
  He also made a malicious call to me:
  'I am coming to get you.'
  Arnold Fanning
  St John Of God.

A young man sits in the day room. He wears a protective plastic face mask, a dressing, which nurses assist him with in replacing frequently. Under the mask his face is mutilated, ravaged by fire. It is unclear if he set himself alight when depressed or if he is the victim of an accident and now depressed by his disfigurement. His hands are damaged also, fingers fused together. The only parts of him that seem to have escaped the fire are his eyes and his teeth; indeed, his teeth look shockingly bright. He notices me at times staring at those teeth, as if to avoid looking at the mutilation.

He approaches me. 'I think you want to talk to me,' he says.

It is true, I do wish to talk to him, and we become friends.

Concentration improving, I begin to express a desire to be discharged and to do something interesting and useful. I go for the first session of group therapy, sit and study the list of rules:

1. Punctuality is required by all who attend the group.
2. Smoking is not allowed during the group session.
3. Admission to the group is on the understanding that all members will make a contribution to the session.
4. Sexual relationships are not permitted between group members.
5. Matters mentioned in the group are strictly confidential and are not to be discussed with non-members.
6. Members must not leave the group.
7. A direct question must not be addressed to the therapist.

A patient I had been talking with quite often has now been discharged, and I think of phoning her; it occurs to me that we could remain friends outside the hospital. She has left me her phone number, a landline, and when I call it a man answers.

'Who is this?' he wants to know, and when I tell him he asks: 'How do you know her?'

He listens as I explain how his wife and I were fellow

patients in St John of God's. Then he tells me not to phone again and hangs up.

Finally, my mood becomes stable and I am discharged, to continue my care as an out-patient. Again my belongings are packed into black plastic bin bags, and my father drives me home in the red Ford Fiesta. Home once more is his small house in the quiet estate in the suburb near the sea; home, after three months away.

6. 'A More Arnoldy Arnold'

Summer, 2000, over a year since my discharge from St John of God's. In that time I've completed a rehabilitative course for people in recovery from the effects of acute mental illness; I've started making videos as part of a community employment scheme; I've been playing tennis with Cathy, who has also been discharged; and I've been swimming, often, at Killiney beach. I've also finally arranged to go to the artists' residency in Virginia in August.

But life feels curiously flat: it is as if I am not fully experiencing it, like I am trapped in a bubble, separated from the world. I don't feel depressed, but I sense something is wrong with me, profoundly wrong, and yet I can't quite understand what it is. I just don't feel fully *real*.

Before the invisible walls of the bubble descended, I completed my screenplay about my breakdown and gave it to a producer. She in turn has given it to a film director, Jer, who likes it. Jer and I meet often in a pub in Kilmainham and talk about our plans for the film, potential producers and funding opportunities, all over pints of Guinness and long, competitive games of chess. He nearly always wins.

Cathy and I discuss the flat feeling I am experiencing, the feeling of not wanting to do anything, not being able to write, the feeling of being in a bubble. More and more, I wonder is it the medications that are doing this to me. Cathy tells me about a private therapeutic practice on the southside that takes a more patient-centred approach to psychiatry and where there is less emphasis on medications. Cathy thinks they can help me.

After much procrastination I begin to attend counselling sessions there with Alfred, a middle-aged, Mitteleuropean psychoanalyst. The sessions do not go well: I find it hard to open up and express myself. Exasperated with my lack of progress, the analyst steers me to his colleague, Dr Kirby.

On the registration form that I fill in when I consult with Dr Kirby, I declare that I have 'manic depression' and list all the medications I am currently on: Lamictal, an anticonvulsant; Serenace, an antipsychotic; Stilnoct, a sleeping pill; and Cogentin, a medication to help with the side-effects of all the other medications.

Dr Kirby listens intently as I recount my personal history and the events leading up to my breakdown in Annaghmakerrig. He says he's seen it all before: people who had no history of mania before going manic on antidepressants.

He suggests I stop the antipsychotic, the sleeping tablet and the side-effect medication, and reduce the dose of the anticonvulsant, as I might go high if I discontinued it completely. Hearing his take on my illness and on the medication affects me profoundly: it seems to fit exactly with my experience: the pounding heart and the rushing euphoria I felt after resuming the course of antidepressants while in the residency. It is, also, what I want to hear: I am not bipolar; it is the medications that are making me unwell. Talking to Dr Kirby confirms a suspicion that I do not need to be on meds and that the feeling of being in a bubble is caused by them.

In August I arrive at the Virginia Centre for the Creative Arts, a small artists' colony attached to a university campus. I am full of aspirations to write again.

But I can't write. Since finishing my screenplay I haven't had any new ideas, and now, sitting every day in my over-air-conditioned and sterile studio, I face a blank page and cannot fill it. My mind is simply not functioning properly, and creativity is impossible.

To try to stimulate something in my mind, I go on long walks around the grounds and the surrounding area and try writing in different places, but nothing works; the pages remain blank.

I'm sitting out on the lawn, chatting to other residents, when a woman arrives: thin, sallow, raven-haired, angular, pretty. She observes an artist she is friendly with lolling on the grass nearby, half asleep.

'I'm going to poke her with a stick to let her know I'm here,' she announces, and goes over to do just that. This makes me smile.

Her name is Jennifer, she is my age, a painter and art teacher, a New Yorker, Jewish, and full of electric energy. We end up talking together often – on trips to the supermarket for ice-cream or beer, on walks around the residency, at the pool, at meals. With other residents we walk down country lanes, long, rambling walks full of talk of art and writing. At the side of the road, goats graze in scrubby fields. One goat has its horns caught in the wire fencing. Thinking little of it, I go down the bankside to the fence and gently release the goat. It waits patiently as I do so, then runs off to join its companions. When I turn back to walk up the bank I see Jennifer has been watching me execute this release and is smiling.

On a darkening evening, walking alone, we go down the driveway away from where the other residents usually walk; the air seems hotter than ever, the humidity pressing down from thick, purpling clouds overhead. We have come this way deliberately, to avoid the dogs that have been disturbing our walks on the roads that pass houses and farms on the other side of the residency. But we are aware, too, of our separation now from the others. 'I'm sorry you're not able to write,' she tells me.

We talk, at ease, and she is a kind and sympathetic listener. I find I am not ashamed to tell her parts of my story: my unemployment, and living in my father's house. It feels as though she does not judge me for these things. She notices that I repeat myself often, forget what I have already said. Finally, and not unkindly, she says: 'No offence, but you have a really bad memory.'

This makes me stop walking and consider. It is true. My memory seems impaired; I put it down to my brain being wounded, damaged at some level. Or it could be caused by the meds, another side-effect. Either way, Jennifer deserves an explanation, so now I take a risk and tell her about the breakdowns, the medications, the hospitalizations, the fear I have that my brain is irretrievably altered or damaged by the trauma it has been subjected to and endured and the medications inflicted upon it.

Jennifer listens patiently. She does not, on hearing these things, appear frightened of me, nor disgusted, nor embarrassed. She does not judge, and she does not make me feel inadequate or ashamed; instead, when I have finished my account, she asks gently and warmly: 'Can I give you a hug?'

To this I nod.

Jennifer hugs me, pressing her body to mine, tight. At first I am still and awkward, resisting intimacy. Then I relax, and allow myself to be hugged, and hug her back. It feels like the first time in a long time that I have been accepted by another for who I am.

She leans back and looks at me. We are still holding one another, and now we move closer again and kiss. We kiss for a long time. Then, as if on cue, there is a flash of lightning overhead, a cymbal crash of thunder nearby, and the rain that has been threatening so long is suddenly unleashed and gushes hotly from the skies above us and engulfs us.

Jennifer laughs, kisses me one more time in the rain then grabs my hand and pulls me. We run quickly back to the residency through the downpour, laughing and kissing all the way, and tumble in the door, giggling. Another resident is incredulous at the sight of us, soaked to the skin as we arrive, but still laughing at our state, delighted to be so, together, holding hands.

'Do you want to come to my room and make out?' asks Jennifer. With that, we become lovers. ✗

All this time, I have been following a schedule of reducing the dosage of my meds. But the inability to write, the poor memory, the lingering sense of not being connected to the world – all these things continue to frustrate me, so I abandon the schedule and simply stop taking all the meds completely. The fact that I have experienced neither mania nor depression while reducing the meds has reassured me that it is safe to do so; also, I think it is worth the risk, as I will return to Ireland and see Dr Kirby shortly. I hope now to be restored to myself completely, and quickly.

After the residency is finished, Jennifer and I rent a car, pile all the paintings she has completed during her stay into the trunk and drive together to New York. We spend the few days before my flight home in her apartment on Canal Street. It is a large, converted industrial space, a third-storey loft that she is subletting from friends who've moved to the Midwest. We don't socialize with her friends or family; after all, we are not making any plans for the future and we assume that this has merely been a summer affair.

Back to my father's house, back to unemployment and no sense of direction in my life, no motivation. The excitement of the brief happiness I felt in Jennifer's company is replaced by apathy.

I tell Dr Kirby about my summer and my decision to come off the meds completely; I feel I have done the right thing because I am neither manic nor depressed, but I tell him also that I don't know what to do next and feel unmotivated in life. Dr Kirby suggests that I should return to the States, to reconnect with Jennifer and to find work. 'You could probably get a job teaching English to Spanish-speaking people,' he says.

I explain I don't feel confident enough to teach.

'Stop living the life of a sick person,' he admonishes me. 'Stop living the life of a psychiatric patient. Embrace an active life and see yourself as a healthy person.'

But it seems impossible: I think of myself now as damaged, irreparably.

Once the meds have finally left my bloodstream, there are withdrawal symptoms, feelings of anxiety, being spacy, and cravings for the meds themselves. This makes me feel that I'll never leave the effects of mental illness behind me.

It seems I am not eligible for any kind of visa that would allow me to live and work in the States. This disheartens me, and when I return to Dr Kirby I am in a low mood. He suggests I try a new class of antidepressant, for a short while, to get me over the bump of coming off the meds so quickly. There is a risk of me going high on the drug, so he will monitor me while I'm on it. Dr Kirby also suggests I look into doing a course in back-to-work skills, and that I should move out of my father's house as soon as possible. 'Your father is also sitting around all day doing nothing, and this can only have a depressing effect on you,' he says.

What he says is true: I need to act, to move, to do something to change my life. But I can't figure out what is to be the first step, with no job, no way of affording my own place to live, no real plan or idea for the future.

I am drifting, drifting, drifting; and then Jennifer phones me. 'Hi!' she cries out, and that happy greeting fills me with joy, happiness at hearing her voice again.

She is phoning from her parents' weekend house in Long Island, and I can hear the smile in her voice. Her sister is there, too, and her nephews; there is a lot of noise in the background, so she has to shout to be heard. Her voice sounds bright, happy, energetic, and I realize I am delighted she has phoned. I had been forcibly pushing her out of my mind, thinking a further relationship was impossible, instead of exploring my feelings for her fully. Now she suggests that she come to Ireland to visit me. Breathless with excitement, we arrange her trip there and then.

Jennifer arrives a few weeks later, in mid-autumn. We go to Kerry, where I have borrowed a relative's house near Annascaul for a few days. Then we drive back to Dublin, and as a surprise I treat us to a weekend in Paris. There we attend a retrospective of her favourite artist, Philip Guston. The trip goes well, and I begin to sense that something is stirring in me: a return to life, to connection with the world. We don't yet talk about long-term plans, but we agree that I will travel to visit her in New York, somehow.

In the meantime we talk regularly on the phone, we email and we write long letters; hers are always illustrated with a small flower motif, mine with a symbol that involves a smiley face with a shamrock protruding from its head. Our conversations are long and intimate; slowly, we are falling in love.

Now, I feel energized, alive, more connected to myself and to others. It was, I conclude, the medications that were causing all the absences and disconnections in my life. I see no further need to take the antidepressant Dr Kirby suggested; now, I am finally off medications completely.

On my media course I write and direct a short film. It is crude and amateurish, but is the first creative endeavour I have completed in a long time. Thinking of ways to get back to a more active participation in life, I start volunteering with a service for the blind, recording audio books, and I complete a course in arts facilitation for people with disabilities.

There is now a sense of readiness, and of feeling able, competent. As a way of spending time with Jennifer, I intern on a film festival in New York and get funding to cover my costs for the trip. She in turn visits me again, and we travel to the Aran Islands together. There I feel vibrant and alive, cycling in the rain to the ancient sites between drystone walls, feeling genuine happiness for the first time in years.

When Jennifer returns to New York I tell her over the phone how I feel more vital, spirited, connected, more like *me*, since coming off the meds. She considers this a moment then exclaims:

'A more Arnoldy Arnold!'

This makes me smile. 'That's it exactly.'

All the travelling back and forth, the distance between us, begins to grate.

'You better get your ass over here soon,' she tells me.

'I want to.'

'I mean it. I'm not sure I can do this long-distance thing any more.'

'Me neither.'

'You're going to need money to get started over here. New York City is expensive.'

Knowing I couldn't take the stress of working on a film or theatre production yet, I end up in two casual jobs. I work mid-week in a bookie's office, taking small bets off mainly unemployed men in a working-class district near my father's house, feeling vaguely guilty for doing so; weekends I spend waiting tables in a golf club in County Wicklow, where I am always surprised that the well-heeled clientele don't leave better tips.

In this way I quickly build up savings to fund my trip to the States.

In the middle of the summer, Jennifer and I take a holiday in Italy. We travel to the village of Manarola, part of the Cinque Terre on the coast of the Ligurian Sea. We rent a small apartment up a steep hill off a narrow street. By day we swim in the coves and walk the cliff routes, and in the evenings we search out restaurants to eat seafood. There are arguments, too, and a huge row, a row about nothing, about whether to have breakfast or lunch after getting up late. Exasperated, I leave Jennifer sitting in the restaurant we are arguing in and return a little while later to find her still fuming; this argument takes several hours to recover from.

Later we make love in the apartment before going out to dinner. The daylight is fading, an early hint of autumn. The shutters are open and a surprisingly cool breeze blows into the room and across our naked bodies. The dark and the cold make me feel surprisingly alone, even as I am embracing the one I love, and I feel doubt suddenly over committing to the move to America, a remnant of the argument earlier.

That evening, as we walk back to the apartment after dinner, skirting the cliffs as the sun sets red over the still sea, I regain my equilibrium, my certainty that what I am doing is right.

By the end of the summer, when I have saved enough, I book my flight to New York. In order to look convincing to the immigration authorities, I buy a return flight and get letters from my Irish employers stating I am in employment and on holiday. My real intention is to stay on indefinitely, and to work.

In September, with my backpack and guitar and a few notebooks, I board my flight and take off for New York, feeling mentally well at last and ready to start a new life.

PART II

7. The Ocean

A couple of hours before we are due to touch down in New York, the pilot of the plane comes on over the intercom and says: 'Due to terrorist activity in New York City, this flight is being diverted to Gander International Airport, Newfoundland. North American airspace is now closed.'

There is an audible intake of breath in the cabin, followed by an urgent whispered chatter. No one knows what is going on.

The plane taxis to a parking spot in Gander, now only occasionally used as a refuelling stop. Looking out the cabin window, I see dozens of other planes parked on the runway, and more descending to land.

'Okay, folks, we have to wait a while to get you off the plane,' the pilot informs us wearily over the intercom. 'We need to wait until a boarding ramp becomes available.'

We wait for hours. Some of the passengers have cell phones and radios, and news begins to trickle in. I think of Jennifer on Canal Street.

With other passengers, I queue to borrow a phone. When my turn comes, I can get through to no one I know in New York: not Jennifer, nor her sister, nor her parents or friends.

There's a sudden silence in the cabin, a change in the quality of the sound, and everyone freezes, sensing something is wrong and dreading what could follow. But it is just the air-conditioning being turned off; the doors are open and we can finally disembark.

We are taken to a community centre in Gander. Local

residents have brought bedding and food for us; there will be no flights leaving Newfoundland for at least five days. Even then, we won't be flying to New York, but back to Ireland. There, we will have to rebook our flights back to the States, and I will have to go through immigration clearance again. The letters from my employers stating I will be returning to work will be perilously close to being out of date by the time this is all sorted out.

Fixed on a wall above us is a TV showing the scene from Manhattan over and over again: two planes crashing into the Twin Towers and their subsequent collapse. No matter how often we see it, it is difficult to stop watching.

I join the queue for the payphones, and manage to get through to Jennifer. Relief floods through me as I hear that she, her family and her friends are all well. I explain my situation with the flights, and the need to go through US immigration again if I fly back to Dublin. 'But it's okay,' I tell her. 'I've decided to make my own way down to you.'

'How?'

'There's a ferry I can get from Port aux Basques to Nova Scotia, and then I can take trains down to New York.'

'Are you sure you want to come?' she asks me.

'What do you mean?'

'Are you sure you want to come to New York now, when all this is going on? It's so fucked up.'

Exhausted and stressed, I hear this as a rejection of me, but I am determined to keep going with my plan to see Jennifer; it is imperative that I be with her, after all this effort and all the planning we've done.

'I'm sure,' I tell her.

We make arrangements. Jennifer is going out to her parents' weekend house; I will travel first to Montreal, where I can stay with some of her friends and get some rest. Then

I will go to New Haven, where Jennifer will meet me, and we'll get a ferry across to Long Island.

Our luggage is not brought to us; passengers will have to retrieve it on their return to Dublin. But I'm not going to Dublin, and I feel a twinge of sadness over losing my guitar, which I've owned for thirteen years.

I leave the community centre, cross the road to a shop and buy a pack of cigarettes. I haven't smoked in more than a year, but I am getting increasingly anxious and edgy and feel a cigarette would help. After a few I calm down; then I eat, and then I hitch a ride to Port aux Basques. The driver tells me about local life, hunting and fishing.

'What do you hunt?' I ask him.

'Moose,' he replies. 'Mainly moose.'

We drive on, for hours, across the island. Then I cross the sound on the ferry to the mainland. It's a seven-hour crossing, and I'm tired from the journey so far, but I stay up, watching the sea as we travel. On the mainland I catch a train, and then another. I lose all sense of time and distance on this long trip, and am anxious over missing connections or getting lost, so I don't sleep. Nor do I stop anywhere to rest up but just keep moving, through the night when necessary. The important thing is to keep moving.

A fellow passenger lends me a cell phone, and I call Jennifer at her parents' house to update her; I also talk to her father, Bob, who is concerned for me. But I am more concerned about him, with his job in midtown Manhattan. I tell him not to go back there: 'Everyone knows there's going to be a second strike!' When I hand the phone back to its owner she looks at me in shock.

My train finally arrives in Montreal; it is early morning, what seems like several days after arriving in Gander. Immediately outside the train station I see a scrawl of graffiti on a wall: 'The Capitalists got what they deserved.'

In my exhausted state, the words affect me deeply, and in front of the graffiti I begin abruptly to cry.

Jennifer's friends are hospitable and friendly to me, a stranger, arriving in their midst. They bring me to a museum and to dinner, and to do practical things like buy clothes to replace the ones left behind with my luggage in Gander.

The next morning, after a much-needed night's sleep, one of my hosts checks in with me as I wake and tells me he is going out to shoot.

'Oh,' I say drowsily. 'Moose?'

He looks puzzled, and I remember he told me he's a filmmaker.

Once I've caught up on sleep, I set off again, by train, from Montreal. At the US border there is closer scrutiny of my credentials, but everything is in order and my passport was stamped in Dublin, so I am allowed through.

It's peaceful in the small town-centre park in New Haven where I meet Jennifer; we hold each other, sitting on the grass, and kiss, and reassure each other that everything is going to be all right.

On the ferry to Long Island, the tiredness catches up with me again. I am fractious, irritable, argumentative. I remember what Jennifer said to me on the phone when I called her from Gander, and bellow to her over the sound of the ferry engine: 'So, you didn't want me to come to New York?'

'I just wanted to make sure you knew what you were getting yourself into,' she replies, shouting also to be heard.

But the fury I feel continues as we travel on across the sound, and I don't let up, needling her until she grows exasperated and then angry with me. She and I are still fuming when we arrive at her parents' house in the Hamptons. Her father, sensing something amiss, asks: 'Are you sleep-deprived?'

His words frighten me: I think of what sleep-deprivation has meant in the past, what it has led to, what it has done to me. It makes me reflect on my behaviour of the last few days, the babbling talk, the tearfulness, the irritability with Jennifer; now I feel suddenly worried I may be going manic. Then I dismiss the thought: I am not bipolar; it was the antidepressants that made me high in the past.

'Yeah,' I say to him, 'I'm sleep-deprived.'

There is rest then, proper rest, in a cosy bedroom upstairs in this wooden house not far from the sea. Jennifer is with me, and we make up after our argument, and she convinces me, now I am calmer, that she does indeed want me to be here in New York, and to stay with her in Manhattan.

The next day we all go to Amagansett beach, a short walk from the house. Jennifer watches as I head for the water, thrust myself through the crashing waves and then strike off, swimming into deeper water. The foaming water cleanses and energizes me after days of cooped-up travel, and as I come out of the water the sun beats down on my bare skin. I walk up the beach to where Jennifer stands waiting for me. She hands me a towel and I dry off, turn back and look at the beautiful ocean. I am grinning.

'I've never seen anyone so happy,' she declares.

It is true: at this moment I am the happiest I have ever been in my life. Fit, healthy, swimming in a beautiful place, in love with and loved by a beautiful and creative woman. I turn and stare at the ocean. I feel calm. I am well now.

8. The City

Jennifer wakes me in the middle of the night.

'I had a nightmare,' she tells me, crying. 'You were back in hospital.'

It is a deep-rooted fear in her: that my madness will return.

We're in Jennifer's loft apartment on Canal Street, near the East River. It's autumn now, and I'm finding my way in the city.

I manage to get various odd jobs: walking dogs for their owners, moving furniture, catering. Jennifer puts me in contact with Leonora, a woman who runs an artists' studio downtown, where I get regular and well-paid employment as an artist's model.

Every three months or so, when my holiday permit expires, I cross the border to Canada and re-enter, to get my passport stamped with a new date. Jennifer's father is a lawyer, and contacts of his help me to secure an O1 Artist Visa. It doesn't make it any easier for me to get a job, as the only income I can declare to the authorities is that which comes from my writing, but it does mean I can legally reside in the States for three years, set up a bank account and generally feel more secure.

Bob then helps me get a steady part-time job in a private security and investigation firm in the financial district. They will pay me a weekly wage out of the petty cash. This is a real help, but Jennifer and I still talk about the visa situation often, the limited work available to me on it, how I am still working illegally. I suggest to Jennifer that to get a Green Card, I could marry a friend of hers, who is gay, for convenience.

'If you're going to marry anyone, it's going to be me,' she replies. It is meant as a joke, but the topic of a permanent future together, of marriage, has been broached. Now we talk of marriage more frequently, and not always in jest.

Walking the beach at Amagansett, Jennifer and I decide that as we both love the ocean, we would like to get married facing it. I want to be with her all my life to come, and raise a family with her. We will be happy, I have no doubt.

Life in New York is good. There are literary readings in bars and cafés, and bookshops like The Strand and St Mark's, where I buy US editions of books I couldn't find back home. On weekends, Jennifer and I cycle to Brooklyn – I've bought a second-hand bike – and we have brunch, go to gigs in quirky bars. I've joined a YMCA with a gym and pool, and I go there three or four times a week, swimming a thousand metres every session, getting strong again. Jennifer and I cook for each other with ingredients we buy in Chinatown. She spends most of her time in her studio in a collective in the East Village; I like to go there and watch her work on her large abstract paintings. She has a show, too, a solo show, in a good gallery downtown; after the opening we celebrate with a dinner with her friends and family, splurging on an expensive meal.

Jennifer's parents frequently take us out to dinner, then a Broadway show, then dessert or drinks afterwards. Many weekends we go to their house in the Hamptons, walking the beach at Amagansett, enjoying the fresh air and views of the ocean.

I make new friends in New York, and have a social life apart from Jennifer. There's Jim, a short-story writer, a gay man about my age, who lives in a tiny apartment uptown and works in admin in a hospital. Rick, who is a little older, is caught up in a complex relationship with a woman in her seventies. He and I go to bars and talk about sex and relationships all night. Outside the Irish Arts Centre on the Upper West Side, where I get occasional work in the bar, I meet Phil, an Irish actor, and I spend a lot of time listening to his dreams of making it big in America.

Wanting to be more creative, to get my ideas flowing, I join the Barrow Group theatre company and participate in their six-week acting course. When they learn of my production experience they hire me to stage-manage a one-man show they are producing. In a small venue uptown I operate the lights and sound during performances, and the actor pays me a hundred dollars cash in hand each time. It's a good show, and it feels gratifying to be finally back and working in a world I know and love.

Now I start writing in earnest again, working on two new plays. *Those Powerful Machines*, meanwhile, is workshopped in a playwriting group uptown, then given a public reading at the Barrow Group's theatre space in the Meatpacking District. The Irish Arts Centre takes an interest in the play; it goes through a period of development and workshopping there, and I rewrite it further in anticipation of production. Finally, I am getting my creative life back on track.

There's another change in me: the anger is gone. At work I get on with my colleagues and am invariably polite and good-natured; I'm patient during commutes, while waiting in queues, doing errands. And I no longer get angry with myself – no longer hit myself on the head as I used to do, nor call myself names when I make mistakes or do something wrong. I feel calmer and, seemingly, a better person than before.

Except when I row with Jennifer. Then, the old rage comes boiling up and erupts out of me once more.

There are many triggers for our arguments. Since 9/11 Jennifer has become more interested in political activism, and now when she returns to the apartment at night it is often after some meeting that has got her riled up. She sometimes does not know what to do with the anger she feels; it spills over and becomes directed at me.

She accuses me of being a racist, and nothing I can do or say can persuade her otherwise.

'You should do an antiracism workshop,' she tells me.

'I don't have a racist bone in my body,' I reply.

'Everyone is racist. I did a racism workshop and I found out a lot of stuff about myself. You should do one, too.'

This exasperates and irritates me, and all the anger I felt in my twenties comes flooding back and I unleash it upon her. We end up roaring at each other and hurling objects around the apartment.

'Fine!' she invariably screams at me, red-faced, furious, when things reach this stage. 'Let's break up.'

It takes days to make up after these rows. There will be wary, moody silences, I'll go to work and she to her studio, then some time during the day or the next day my work-issued cell phone will ring and I'll take it out and hear her say, 'Sweetie!' in that familiar loving tone of hers, and I'll know: we have made up once more.

Before I left Dublin, I told Dr Kirby that I would like, when in New York, to continue with psychotherapy, feeling that there were many issues in my life yet to be resolved and understood. Once settled in the city, and with a regular income from my office job, I start regular therapy in a practice in the West Village. My therapist, Martin, is thin, balding, younger than me, and possesses a delicate, gentle manner that puts me at my ease.

Although Martin and I try to explore my past, and the legacy and causes of my breakdowns, often I come to him wanting to talk about the latest argument with Jennifer.

Frequently, she and I argue about the nature of our relationship, whether we should experiment more sexually. Jennifer thinks she wants to be in a polyamorous relationship. 'I need to explore my sexuality,' she says. 'I need to be with women sometimes.' She also wants to go to sex parties, and doesn't understand why I don't. 'You're a writer, you should want to experience new things,' she tells me, kicking off an argument about sexuality, polyamory, monogamy, commitment, and whether or not I am sexist, homophobic, misogynistic. She regards the jealousy I know I'll feel if she is with another as a sign of weakness, patriarchal possessiveness and oppression.

At times, when Jennifer and I argue, I confess to Martin, it feels like I am replicating the behaviour and attitudes of my father, being conservative and unyielding, stubborn and inflexible and harsh, determined above all to win the argument. My demeanour when we begin to argue is cold, calculating, even robotic, in the face of Jennifer's tempestuousness. Then, eventually, I'll explode in rage. This is the rage I felt was contained in my father and was afraid would be unleashed upon me.

In the summer of 2002, Jennifer spends several months at an artists' residency in Vermont. On her return it takes a while for her to feel at ease in my company again: she has got used to being by herself. There is a period when we exist like housemates; then gradually we return to being lovers.

Her parents bring us to a party in a red-brick townhouse in the West Village. The house is full of fine antique furniture, ornaments and paintings. There are canapés served by bow-tied caterers, and good wine. It is a convivial group of people milling around, polite, friendly and engaging. But standing at the fireplace, gazing into the fire, then catching sight of my reflection in the mirror above the fireplace, I am drawn back to the dark past: the hospitals, the breakdowns, the madness, the misery and shame of it all, of being stuck back, unemployed, in my father's house and getting nowhere, then helpless in the bubble of illness and medication. Thinking of all the time that has been lost, the damage to my friendships, family relationships and career, as well as my writing progress, I am suddenly overwhelmed with sadness and self-pity and start to cry. No one notices – I have my back turned to the room – and after a while I regain my composure and return to the party.

During the winter, for no apparent reason, I experience a period of utter debilitation and exhaustion. This is different from the depressions of the past: it is mainly physical. At work I find myself nodding off at my desk in the middle of the day. On a day off I go to Central Park, to see it in the snow, and when I am deep inside I realize I am too tired to make my way out. Huddling on a park bench to rest, I wait a long time in the freezing afternoon until I can find the energy to move on. This period of exhaustion does not last; a few weeks later it lifts as mysteriously as it descended, and my life in New York continues as normal.

There's a habit I've developed of muttering inaudibly to myself; my lips move on these occasions, where, mostly, I am expressing a minor irritation at something.

'For fuck's sake,' I mouth at such times, visibly but not audibly.

Jennifer notices this, and it worries her. She thinks I am talking to myself, and that the only people who do so are the mad, the mentally ill.

*

We visit Jennifer's elderly aunt, who lives in a retirement home in Florida. Sitting by the pool of a hotel having lunch with us, this aunt says something I find vaguely annoying; unconsciously, I mouth, 'For fuck's sake.'

Later, alone in our hotel room, Jennifer falls silent. When I ask her why, she suggests we go out for a walk. We sit on the beach outside the hotel in the gathering dark and watch the ocean in silence.

'You were doing it again,' she finally says.

She is talking about the lip-moving, and I remember: my irritation at lunch, my reaction. I didn't realize it was obvious. For once, we don't start arguing over it; this time, Jennifer is subdued, withdrawn, sad and, I realize with growing concern, frightened. Of me. Of my potential for madness. That night we go to bed without talking. We fly back to New York the next day strangely uncomfortable and muted with each other.

The rest of the winter is an unravelling of our relationship. Jennifer simply withdraws from me. When I arrive home into the apartment in the evening I find her listening to music, the same Norah Jones album every time; and every time, on my arrival, she turns off the music, glares at me in silence for a moment, as if I have interrupted her in some important private act, and goes into the other room. When I beg her to talk to me, to talk it all over, she refuses. This is completely unlike the way we used to argue; this is complete disengagement, a shutting out. It unnerves me, and I can do nothing about it.

At the suggestion of Jennifer's own therapist, we go to counselling together. This comes as a relief to me: I think we can work through our problems together. At our first session, however, it becomes clear to me why Jennifer has agreed to go: she wants a platform through which to negotiate our separation. Moreover, she wants a forum for her grievances and a witness who will support her.

There are many grievances, culminating in what she thinks is my biggest failing: 'You don't care about things strongly enough, you're not passionate about anything.'

It seems she is implying I am sleepwalking through life. For a moment I wonder if she is right: has my history of breakdowns and medications rendered me permanently zombie-like, the bubble a permanent state? But it is not true: I feel alive again. Hearing the accusation makes me angry and I defend myself, declare all the things I am passionate about.

In the next session, we discuss the volatile arguments that have characterized our relationship, and I admit to feeling triggered into rage that is out of proportion to the issues being argued over. The therapist seems pleased at this admission.

'That's right,' she beams, as if she has achieved victory in some debate I didn't know we were having. 'You regress.'

It seems she is taking Jennifer's side against me at this juncture, using a judgemental term, and I take umbrage at this. To my amazement, Jennifer jumps to my defence.

Sensing a change in the dynamic between us, the therapist is all pragmatism suddenly; she wants to discuss what is to happen now that we are at the point of breaking up. She talks about the timing and the practicalities of my departure from Jennifer's apartment. Jennifer is mute throughout this; I assume she is considering it all seriously, and when the session ends I assume that she and I will shortly separate.

Outside on the sidewalk I feel dazed. Our relationship is officially over, it seems. Jennifer walks a few steps ahead of me, hunched over slightly, then stops walking. For a moment we both just stand there, Jennifer with her back to me, and then she turns and I see that she is crying. Taking a few urgent steps, she rushes to me and presses her face to my chest.

'Oh, sweetie,' she says, and she says it with love and then throws her arms around me and hugs me tightly.

There on the cold winter sidewalk we agree to give our relationship another go, to commit to each other once again. Not fully understanding how or why it has happened, I am grateful that something has fallen into place between us, and now we are able to love each other once more.

When I return to my own therapy with Martin, I find myself talking less about Jennifer; instead, I talk about my own history, family background and upbringing, the dynamics that made me who I have become and perhaps led to all I have recently been through.

9. The Past

There's a family story I often heard growing up. Two years before I was born, when my sister was four years old, my parents held a Christmas party. The adults were all in one room, drinking and talking; the children, playing, in another. There was a Christmas tree in the room where the children were playing, and near it were some lit candles. My sister recalled how a little girl's dress brushed the candle and went on fire; then, as she thrashed around, the tree caught fire, too. My sister calmly went into the other room to tell the adults. There was a hiatus then, between when they heard her report and when they acted. Did they disbelieve her, or did they just misunderstand? I picture them all drunk, and laughing, my sister trying to convince them, then finally doing so. Only then do they spring into action and address themselves to the fire, the burning child.

Later the adults told this as a funny story; my sister, however, found the incident disturbing and haunting. The story was told so often, I listened to it so frequently, that I imagined I had been there, too, could see myself there; could see the child on fire, the tree in flames. Into the scene, I placed myself.

That party occurred in London, where my parents lived at the time, and where I was born, in 1969. A year later we all moved back to Ireland, to live in Tralee, a market town in County Kerry, where my parents were from. We lived in a bungalow in a suburban part of the town. My father worked for an advertising company in Dublin, over two hundred miles away. He lived in Dublin during the week and returned at weekends, almost always bringing me a gift. Whenever he arrived in Tralee without a present, I cried.

'Do you only want to see me for the presents I give you?' he said on such occasions.

Too young to react or respond, I stared at him in silence, nonetheless aware I had somehow done wrong and disappointed him.

When I was still quite small we moved to Dublin. Our estate was a new one in Blackrock, not fully completed, adjacent to a still-functioning dairy farm and a small forest, where I used to spend hours climbing trees.

We spent two weeks on holiday in Kerry every summer. At the beach my mother would paddle but not swim; she had a paralysed leg, a relic of a childhood trauma that was never explained to me. After paddling she would sit and watch us in the water. My father and sister were good swimmers, but I was scared of the water. As a toddler, standing in the shallows, I had been knocked down and engulfed by a wave; now the sensation of being underwater frightened me, and learning to swim in the sea was impossible.

Some years we'd go camping. Early in the mornings, we picked mushrooms and cooked them on a portable gas stove, the funky smell making us ravenous. We'd stuff ourselves on mushrooms and bread fried in butter or beef dripping, my father's favourite.

My father brought me fishing, took me to Fenit pier, where I cast my lure or bait over the side of the jetty, hoping to catch a mackerel or a bass. He took me to rivers, too, silent black waters slowly easing by as I cast my spinners into the dark depths while being eaten by the midges.

The house in Blackrock was full of books, lined up on

bookshelves my father had constructed himself from planks and scrap wood in the garage, which he had converted into a workspace. Row after row of the orange spines of Penguin paperbacks, or Pelican blue, as well as black classics, and older, hardback classics, and larger-format art books, cookery books, and books about archaeology and natural history. Later my father bought us a full set of Collier's encyclopaedias, an extravagance. They sat on their own shelf in the living room. When my father took down a volume to consult, we would ask him, invariably, interrupting his reading: 'Whatcha looking up?'

But he never answered.

My father worked in the back garden weekend after weekend, over a number of years, to install a raised bed, a pond and a patio. The garden became a cluttered and cosy place filled with trees and shrubs and flowers; apple, pear and cherry trees, raspberry and loganberry and gooseberry bushes, strawberry plants as well as herbs, vegetables and various ornamentals. The patio was a heat trap, where we'd sit out until late in the evening all summer.

My mother loved to cook and fed me with treats: almond slices, fairy cakes, brandy snaps and, my favourite, devil's food cake. As I got older she taught me to cook, and we'd spend afternoons in the kitchen together, both wearing aprons, as she made the evening meal and I got on with baking cakes.

At the weekends there would be games of cards, the dining-room table extension pulled out to accommodate grandparents, neighbours, uncles, aunts, cousins, family friends – eight or a dozen of us all sitting at that table betting coppers over hands of gin rummy, using two or sometimes three packs of cards at once, the pot rapidly growing as we gobbled the sweets my mother laid out in wooden bowls:

American hard gums, wine gums, Liquorice Allsorts. Invariably, I'd win the final round of these epic games, the largest round, with the biggest pot of coppers, money that could buy me a book or a new Airfix kit.

My free time was spent making model airplanes, reading, drawing, cycling, fishing. The west pier at Dun Laoghaire was my main fishing spot, and I would catch enough mackerel or plaice or pollock during my days there to bring home a decent supper. My cookery skills developed so I could cook the fish I caught, too, the recipes gleaned from my father's hardback edition of Robert Carrier's *Great Dishes of the World*, or a paperback edition of Elizabeth David's *A Book of Mediterranean Food*, or my mother's large and food-stained copy of a *Good Housekeeping* cookery compendium. Mackerel, however, was always cooked the same simple way: fried fillets, served with buttered brown bread and wedges of lemon, sometimes very late, if I had been out fishing all evening. The whole family sat down for these late-night fish meals I prepared, and relished them.

At primary school I was a cheeky, insubordinate, unruly, restless and scrappy child, frequently in trouble for what we boys called 'dossing' or 'messing' at school, and as frequently infuriating my normally gentle mother with my bad behaviour. When I went too far she would lose her temper, take me by the arm and whack my bare legs with the head of a wooden spoon to discipline me.

On one occasion, she asked me to do an errand, and I refused, going out instead to meet a friend who was waiting for me outside. Halfway down the driveway, to impress this friend, I turned and put up my fingers in a 'V' of defiance to the house just left behind. But I had calculated my timing badly and saw that my mother was just inside the door, watching my departure from the hall window. Now she opened the door and crooked her finger outside and beckoned me in; I knew there was no option but to return. Leaving my friend behind me on the driveway, I trudged back inside the house, there to receive the worst beating ever with the dreaded wooden spoon.

When I was in my final year of primary school, I became more popular with my classmates. This was because of something I wrote, which they couldn't get enough of reading: a comic book called *The Thing*. It was populated with monstrous caricatures of all the teachers in our school, as well as more flattering representations of my classmates. They were the heroes of my stories, always persecuted by the teachers-as-monsters.

The main monster in the story was 'The Thing' itself, a creature who was recognizably Mr Foley, the most popular teacher in the school. He fancied himself as a bit of a lad: wore open-necked shirts, a medallion around his neck and a bomber jacket, drove a sporty red Alfa Romeo and had a young, pretty wife who we occasionally glimpsed at the school gates. As The Thing, he was the monster the boys in the comic had to fight; it was a representation of our longing to be in his company.

Mr Foley eventually became aware of *The Thing* and his recognizably starring role in it. He was delighted, and made me the class pet. Now I was the envy of the whole year. Mr Foley would send me out to the shops during school-time to get his daily copy of the *Sun*; then I'd hang out with him at his desk at the top of the classroom, chatting, as all the other boys looked on jealously.

My reading was voracious. We visited the local libraries in rotation: Dun Laoghaire, Dundrum, Blackrock, Deansgrange. In the bookshop on the top floor of the shopping centre in Dun Laoghaire, I bought books with my weekly allowance of pocket money.

When my father got a new stereo for the living room, I inherited his portable record player. He gave me some of his old LPs, too. I spent long hours in my room listening to *Scheherazade* by Rimsky-Korsakov and reading. After lights-out, I continued reading with a torch.

My father spent huge amounts of time painting and drawing. After dinner he'd set up his easel in the garage, place the piece he was currently working on into it, and then, palette to hand, continue working on it. His paintings were based on the sketches he collected in his sketchbook; he always brought one with him wherever he and our family went, frequently stopping the car to capture a scene or a landscape.

On weekends he and I would load up the car, he with his sketch pads, charcoals and pencils or watercolours, me with my fishing gear. We'd pick up his friend Michael, a professional artist, and then head down the country. We'd find a spot by one of the canals, in Meath or Kildare, and I would be plonked down at the bankside with my rod and reel and float and hooks and maggots as bait to fish, while he and Michael pottered off to go sketching.

Hours would pass in solitude as I fished for perch and rudd and bream, completely mesmerized as I waited for the top of the rod to jerk or the tip of the float in the water to bob. After catching a fish, I'd unhook it and lay it on the grass on the canal bank for a moment, admire its fine colouring as it gasped; then I'd place it gently back in the water and watch it dart away. Then I'd rebait my hook with a wriggling maggot, cast my float into the water again, and go on fishing, for hours and hours more.

The day would pass like this, totally free of boredom, and then, finally, my father and his friend, sketchbooks under their arms, would heave into view, retrieve me, and we'd all pile into the car and head to a canal-side pub. There we'd have some food, and I'd get a fizzy orange or Cidona while they got down to drinking several pints of Guinness each and grew a little boisterous. In the early evening we'd return to the car, and my father, very slowly, cautiously and carefully, now he was inebriated, would drive us all back to the city.

At home the following day my father would begin a new painting based on the sketch. Once it was finished, it would be hung on one of the walls in the house until, eventually, every spare space in every room and all the way up the stairwell, the hall and the landings had one or more paintings on display.

I knew that my father had briefly attended art college in London. It was not clear to me why he had not completed his studies, but I understood this to be a bitter memory.

One night, we sat in the living room watching a TV programme, a BBC documentary about a successful artist. When this artist spoke about his early career, how he spent all his time at his art, my father grew sullen and muttered grumpily at the screen: 'Ah yes, but how did you pay the rent?'

The implication I took from this was that paying the rent as an artist was something my father had been unable to do or had decided was impossible; but I could only speculate, as he never spoke to me about it.

I, too, spent hours drawing – pictures of airplanes and spaceships – but when I brought these to show to my father, he was not interested. My grandfather, my father's father, had been a playwright and amateur theatre producer and director while working as a secondary-school maths teacher in Tralee. Playwriting, my father sometimes implied, was the tradition I should be following in: the written, not the visual.

This jealous possessiveness of the artistic role did not apply to my sister, however: he taught her to sketch and paint, and later encouraged her to go to art school.

We went to Mass as a family, driving to the church in Blackrock. My mother would follow the service closely, observing all the rituals; I would follow suit, devoutly. My father sat by himself at the end of the pew by the aisle, quiet and still. Instead of taking part in the Mass, he simply read his King James version of the Bible to himself. His mother was a Presbyterian from Belfast who had married his father, a Catholic, at a time when such things were frowned upon.

In time, we stopped going to weekly Mass as a family; no reason was given for this, and there was no discussion about it. Now we attended only Christmas and Easter services together. But I remained pious, and as a teenager I walked to the nearby parish church at Newtownpark Avenue. I prayed and followed the rituals by myself, and read the Bible – the revised standard version, given out at school. I even went to church mid-week, when it was spookily devoid of worshippers, there to pray by myself.

I was sent to a Christian Brothers secondary school not far from my house. On my first day, I was dismayed to be put in the lowest stream. My friends from primary school went into higher streams, or had gone to other schools, and I felt alone in the class I ended up in. My classmates were even bigger dossers than I was, and received no educational support or encouragement from our teachers. We had, it seemed, been given up on as no-hopers; we were disciplined rather than educated.

School became something to dread.

*

My paternal grandfather died around the time I started attending secondary school. After we all came back from the funeral I noticed a change in my father. Now, rather than go into the garage to work on his latest painting, he sat for hours in his armchair by the fire, legs stretched out before him, eyes shut, hands on his belly, unmoving. His face became a stiff mask at such times, his mouth permanently drawn down. He was not asleep, but nor was he fully awake to the room, to us, to me. His eyes would blink open when he heard something that did not please him; at such times he would look around, then his eyes would slowly close again, lizard-like, and he would withdraw into himself once more.

My father became angry at me often now, at unpredictable times, for unpredictable reasons; anything could set him off.

On a shopping trip to the city centre, my father and I waited outside a shoe shop while my mother and sister shopped inside. I wanted to go to the model shop and buy some Airfix with my pocket money.

'When can we go look at Airfix?' I asked my father, not for the first time during the shopping expedition.

He briefly fixed me with his gaze, then turned his head so that he no longer faced me, a habit he had recently acquired. His face hardened and reddened, sinews in his neck tightening, and he jabbed a finger, first in my direction, then at the shop window beside us, and said between clenched teeth:

'You see that window? If you don't stop your whingeing, I'll put your head through that window.'

I froze in fear at this; I was sure, even though it was a Saturday afternoon on Grafton Street in the centre of Dublin, and despite the crowds around us, that he meant it. Remaining silent and holding myself still, hoping not to provoke him further, I forced myself to wait patiently while my mother helped my sister find her shoes. When, finally, they came out with their purchase, we did indeed go, as a family, to the model shop to pick out an Airfix for me to buy, and I relaxed; all was again well with the world, with the family.

I was sent to clarinet lessons in a nearby comprehensive school to do graded study, but the guitar was my favourite instrument, and I taught myself to play on a second-hand one I'd bought in an antiques market. While all my peers at school were listening to David Bowie, the Boomtown Rats, Depeche Mode, Gary Numan or the Smiths, I listened on my LP player in my room to Delta blues men like Skip James, Robert Johnson and Charley Patton, learning to play their songs fingerstyle and singing along. Most weeks my parents' friend Donal would come to our house and bring his guitar. We would have a sing-song, he singing Irish and American and English traditional songs, and I working through my rapidly expanding Delta blues repertoire.

At times, my father's darkness would lift and he would quite suddenly become animated and cheerful once more. He might then suggest a barbecue, and relatives and friends would come and he would cook out on the patio for the large group. Or he'd consult his cookbooks and propose a home-made Chinese meal, and we'd all drive into the city centre on a Saturday morning especially, to shop for the ingredients in the Asian supermarket there. All of us would participate in the cooking of the meal, cooking one dish each. We'd spend the evening eating with chopsticks and drinking lap-sang souchong tea, following the rituals and procedures gleaned from books my father read, which in turn were based on cookery series on the TV. My father's own dish would be the star of the meal, the centrepiece, usually sweet-and-sour chicken or pork, a bit of a palaver to make; mine was a loin of pork cooked in a broth, pressed, sliced and served as medallions.

During these periods, my father would be energetic and good-humoured and unthreatening. But he and I still did not spend time alone together by choice, and did not talk much; I was wary of his temper and his shifting moods.

On one rare occasion we did find ourselves alone, we went for a walk to get chips, and he spoke quite unguardedly of his father, my grandfather, who had died a few years previously. As a young boy, my father had been summoned out of class and told to 'Go down the town.' He did so, and found his father lying face down in a gutter outside his favourite pub. My father had to revive him and get him on his feet and back to home.

'Terrible thing for a young lad to see,' my father said, still not making eye contact with me but gazing off as if at an image of the scene that clearly haunted him still.

We walked on, bought chips and returned home. My mother was at the door, as if anticipating our arrival, held it open for us, saw us talking.

'Look at you two, chattering away,' she said brightly, beaming at us, delighted to see this oddity, perhaps a sign of a rapprochement. But we fell silent, my father and I, self-conscious, and the silence again grew between us and lasted and endured, punctuated only when he issued me instructions, admonished me, criticized me or threatened me.

Mostly, he delivered instructions via my mother.

'Your father doesn't want you going to discos, he doesn't like the disco scene,' she'd tell me.

This was a rule: I was not to go to discos with my friends.

'Your father thinks you should find a sport, get out more. You look like you need to get stronger.'

This became for a while his obsession: I was weedy, not

getting out of the house enough, spending too much time with books and Airfix models.

Not looking at me directly, he said: 'What about swimming? Look at Johnny Weissmuller. He was small like you, then he took up swimming.'

Johnny Weissmuller played Tarzan in 1930s and '40s films my father would have seen as a child, and was an ox of a man, but I was afraid of water.

'I won't make you get out on a rugby pitch,' my father went on, 'but you have to do something.'

But I did do something, I didn't just sit around the house all day, reading: I had become obsessed with tennis, and every summer played as much as I could. My friend Johnny and I watched Wimbledon, then went to the vacant tennis courts in the nearby comprehensive and played for hours and hours, epic five-set matches. My father showed no interest in my tennis-playing, however.

Johnny lived just around the corner. We fished and cycled and played guitar together. In the winter we took up home-brewing and concocted barely drinkable wine, beer and stout to give to the adults, meanwhile drinking as much as we could. We were aged fourteen or fifteen, and the adults seemed to think this a suitable hobby, as it involved skill and craft, just another form of cooking, as it were.

After school one boy waited for me at the bus stop. He was from the nearby technical school, which we in the Christian Brothers regarded as 'rough', and he was bigger and broader than I. For some reason, he took a dislike to me. I now had a southside Dublin middle-class accent, and maybe he considered it, and me, 'posh', or just took note of how small I was and so an easy target; either way, he always took time to pick on me.

I was at the bus stop when he hunched down in front of me; bulky, squat. He forced his face into mine.

'See this?' he said.

In front of my eyes, he held his clenched fist; I braced for it to jerk forward and strike me. But instead he blind-sided me with a blow from his other fist to the side of my head.

Reeling, my ear ringing, I staggered up and boarded the bus that was just pulling away, and I went home.

I told no one of these encounters.

I brought my dog Shelly for walks that took many hours, going through the suburban housing estates and back lanes and then out to the end of Dun Laoghaire pier and back. During these walks I'd think up stories in my head, and when I got home I'd sit at my desk in my room in front of the old Remington Noiseless typewriter my father had given me and bang out short stories, using two fingers to do so, clattering away at the keys; for I had moved on from making comic books and now, in creating these short stories, I thought of myself as a real writer. After a while I had accumulated several hundred pages, a drawerful, and when I ran out of typing paper my father brought me more from his office, encouraging me. Meanwhile, he also encouraged me to think of journalism as a career, and steered me towards contributing to the school newspaper; I volunteered to do so and ended up writing a fishing column. But I wasn't really interested in journalism, and continued to put most of my energies into my fiction.

My mother was short, slightly stout and gentle in manner, unless provoked by some instance of insolence from one of her children, at which times she would become furious. She wore dresses that she constructed herself from patterns she bought in fabric shops. Once a month, she went to the hair-dresser's in Deansgrange Road and got streaks added to her cropped hairdo.

In the afternoons my mother liked to spread out on the sofa in the living room in front of the fire, feet up on cushions, slippers off, glasses on, and read novels by the likes of M. J. Farrell and Kate O'Brien – Irish women of an earlier era. On such afternoons I liked nothing better than to sit by her side on the sofa, still in my school uniform, feet up on the cushions also. She put her arm around me as she read, and I read, too: P. G. Wodehouse, or J. R. R. Tolkien.

The curtains of the large living-room window were open all afternoon, so we had a view of the patio and the back garden, the encroaching evening. The light faded on these occasions until it reached a point where the room was in near-darkness. That was the cue for my mother to set aside her book, place her reading glasses in their case, slowly rise and smooth out her dress, put on her slippers and go around the room turning on all the lamps in turn: those on the bookshelves and stands, and the standard lamp in the corner. Once the room was lit, she could then go into the kitchen, take down her apron and start to cook the evening meal.

Sitting alone then for a while on the sofa, still warm from her embrace, I would slowly realize that my stomach felt bad. Anticipating the evening ahead, the meal to come, I was growing tense, distracted. I put down my book and turned on the television and began to watch the old black-and-white comedy films broadcast during the children's hours on the BBC: Laurel and Hardy shorts, Buster Keaton, Charlie Chaplin and, my favourite at the time, Harold Lloyd. These made me forget my worries for a while.

The key rattled as it was slotted into the front-door lock; I tensed again at the sound. My father and sister had returned, he from work, she from art college. My stomach tightened and I switched off the television, went into the kitchen – now filled with steam and smoke and the noise of the extractor fan – and began to help my mother by setting the table.

My father changed out of his suit upstairs, then joined us downstairs. He was not much taller than me now, in my mid-adolescence; thin, wiry, a hard and unyielding man in a hard and unyielding physique. His hair was darker than mine, almost black, but we had the same brown eyes, and his nose was as prominent as mine, and I resented this unwanted family inheritance. Unlike me, he had a prominent, strong jaw, which gave his face a classical mien; often he would shave that jaw closely again on his return from work and treat it with talcum powder, so that he was clean-shaven and pale-skinned when he sat down to dinner.

Meals were eaten mostly in silence, but now and then my father might make a pronouncement.

'I don't like the look of that spot on your nose.'

This caused me to flush red: I had burst a large spot on the side of my nose, then picked the ensuing scab, and now the resulting mess was indeed disgusting to look at, swollen, inflamed and flaking, spreading ever wider across my skin.

Somehow, now, I began to argue with my sister over this.

'Ah, stop your bickering,' my father commanded me.

'She started it,' I replied.

'Stop your whingeing.'

But I resented the injustice of being singled out and humili-ated, and my father lost his temper at my muttering, became enraged, his face strained. He jerked his body towards me and I shrank into myself, but there was no blow, despite my bracing for one. Instead he jabbed his finger in my face, then pointed aggressively at the dining-room wall behind me.

'You see that wall?' he demanded, teeth clenched, red-faced. 'If you don't stop your whingeing, I'll put your head through that wall.'

My mother said nothing.

Remaining very still and silent so as not to provoke him further, I waited for him to withdraw.

My best friend in school was Boylan, a crop-haired mod who affected a cockney accent in homage to his musical heroes; we spent much of our free time together. We went to the shopping centre near school for lunch, where we shoved soggy chips into the sugar bowls in Bewley's restaurant as a prank, bought the latest comics, went to the amusement arcade across the road to play *Pac-Man*, *Galaxian*, *Centipede* and *Scramble*, and talked endlessly. With my bobbed, fringed hair and prominent nose, he said I looked a little like Keith Moon, the drummer from The Who, his favourite band, which was praise of a sort. Boylan, in my mind, was the coolest boy in class, and I loved spending time exclusively with him, he in his tan trench coat, black-and-white scarf and flashy shoes.

There was a winter of heavy snow. School closed down for the duration and, as Boylan owned a beautiful wooden toboggan and lived in Foxrock, with its hilly streets and golf course, we took to spending every day of the closure up in his neighbourhood, sledding.

After the thaw, the school reopened and we returned to classes as normal. On my first day back, however, on walking into the classroom, Boylan shouted out quite loudly to the other boys, glancing in my direction.

'Jew!' he shouted.

He was referring to me.

'Jew! Jew! Jew!' the other boys chanted in response. Puzzled, and also completely rebuffed by Boylan when I tried to approach him and talk, I took my seat instead, embarrassed, slighted and humiliated.

Quickly, the habit of calling me a Jew took hold of the class. Now, every time I spoke or got up to go to the toilet, or in any way made myself conspicuous, Boylan would mutter, 'Jew', under his breath, and, if there were no teachers paying attention, the rest of the class would pick up the chorus:

'Jew! Jew! Jew!'

For the final two years of secondary school I was moved up a stream, and so I was now doing Honours subjects for my Leaving Cert. I was unsure what to do once I finished school, however; my father wanted me to study journalism, or become an apprentice journalist, but for a long time I considered some sort of career in the fishing industry. University did not seem to be an option.

My deskmate was Declan, whose house I went to on weekends; there I'd watch him as he tinkered with his motorbike, trying to get it running again, and later we'd hang out in his room, listening to James Taylor records. We'd talk about bikes, and music, and girls, but I had no success on the girlfriend front during my school years.

The only way I knew it was possible to meet girls was to go to a disco, and Declan frequently suggested I go with him to the one in the rugby club at Donnybrook. But this, of course, was forbidden by my father. One evening, keeping it a secret from my parents, I waited until bedtime, went to bed as usual and put pillows under my blankets, as I'd seen done on TV; then I climbed out of the bedroom window and retrieved my bike from where I'd hidden it in the garden earlier that evening, and set out cycling the five or six miles to Donnybrook.

Declan was quite drunk by the time I got to the pub where

we'd arranged to meet. He staggered as he walked with me the short distance to the disco. Once inside, I felt my heart pounding in anticipation of meeting a girl, but as soon as I took off my windcheater Declan visibly recoiled from me and looked repulsed.

'Ugh!' he exclaimed. 'Body odour!'

I felt myself go red with shame. I had not bathed before I came out, because I didn't want to alert my parents I was doing something out of the ordinary: it was not a bath night. Nor did I ever wear deodorant: such cosmetic fripperies were frowned upon in my household. After my long, urgent cycle to get to the disco on time, I was sweating, sticky and stinking. Mortified, feeling everyone was now staring at me, I put my windcheater back on, left the disco, got on my bike, cycled all the way home, climbed back through my bedroom window and went to bed.

Declan did not invite me to any more discos.

During the summer after my Leaving Cert, I found out I had been accepted to study Arts at University College Dublin. Excited, I went to tell my father the good news.

He was sitting outside, reading on the patio; it was a fine, sunny day. Breathlessly, I told him I had got into university, and waited for him to congratulate me.

'You're joking,' he replied.

I stood beside him on the step to the patio, waiting for him to speak again. But he remained silent, returned to his book once more and continued reading, and ignored me. Finally, I left him, and went to my room.

I spent the summer reading in preparation for my English course and got through most of *Ulysses*. Feeling that I could never be a real writer like James Joyce, who had profoundly impressed me, I went to my room and opened the drawer that contained my writing, gathered up the hundreds and hundreds of typed pages I had accumulated over the years. Then I went outside and stood at my father's incinerator in the back yard, where he got rid of his garden rubbish, and burned all my stories, all my writing, watching the smoke drift up and be blown away and feeling nothing, watching it all turn to ash.

My mother was frequently absent from the house at this time, and it was unclear to me why. She would simply disappear for days and nights on end. We would all muddle through at such times, doing more housework and not commenting on her absence. Then she would be back, and everything would return to normal.

If there ever was a comment on these absences, it was delivered ambiguously. 'Your mother is having some tests,' my father would say, but would offer no further explanation.

It was all so normal to me, this lack of openness, of explanation. I thought little of it, and because I had been in the habit of not talking to my father about anything intimate or important over the years, I found it impossible now to have a conversation with him about what was going on with my mother.

The rest of the summer after my Leaving Cert, my father did not mention my acceptance into university, and when my mother spoke of it, proudly, he remained silent until she changed the subject. When it came time to enrol, and pay the fees, I was finally forced to talk to him directly. He took a moment, not looking at me, and replied: 'You only come to me when you need some money.'

There was a certain truth to this, and I thought my place in university was not to be; but silently he rose and went to the living room, wrote the cheque and handed it to me, and I was able to begin First Year Arts at University College Dublin, studying English, geography and Greek and Roman civilization.

In university I found an escape from my increasingly stifling home life. Home was a place to sleep, and where I ate the Sunday dinner; otherwise, I managed, somehow, to avoid my family, and failed to notice if anything was amiss, or changing.

The university drama society became a surrogate home and family for me. I had several acting roles in plays, light comedies mostly, and I played clarinet in a musical at Christmas, and later directed a play myself. Other times I helped out building sets, painting furniture, putting up posters for productions around the campus or just running errands. When not actually involved in a production, I hung around the Dramsoc office and performance space talking to people, watching rehearsals and auditions and learning about the workings of theatre. Just down the corridor was an amusement arcade, where I played my favourite video games. Then it would be back to the library to study, or to lectures.

In the library, I gave myself an education in drama history separate from, and more detailed than, what we got on the English course. But my own writing was in complete abeyance at this stage; since the story-burning, I had become convinced that I had nothing worth saying in words, that every other writer had already achieved everything I could ever hope to do and that there was no point in even trying. If, in a moment of enthusiasm, I did attempt to write something other than an essay for one of my courses, I quickly convinced myself that it was worthless.

*

In my second year of university, my mother was absent for a longer period than normal. It was decided that we would all go and visit her, but it remained unclear where we were going.

My father, sister and I got into the car and drove towards the city centre. At a junction not far from where my father worked, we took a left turn into a tree-lined street, past fine Edwardian houses, and turned into the driveway of a large institution, a red-brick Victorian building. There was a sign at the entrance with the insignia of a religious order, but I didn't take in the details fully: I was still unsure of where exactly we were.

We entered the building. A reception desk, corridors leading off a vestibule, staff dressed in white, light reflecting off shiny floors, but a strange darkness to the place. We went down a corridor and, suddenly, with a jarring sensation, as if I had just dropped from a height, or conversely, been set afloat above the ground, awareness shuddered through me: we were in a place for cancer patients. Cold dread seeped through my body, making me virtually numb, deaf, dumb.

My mother lay before us in her room. My sister and father spoke to her quietly, but I felt as if I were floating free in another part of the room, not fully there, unable to speak or hear what was being said, and confused.

We visited my mother often in the coming days. My father, my sister and I sat in my mother's room while the television played. Little was said. When left alone with my mother I simply stared at her, and she stared back. She had lost a lot of weight, and looked fragile and paper-skinned, her lips dry and at times covered in a film of purple crystals that I was afraid to ask her about.

Still, I did not talk to my father about what was going on; I could not bring myself to do so. For we were both ashamed to speak of anything important or intimate together; years of habit, of distance, of silence, had set us apart.

Silence. Silence. Silence.

My own fear did not help: I was so afraid of my mother dying that I did not want to ask questions, in case the answers I heard were ones I could not bear. Even if my father had wanted to talk to me, I would not have been receptive.

We visited my mother late one night, with a sense of urgency, emergency even. My father spoke to the people in white uniforms at the reception desk and I stood by his side, not hearing, frightened. He turned to me after they had finished speaking.

'She's not going to make it,' he said. It was the most he had ever said to me about her condition.

But somehow my mother got through that night. Eventually, her cancer went into remission, and she came home. She regained a little strength and vitality, resumed elements of her normal routine.

In the college library, where I worked part-time as an assistant, shelving books, I lived in dread of the announcements that came over the Tannoy system calling students to reception for an urgent phone message. I expected one to come for me any day, informing me my mother had returned to the hospital, or had died.

My mother seemed to drift about the house now in a way she didn't before; she seemed less grounded, a gossamer thing. She stood in the garden and I stood at the steps to the patio and she gazed right at me and through me; it was unnerving, and I retreated back into the house.

But with time, a sort of normality returned. At college I had to prepare for my second-year exams, and at home it appeared my mother was improving. I was also planning a trip to New York for the summer on a J-1 work visa, and she helped me with my plans, talked about the trip with enthusiasm. I relaxed my vigilance and no longer expected a sudden call announcing disaster. I allowed myself to believe that all was well, based on what I observed: my mother going about her normal routines, frailer than before, to be sure, but seemingly well. It would be, I reasoned, completely fine to go away for the summer; and, on my return, I would make an effort, finally, to talk of important, adult things with her, in a way I had not done before.

My mother had arranged for me to stay with her relative, Pat, and his wife in Queens. Shortly after I arrived, they went on holiday, so I was left alone in their house. Pat had found me work waiting tables in a midtown bar and grill. I worked there most evenings, and at weekends I worked downtown in a bookstore on Spring Street.

Returning home to the house in Queens late at night, I'd pick up the copy of the *New York Times* that was delivered every day and read it, lying on the living-room sofa. Once I'd finished, I'd drop the paper on the floor and then go to bed in my basement room. After a few weeks of this there was a substantial pile of newspapers covering the living-room floor. My plan was to do a complete clean-up the day before Pat and his wife arrived back.

Over a month earlier than planned, Pat returned unannounced, and without his wife. He stood at the entrance to the living room and stared at the newspaper-strewn scene, utterly aghast. There was no way I could placate him; he informed me that I had to leave first thing in the morning.

My college friends had gone to Boston to seek work, so that seemed the logical place to go now. When I phoned them, they assured me there would be a place for me to stay with them and that work would be easily found. New York had been a lonely place for me that summer; I had a few casual acquaintances, but nobody I could count as a friend. I had attempted to alleviate this loneliness by phoning my mother, reversing the charges from public payphones. On receiving these calls, not noticing the desperation in my voice, she would urge me to hang up quickly so as to not rack up charges on her phone bill. Her letters to the house in Queens contained little news, but there were long admonishments explaining that the cost of reverse-charge calls was too high and I must not make them.

But the loneliness would get to me again, and so once more I'd do it; and another letter would come, complaining.

My letters to her were chatty and news-filled, and one of them was sent with a photograph. On the back of the photograph is scrawled: 'Here I am on the 59th Street Bridge three blocks from work on the middle East Side.' In the photograph I stand on the walkway of the bridge in a tight T-shirt bearing a photograph of the blues singer Robert Johnson. The grids of the bridge run past me and the skyscrapers loom behind in a heat haze. My hair is slicked back close to my skull with Brylcreem. My chest and arms appear quite firm – I had been working out in the gym in college regularly that year – and there are the beginnings of a smile on my face. Standing there in the bright New York sunshine, upright, fit, strong and confident, I stare out of the photograph as if to say to my mother: 'This is who I am now; not a boy but a man.' If only I had not undermined myself, betrayed myself, by demonstrating my loneliness and neediness by phoning her so often.

Now, on the eve of my ejection from my relative's house in Queens, I packed my suitcase and set it at the end of the bed in my basement room. The next morning, I would take the bus from the Port Authority to Boston. Excited to be moving on, I eventually turned out the light and went to sleep.

Several hours later I was woken by the sound of the phone ringing on the bureau in my room. Thinking it best to answer, as Pat was asleep upstairs, I reached out in the dark and picked up the receiver.

It was my father, who I had not heard from all summer, calling from Dublin; I stood to listen.

'It's Mam,' he said. 'She's dead.'

The cancer had not been meant to come back; I had been living with this belief for months, and now I was confused. Did my father say more? Did he explain about the cancer, that it had returned and had killed her? Did he tell me the details of the funeral arrangements? Or did he just say those four words before I hung up the phone in shock, stood still for a moment in the dark and let out a howl of pure animal rage?

I went upstairs to tell Pat the news. Standing in the dark hallway outside his room, I watched his silhouette in the bed as I told him my mother had died.

'Jesus, man,' he said, sleepily. 'That sucks.'

Then he fell back asleep.

It was impossible for me to sleep, and there were not too many hours until dawn, so I got dressed and sat up until morning, waited for the first light, then took my suitcase and left the house without saying goodbye to Pat, and travelled by subway into Manhattan. There I presented myself at the office of the organization that had arranged my J-1 visa and explained my circumstances to them. They were very understanding, and there were contingency plans in place for emergencies such as this, so it was quick and straightforward to book me on to a flight back to Dublin, utilizing the return half of my ticket, with no extra fee charged. The flight would depart later that night from JFK.

Still in a daze from shock and lack of sleep, I left my suitcase in the office and in baggy shorts and T-shirt headed out on to the baking-hot streets, taking a subway downtown. There I bought a bunch of music cassettes in J and R Music World on Park Row and played them on my Walkman, loud, back to back, endlessly, in an effort to drown out my clamouring thoughts. The heat pressed down on me, making every step an effort. It felt like I was being squeezed under a smothering, moist, hot mass.

Hoping for a cool breeze, I walked towards the East River. A man had set up a powerful telescope on the boardwalk and for a dollar it was possible to look through it and see the surface of the sun. Stopping for a moment, I duly paid my dollar and looked through and saw it: a black mass of swirls and circles, pock-marked with what looked like craters, strangely solid-looking and defiantly not of this world. It felt very far away and strange and not at all like the source of the heat that was oppressing me now; indeed, in its black solidity, it looked almost cold.

The rest of the day passed thus: heat, and numbness and inner rage. Eventually, it was time to retrieve my suitcase and travel to the airport. A few hours later, still in that strange state of numbness, I flew over the Atlantic in a fog of grief and shock, utterly bewildered, truly and completely alone.

No one knew of my travel arrangements, so there was no one there to collect me at Dublin airport. In the early morning, my second night without proper sleep just passed, I got myself home by taking buses and hitch-hiking the last mile.

For a moment I stood in the patio and looked into the living room. It was filled with people: aunts, uncles, cousins. After I knocked on the window my father came to the door and let me in. I held out my hand and offered it to be shaken, to shake his, something I had never done before with him. He seemed momentarily confused before he took my hand, clumsily, and shook it. Pushing past him then, past everyone inside, with few words, I escaped to my own room upstairs and fell into bed and finally slept.

When I woke, my aunt from Cork was sitting on my bed, watching me.

'How are you, mister?' she asked me, kindly. It seemed I had slept all the day that I had arrived, and all through the night. I had missed the removal the previous evening; they hadn't wanted to wake me, but now my aunt explained it was time to go to the funeral Mass and burial.

My father wanted me to read from the Bible as part of the Mass, but I refused. Although I no longer went to Mass, until my mother's death I still considered myself a believer. But after her death I was full of anger with God, and so I felt it would be hypocritical to read from the Bible.

There were other sources of dissonance between my father and me. It seemed incomprehensible to me that my father could appear so energetic and cheerful, greeting people at the funeral with a smile and a vigorous handshake. To me, that was indicative that he didn't actually care deeply about my mother's death. It didn't occur to me to consider that he had a duty to greet people without distressing them with overt signs of grief; nor that my own state of numbness, walking around expressionless and speaking in monosyllables, could have struck others as equally uncaring.

At the graveside after the burial my mother's best friend came and took my hand and shook it feebly, racked by sobbing, just managing to say that the last time they had met my mother had seemed fine. I remained numb, did not respond, let my hand drop back limply to my side after she had shaken it.

At home, after it was all over, things returned quickly to a state of normality that I found curiously unnerving. My father and sister sat and watched TV most evenings after dinner, and when I stood at the living-room door considering whether to enter and join them or not, they sat and stared at me blankly. I felt unsure where to sit now that my mother was no longer there: normally, I would have sat on the sofa with her. Instead of joining them, then, I retreated, alone, to my room, wondering what to do next.

For a short time after my mother's death I drifted around Dublin, aimless. Most of my college friends were still in the US on their J-1 visas, and when I did meet people I knew I felt awkward and even ashamed explaining why I was back in Dublin; I found it very difficult to talk about my mother's death, and dreaded having to do so. I wanted just to be left alone, not to have to constantly explain myself. At home, too, I felt increasingly awkward and out of place. I decided to return to the US for the remainder of the period I could work on the J-1; at least I'd be among friends there, and occupied. I spent two months working in Boston to make up my college fees, then I travelled around the southern states a while by myself.

The trip passed in aching loneliness and shocked numbness. When I came home for my final year of college, I was unable to sleep properly, and increasingly stressed and anxious. I went to the college health services, who referred me to the college psychiatrist: Dr Malvey.

'You're very thin,' was the first thing she said when she met me. It was true: since returning from the States, I had been eating very little; lunch now was a Mars Bar and a pint of milk, dinner a bowl of chips in the college canteen. Dr Malvey prescribed me some sedatives to help me sleep and recommended I spend some time in the day hospital at St Vincent's, just down the road from the college.

'It's a place you can just be,' she told me, eager to get me away for a respite from my final year of college, from essays and study for my finals. But when I went to see what it was like, saw the patients in the psychiatric ward sitting around, smoking in silence, I didn't stay; I preferred my routine of walking around the empty corridors of college at night and reading in the library during the day.

Somehow, writing became an imperative once more and I managed to complete a new short story. This I plucked up the courage to show to someone: a lecturer in the English department. She had a kind demeanour and was thought to be a relatively cool member of the faculty. We met in her office in the English department a few days after I had given her the story to read, and I was eager to hear her opinion.

Considering the story before her, considering me, she asked: 'Where's the mother in it?'

She had identified the absence in the story I had written, the one I had been unable to fill. Mortified, unable to answer, I left her office shortly after and resolved not to show anyone my stories again.

10. *Henry's Blues*

Twice a week I go to therapy now with Martin, going into my past in depth, often leaving the sessions tearful and shaky. But I feel that Martin is truly on my side, and I can say anything to him. To restore myself after these sessions I go to the YMCA on 14th Street and swim all of it out of me, length after length after length.

My driving licence needs to be renewed. I don't want it to go out of date, so I arrange, with my father's assistance, to get a new one ordered by post. Several weeks later the new licence is delivered to New York; but I find that in place of my photograph there is a photograph of my father. For no apparent or explicable reason he has replaced the photo that I sent him with one of himself. This unnerves me, seeing his face stare out at me from my driving licence, and I spend several sessions with Martin returning to the subject of the licence and trying to figure it out; but I cannot.

I phone my father, a rare occurrence, and find out that an editor at the *Irish Times* has been trying to contact me to get permission to publish one of my short stories; my father, obtusely, has told her that I am away and hasn't passed on my contact details. Again, Martin and I explore my father's motivation in being so unhelpful and uncommunicative with me. The therapy helps me gain perspective on my relationship with my father, and to distance myself from him.

The story is published finally in the *Irish Times* and I wonder what my father makes of it; he does not phone to say. Martin does buy the paper, and reads the story. I tell him: 'I wasn't sure you'd believe me when I told you I was having a story published.'

'I never doubted you,' he replies.

This moves me profoundly: to be believed, to be heard.

Jennifer and I have made plans to get out of the city for July and August, so my sessions with Martin are temporarily suspended and the apartment on Canal Street is sublet. She will go to her parents' house in the Hamptons and spend her time there painting. I have secured a residency at The Barn, a retreat established by the playwright Edward Albee, near Montauk, a couple of miles from Amagansett, on the tip of Long Island, and then another at the Bread Loaf Writers' Conference in Vermont. The plan is for Jennifer to pick me up in Vermont at the end of the conference and for us to spend the remainder of August camping in New England.

In Montauk my routine is to write in the morning, have lunch, then borrow one of the bikes on the compound and cycle the short distance to the beach, where I spend long, idyllic hours walking the shallows around the rocky headland, finding new pools to swim in. In the evenings, I cook and eat dinner and chat with any of the other residents who are not sequestered away working in their studios or writing in their rooms. At weekends Jennifer and I drive around the tip of Long Island, visiting coastal towns and stopping at roadside shacks to eat steamed lobsters served with drawn butter, fries and cold beer.

I'm sitting outside The Barn eating an apple when Edward Albee arrives to collect his mail. I'd like to talk to him about the play I am working on, but I can say nothing. Finally, he fills the silence.

'Is that a pear you're eating?' he asks.

'No, it's an apple,' I reply.

He nods, as if he knew all along it was an apple but that having it confirmed has satisfied his curiosity somehow and made his day; then he goes inside to pick up his mail. It is only after he is gone that it occurs to me that I should have told him that his *Zoo Story* influenced me greatly, and I wince in embarrassment at my awkwardness.

The residency ends and there is a brief interval before I go to Bread Loaf. During this time I stay with Jennifer in Amagansett. We go swimming during the day, take walks in the evening. There are several bikes at the house, and we go to one of the bays and swim there before coming back through the forest, cycling through the dappled light along winding roads, and chatting. At weekends there are elaborate brunches on the patio with Jennifer's entire family, seven of us sitting outside eating lox and bagels and fruit salad and eggs.

It is a good life, but still there are occasions when I get angry, irritable, and Jennifer does, too, and we argue as badly as before. On a hot summer evening, returning from swimming and cycling, a minor source of irritation turns into a slippery, circling, vicious, accusatory row and all the old dissatisfactions and recriminations are aired once again. I become convinced our relationship is now irretrievably finished at last. Up to now I have always been fighting to remain with her, fighting against the conflict. Now, for the first time I consider leaving her. This thought makes me light-headed with possibility and anxiety: I do not know how I could make a life for myself in America without Jennifer, without the support of her and her family. All the rows, the torturing of each other: are the loving times we share together in any way a compensation for all of that?

Somehow, in the days before I go to Bread Loaf, we put the fight behind us. Jennifer drives me into Manhattan and sees me off at the Port Authority bus terminal. In my bag are notebooks and some stories and an extract of a novel to be workshopped. Jennifer and I leave each other on the best of terms, our love fully restored, and looking forward to our camping trip and then our return to our apartment on Canal Street.

At Bread Loaf there are seminars, workshops and readings from morning to night. There are parties that go on into the small hours. There are walking tours with readings through the forest, one-on-one consultations with established authors. There are expeditions with the other participants to nearby lakes to take a swim, and there is a small stream nearby where I go between sessions to plunge myself into its icy waters to try and cool off from the heat of Vermont in late August.

I am feeling at ease to be away from New York and, I realize, away from Jennifer. I am sick of the arguments, after all, and wonder would I be better off without her. There are writers here from all over, and I quiz them now about work and accommodation possibilities where they live, testing the waters, seeing if another life may be possible for me elsewhere. It occurs to me I am free to go anywhere I want to, if I so choose, and when hanging out with the other participants I grow pushy with my own agenda: I am talking too much, too fast, complaining to anyone who will listen about my relationship, my girlfriend, my need for change in my life.

Then I am handed a phone message from Jennifer. It is a simple message about how she is getting on at her festival, but at the end of the message is an endearment, an old token of love between us; when I read it my heart lurches and my emotions swing as I remember that I am in love with her, that I want to return to her and our life in New York, to her smile and laugh, to the intimacy we share, all the activities, the joy of life she has given me: to our future.

It seems impossible I ever questioned our relationship.

I am at Bread Loaf as a 'work-study scholar', paying my way by working shifts as a waiter in the dining room for the several hundred participants and faculty. This means that I am getting up very early, often while it is still dark, for breakfast service, sometimes after having been out all night talking and drinking. The accommodation for the male work-study scholars is little more than a concrete shed set at a lower level than the sloping meadow it sits in, and groundwater seeps into it from the grassy verge outside the door. The carpet, consequently, is a squelching, stinking mess, the room itself cold and damp; coming in at night, I observe a frog sitting on the sodden carpet.

Living in this way, I become wired, strung out. But despite the lack of sleep, it seems like I have energy for everything.

One of the visiting writers has agreed to give me a one-to-one consultation on a short story. In stifling heat, I trudge along the road for the couple of miles to the house he is renting with his family.

The writer likes my story and, my confidence boosted, I set off back down the road with a bit more vigour, trying to get back to the campus and into shade as quickly as possible. It must be over a hundred degrees at this stage. There is still the evening meal to be served, as part of my scholarship duties, so I must rest. Finally, arriving at the campus, I collapse on the grass beside a bench where a group of people are chatting.

Exhaustion descends on me, flattens me; I feel heavy, weighted down. When it is time to go to the restaurant to start my shift, I realize that I can't get up.

'Help,' I say weakly. 'I need help.'

It takes a while for the chattering group to take any notice of me, then they gather around. It occurs to me even at this stage that I could just ask to be pulled to my feet, force myself up, go back to my accommodation, have a cold shower and go to work. But I don't. I give in to it, decide I am experiencing heatstroke and need medical attention: I want to be helped.

'Call an ambulance,' I order the gathered group. 'I'm not feeling well.'

An ambulance arrives quickly and the crew assess the situation. They pack me with cold, wet towels and apply ice. Cooling down, I feel energy return and am able to stand. They want me to go to the nearby hospital with them for assessment and observation but, suddenly clear-minded and alert, my fear of hospitals takes over and I refuse further treatment or care.

When I go to my room, the flooding is worse than ever, water now visible on the surface of the carpet. A sudden fury fills me, and I return to the main campus to talk to the director of the conference. When I find him I complain about the accommodation and demand to be given a room in the main building that I know to be dry and comfortable. He seems quite put out by my manner but grants me the room I want. I go there and lie down, but I am restless, agitated, flighty. The well-appointed room seems stifling and claustrophobic.

Deciding I am not well enough to work, I don't turn up to do my obligatory shift serving dinner in the dining room that night.

In the morning I am summoned to the director's office and he tells me I will have to leave the conference. They have booked me a flight from the local airport to JFK and I am to go straight away. The discussion is confused, confusing; it is becoming difficult to focus, to concentrate, to understand

and be understood. I can't comprehend why I am being told to leave. My memory of last night is cloudy, but my behaviour has evidently become a cause for alarm and I am no longer welcome or wanted at Bread Loaf. Still confused, I gather my things and leave. Didn't I pass the night alone in my new, dry, plush room? And yet: I can't remember sleeping, nor what I could have been doing if not sleeping.

Jennifer's parents pick me up at JFK. I am talking incessantly, impatient to be on the move – so much so that I leave my suitcase at the airport and we have to go back to pick it up.

Back in Amagansett, it is hard to settle. Jennifer, who is driving back from a festival in the Midwest, has found out about my expulsion and phones the house now to speak to me, concerned. She reveals that she has spoken to the director of the conference.

'He asked me did anything like that ever happen to you before,' she says.

'What did you tell him?' I ask.

'I said there was something that happened, years ago,' she replies.

'Why the fuck did you say that?' I snap back.

'Because it's true, isn't it?'

And now I am furious: for it is obvious that she believes me to be bipolar after all, and that I have done something untoward in Bread Loaf, as I did years ago. Without listening to her any further, I bang down the phone, decide there and then to leave her, and go and pack my bags.

Bob drives me the short distance to the stop for the Hampton Jitney, the luxury bus that will take me back to Manhattan; in the time since I hung up on Jennifer I have phoned my friend Rick and arranged to stay in his apartment downtown. As we drive, I think of Jennifer, on her long drive cross-country, expecting to see me at the end of it; I wonder how she will feel when she arrives back at her parents' house to be told I have left. But my heart is hardened against her, full of hurt and anger at her betrayal of me, and I don't care about her feelings any more.

'You seem agitated,' says Bob.

This makes me sink deeper into myself, resentful; we drive on in silence.

Rick is staying with his girlfriend uptown and has sublet his apartment downtown, not far from Ground Zero, to a rock band he assures me will be the next big thing, but they are currently on tour so the apartment is mine for a few days. It's a large and airy place, and I rattle around in its vast spaces, feeling out of place.

My job in the office of the security firm has been put on hold for the summer. I call the office manager, tell her I am back early, and get scheduled for a few shifts the following week.

In the office, I babble non-stop to one of the investigators; he stares at me across his desk, overwhelmed by the torrent of words. I can't stop talking, have so much to tell him, even though the phone is ringing behind me on my desk and it is one of my duties to answer it.

'Answer the goddamn phone!' the investigator finally shouts, and, startled by his vehemence, I turn and do so.

I am soon fired, in any case; Bob, I think, must have spoken to his friend, the director of the firm, and now that I am no longer with Jennifer, no longer part of the family, he feels no obligation to employ me.

Now begins earnest, urgent writing in notebooks, stopping to record experiences, or vent anger or theories about myself, or write down outlines and ideas for new writing projects. One such is *Henry's Blues*, an epic novel I now conceive, with Henry, the protagonist, my avatar. Into his narrative I thread memories, fantasies, grudges, experiences.

Browsing in the medical section of a bookstore, I write out long definitions of hypoglycaemia from a medical book which seems to prove that I do not have, never did have, bipolar disorder.

Before the summer I worked frequently for a catering firm on the Upper East Side; now I go to the couple who run it and ask for full-time work in their kitchen, thinking my previous, unfinished, training as a chef will qualify me to do so. But on a trial day they complain that I am unsuitable for the job; despite my energized state, I go too slowly in food prep. They give me no further shifts so now I am jobless in New York, and with rapidly dwindling funds. When the band returns to Rick's apartment I start phoning other friends, asking for a place to stay.

I don't consider leaving New York and returning to Ireland; I still think I can make it on my own in the States.

At my friend Jim's apartment on the Upper West Side, I complain I find it hard to sleep on the mattress he has provided for me on the floor. Jim suggests I sleep instead beside him in his double bed, the one that fills most of the space available in the tiny apartment. During the night I wake up to feel the bed moving and realize Jim is masturbating furiously beside me; embarrassed, I move out the next day.

I get a place to stay in Brooklyn, in a room on a mezzanine, in a duplex filled with a rotating cast of transient residents. It is made clear early on that this is to be a short-term arrangement and I am expected to move on soon. The day I leave, having arranged nothing for the night ahead, I tell the residents of the duplex that I am grateful for their hospitality and that I will come back and cook them an Italian meal as a gesture of my gratitude. They stare back at me blankly, not fully comprehending, or not relishing the prospect, just wanting me to leave; I do not know why I am so unwelcome.

'Really,' I tell them, trying to endear them to me, 'after you eat my puttanesca sauce, you will be like pussy in my hands.'

> Henry realised no-one understood a word he said. People said he was obtuse when he didn't know how to answer and obscure when he asked a question himself. He began to think of himself as obscure.

Now there are no more friends or acquaintances who will put me up. Several have turned me down when I phoned them, more loyal to Jennifer, whom they knew first, than to me, or perhaps unnerved by something in my voice.

Walking through the Lower East Side, by the river, I stop at a bench and lie down; I have been walking a lot, and I can now walk no further, so I close my eyes, then promptly fall asleep. When I wake it is morning. I hurriedly check my pockets for my possessions, then my feet to see if my shoes are still there: they are. My bag is still where I left it beneath the bench. It does not seem strange to me that I have spent the night sleeping rough in New York City, just a few blocks from the neighbourhood where I lived with Jennifer.

I want to meet Bob; I want to demonstrate to him that I am doing fine without the job he helped me find, without his daughter, without him. We meet in a midtown coffee shop. Bob cannot comprehend why I grin when I recount my circumstances. He insists on giving me five hundred dollars in cash so I can buy a flight home. The gift angers me, because it shows he lacks faith in my ability to take care of myself, make a life independently for myself in America. I shout at him, storm out of the coffee shop, not caring if I ever see him again. But I keep the money.

*

Sitting in a tiny roadside park, still fuming after my encounter with Bob, I prattle to a stranger, and finally demand to know: 'What do you think of me?'

She looks at me oddly. 'I think you have a triple-A personality,' she says, obliquely.

This delights me, and I grin, get up, go on walking, energized anew.

I use some of Bob's money to pay for a room in a cheap, run-down and slightly sinister hotel on the edge of the West Side Highway called, grandiosely and inaccurately, the Chelsea Inn. It's a relic from another era, short and squat and antique among modern riverside highrises, clinging to the edge of the Meatpacking District and harbouring a clientele of dossers and down-and-outs and transients; and now me. But I do not feel unsafe or odd here in this place; on the contrary, I feel safe everywhere: invulnerable, invincible, dynamic, pumped up. I belong here, belong everywhere in the world now.

I go on writing *Henry's Blues*, obsessively:

Father: I don't know what you want from me.

— I just feel terrible, I feel like doing something terrible to myself.
— Oh, stop it, this is getting boring now.
— I just feel I can't go on, you hear what I'm saying? I feel I can't stand it any more. All this & you & all the shit that happened when I was young & the way you treated me and mom, and, and, I just want my mother, I can't stop thinking about her, or, or, sleep, I can't sleep, or settle, I can't stop thinking, I can't stop, I can't stop, I can't.
— This is getting boring.
— It's not. It's me, it's me, it's who I am now.
— It's all an act.

Sitting on the subway, I glance at the passenger sitting beside me, see she is reading a manuscript; we get talking and it turns out she is a literary agent. Talking a mile a minute, I convince her I am an established writer, and I have a novel-in-progress called *Henry's Blues* she should read; she gives me her card and asks for a synopsis and sample. Getting off the subway clutching her card, I am more exuberant than ever: I have successfully pitched my novel to this agent and it is only a matter of time before it is published and is a bestseller.

In a department store I am ejected after arguing with a clerk, and a security guard escorts me outside. Customers stare at me in horror as I pass, bristling with rage, and shout at them: 'There's going to be another 9/11 and you fuckers all deserve it!'

Then I'm chucked out on the street.

All my belongings are still in Jennifer's apartment, and I phone her, agitated and angry, trying to arrange to get them back. We end up arguing over the phone, and I grow increasingly paranoid she will damage or destroy my belongings out of spite, to hurt me.

'Don't break my guitar,' I plead.

'Why would I break your guitar?' she replies, bewildered, confused, hurt.

She doesn't want me to come to her apartment to pick any things up; she is clearly frightened of me.

There is an attempt to return to some sense of normality, routine, the life I had before. Using some of Bob's money to pay for therapy sessions, I find I can't sit still for the duration. Martin watches me in confusion as, a few minutes into the session, I explain that I need to go outside for a cigarette, and then I go out, descend in the lift, go on to the street and smoke, several times during the fifty minutes we have together.

Jennifer agrees to meet up with me in Tompkins Square Park on the Lower East Side. It is a park we have always liked – watching the dogs playing, going to open-air concerts. Now we sit on a bench, uncomfortable in each other's company, while I smoke cigarette after cigarette and Jennifer tries to communicate with me, get me to talk about what I feel, and to make sense of me. But the only reason I have met her, resentful still, is to demonstrate to her that I am independent of her now, I am over her.

Jennifer has brought me a present, and now gives it to me, a hardback book of Snoopy cartoons. Inside she has written a dedication: 'Laughter, laughter, laughter, is the best medicine.'

But this only irritates and angers me further, because I do not consider myself to be ill and I am insulted that she thinks I need some form of 'medicine'.

We walk out of the park and pass by a drifter, a young kid who reminds me of myself sleeping on a park bench a few nights previously. He's begging, so I give him five dollars. After walking a few steps, Jennifer takes my arm to stop me. 'I know that was a really nice thing to do,' she says. 'But you really need to conserve your money right now.'

This I take as another insult; and it humiliates me to know that she is aware of how little money I have in the world. Shaking her off, I leave her standing there on 2nd Avenue and walk off into the city alone.

Walking, brooding, remembering, fantasizing, I conjure a scene, write furiously:

- But it's not, you understand, I feel like doing something,
  I wrote you a suicide note.
- Ah, stop it.
- I saved up all my meds & a plastic bag.

— You just need to go back to hospital.

— I want to hurt myself, you understand, to end, just end, be nothing.

— Then do it. Stop boring me with this stupid act.

— I just want to be with my mother.

— Ah, this is – His father turned and turned on the TV. A test signal lit the room. Without trying another channel, he left and went upstairs. Henry remained a while, watching it, then went and flicked through the stations. Some Eurotrash, some TV Sales, some live football. A movie was running the credits. He told himself he'd put his fate in the lap of the Gods, any God, any God at all, the God of his Pagan ancestors if need be, said this to the empty room. Aloud then he said: 'If these credits are the end of the movie, I'll go upstairs and kill myself. If it's the start I'll watch it to the end then go to sleep and try again to live another day tomorrow.' The credits revealed after a moment to be the opening credits of a movie.

Still wanting to get Jennifer to see my point of view, to make her accept she was wrong to betray me, I phone her and convince her to come to a therapy session with Martin. During the session, Martin and Jennifer observe me in a glum, shocked, bewildered silence as I vent my grievances.

Out on the street I light up a cigarette, grinning. Jennifer is silent, and we don't even bid each other farewell as I swing around, hurry away, eager to be on the march through Manhattan again, not caring when I'll next see her.

Jennifer's mother, Vera, now becomes the only member of the family I still speak to; she helps coordinate the retrieval of my belongings that are in Jennifer's apartment. During one phone call she tells me she has got me a pair of tickets for an off-Broadway show, a Beckett and Albee double bill of one-act plays. During the performance, I laugh loudly during the Beckett play, seeing humour everywhere; the other audience members grow annoyed. But everything to me is funny; I cannot understand why no one else is laughing, and keep twisting around in my seat as if to scrutinize everyone else and ascertain why they are not laughing along loudly, too.

To make some money, I call in to Leonora at the artists' studio looking to get some modelling work. Observing my wiry body, which is now stick-thin and quite firmed up after a summer of swimming in the ocean, she suggests I do a session with a photographer instead of the regular life-drawing class.

'I can see every sinew on you,' she says. 'This photographer I know will love it.'

The session is set up, and I will be paid a higher rate than normal, as it is a photo shoot. The photographer is a young woman who exclaims in excitement when I strip off in the outside yard where the photo shoot is taking place. Quickly, I move from pose to pose, pushing my body to ever more extreme contortions so she can see the muscle shapes clearly; she snaps away under the pounding midday sun. I go into plank, into handstands, into push-ups, forcing the hardest shapes out of my body for her camera.

Finally, I can collect my belongings: not from Jennifer's apartment but from that of her parents. They live in a condominium on the Lower East Side, but they are not there when I go to collect my things. Instead it is the doorman who lets me in, and who stands by, a little embarrassed, as I go in to remove the black plastic bags that contain my clothes, as well as my laptop and guitar.

This doorman has seen me come and go from this

apartment building many times, on happier occasions: for dinners, for Hanukkah, for Passover, for birthdays, for Christmas lunch. Now he watches without comment as I gather up my things and looks bemused and embarrassed as he helps me bring all the bags and other items down to the street, where I hail a taxi, load them all in the back and bring them to my hotel.

The hotel is a sanctuary, a quiet place I can lie on the bed with the window open, a faint breeze coming off the Hudson River outside to cool me; rest a while, if not sleep. Bounding down the corridor, back from the street, heading for my room once again, I pass by an open door and glance inside. Another room, identical to my own, and on the bed a guy and a young woman, huddled, concentrating over something on the mattress. The woman looks up as I pass and catches my eye; she is younger than I, curly-haired, pretty, sallow, quite lean, and with an air of hunger and desperation about her.

They are dividing up drugs between themselves, it would seem; I leave them to it and walk on.

Too jumped up for sleep, I lie down a while on the bed, that Hudson breeze coming in through the window, billowing the dirty curtains and cooling me down in the otherwise torrid room.

There is a soft knock on the door, and I get up and open it; the sallow woman stands there. She says nothing, steps into the room. Suddenly aroused, I step by to let her in.

Now it is agreed, with minimal discussion, that she will have sex with me if I will give her enough money to pay for her drugs. That she is not a prostitute and I am not her client is made clear also; she just needs some money, quickly, and would appreciate my help with this, in return for helping me with needs of my own.

167

Eagerly, feeling lust rise in me with almost animalistic force, I walk down with her to the streets and then a nearby ATM.

'How much?' I ask.

'Sixty dollars,' she says.

'Forty okay?'

'Yeah.'

We walk back to the hotel, heat weighing us down. In my room, I immediately undress. She does not, but stands dressed in her loose, light dress still.

'The money,' she says, holding out a thin hand; I give it to her.

She turns, leaves the room, pads down the corridor without another word.

Somehow, I trust her to come back. She is just going to pay for and maybe take her drugs; she needs to get high before she can fuck me. But that's not the real reason I trust her: I trust her because I am convinced we have made a connection, a bond, that she likes me, and that she does in fact want to come back.

The door pushes open a few minutes later; she has returned, to find me lying calmly on the bed in my boxing shorts. She sits in front of me, beneath the window, and pulls that lightweight dress over her head and discards it, wriggles out of her underwear, and lies down. She is painfully thin, head to toe, and there is little shape or structure to her body; her flesh seems too soft and formless for her years and her skin seems strangely loose, hanging over her flesh. A strange, sharp smell emanates from her, and I find it, and her, suddenly immensely arousing.

Before we commence, she asks me, facing me from where she sprawls naked: 'How do you want to do it?'

'Like we are on a date,' I reply.

'I'm not going to kiss you,' she replies.

This makes me nuzzle her and attempt to kiss her, but when my lips touch hers and my mouth opens, her mouth is limp, paper-dry and unmoving. Pulling back, I give up on this attempt to kiss, to pursue the intimacy that does not exist. I pull off my boxing shorts and put on a condom. She lies on her belly and I begin to fuck her from behind in the airless room.

It is wordless and mechanical and strictly transactional sex, she a completely passive and limp partner who receives my thrusts without a sound; but when I have come, and lie back gasping, I feel I have just gone through the most gratifying and satisfying sexual experience of my life. It is as if my nerve endings are over-energized, hyperactive, more alive than ever before, and acutely sensitized to pleasure.

She gets up off the sagging bed and gets dressed, and goes without a word or a glance at me, and I just lie there, grinning inanely, as if I have achieved something of note.

Still I do not sleep, but brood on my situation. It seems to me that I have been let down and betrayed, not just by Jennifer and her family but by my New York friends, employers, by the citizenry as a whole, by all of America; no one has come to help me in my hour of need. I resolve there and then to leave, leave, as it were, on a high of pleasure, before things can get worse, facing up to the fact I am no longer satisfied to be cooped up in this dingy hotel, with nowhere to go and nothing to do. Also, I feel ambitious now: I am going to write great things, do great things, make money doing interesting jobs. But not here; it is simply impossible to do any of these things in America. Therefore, I will go.

An idea occurs to me: I will do postgraduate study, and explain to the world all my theories linking what is called 'mental illness' to diet:

Apply – NUI-UCD: MPhil, MA, in Geography

1. Geographical distribution of 'Schiz-Bi-P'
2. Historical growth/ spread of 'Schiz-Bi-P'
3. Incidence of 'Schiz-Bi-P' in Jew/ Gael/ North African Diaspora
4. Is there a geog weight of 'Schiz/Bi-P' in meat/ dairy-consuming countries with Gaels, Jews + North Africans?
5. Is there a hist. weight of 'Schiz-Bi-P' in post-1950s era? (growth of wealth: meat + dairy consumption)
6. Combo: is there geog + hist. weight of Bi-P-Schiz' diagnostic in J/G/A Diaspora?

Research:

Protein? Enzyme? Gene? That near-Eastern Indo-E (?) racial source lack + that makes them:

1. Lactose intolerant (?)
2. Prone to alcoholism (?)
3. Subject to hypoglycaemia and therefore misdiagnosed 'Bi-P/Schiz'

With what is left of Bob's gift and the money I got modelling, I manage to buy a one-way ticket to Dublin. Despite the fact I haven't phoned even for a chat in a while, and that I am still angry with him, I now phone my father and ask him for a lift when I arrive in Dublin airport the next morning.

Arriving at the check-in desk, I am told my baggage is in excess of the weight allowance and I have to pay a hundred-dollar surcharge. But I do not have the money: I gave my last fifty dollars to the driver who brought me to the airport.

'Can I use your phone?' I ask the check-in clerk; she allows me to use the courtesy phone, and I phone Vera, the only person left in America who might be willing to help me. I get through to her and explain the luggage situation, tell her the fee can be paid over the phone by credit card, and leave her in awkward silence to consider, until finally she agrees to pay.

As the plane takes off I am grinning, my foot tapping, my leg jumping; it is hard to sit still. I tell the air hostess I am hypoglycaemic, allergic to certain foods, too, and I need a special diet. Refusing the food offered, I demand an alternative; the air hostess tells me to calm down, and I am observed closely and warily for the rest of the flight.

It is smothering for me to be trapped in the plane so long, the flight seems interminable; but I feel glad, genuinely joyful, that I have ended it all definitively with the woman I had wanted to marry and have children with, who I had wanted to spend the rest of my life with, who I had loved more than any other woman in my life up to this point. I feel nothing but euphoria, ringing, pounding through me, as I cross the Atlantic and return to Ireland.

11. The Railway Tracks

I stand at the doorway of my father's house in the suburb by the sea as he and my sister go out on their way for a walk. I am smoking, I seem always to be smoking these days, and I am half smiling, giddy.

My sister asks me: 'What are you up to?'

I do not look at her, but stare out, gazing at the houses and trees in the estate.

'Just smoking,' I say.

'No, I mean, generally, what are you up to these days?'

The smile does not falter, the gaze does not shift from the street: I am doing my best to act as if she is not there.

'Just smoking,' I say again.

She gives up and goes for her walk.

I've decided not to look for a job. After all, the agent I met on the subway is even now considering the extract and synopsis of *Henry's Blues* that I managed to send her, and she will recognize it as a work of genius, recognize me as the next big thing, find me a publisher. I'll have a bestseller and be rich; no need for a job then, which would just be an encumbrance. I will need a little cashflow in the meantime, so I will claim disability benefits to tide me over; for am I not hypoglycaemic? The all-too-frequent crashes, being suddenly laid low, exhausted; then the return, equally rapidly, to my over-energized state: it must be fluctuating blood sugar. What else could it be?

In early October I have the first consultation with a new

GP, a kind, attentive man slightly younger than myself. I have come armed with my copy of *Hypoglycaemia for Dummies* and a notebook of cramped notes detailing all my symptoms and ideas about the condition, about me. As I explain myself, my history, and the misdiagnosis of bipolar disorder, the GP at one moment mishears or misunderstands me; taking umbrage, I stand up, intending to storm out, and he has to reassure me, placate me. Calming, I sit again and we work out a plan to do a full physical examination, including blood tests.

I weigh eight stone two pounds.

The blood tests for hypoglycaemia do not indicate anything untoward. Nonetheless, I am deemed unfit for work and so I am able to get the sick certs I need to claim disability payments. Now I have an income.

There's a workshop for actors, writers and directors I've heard about that meets weekly, and I start to attend the sessions. In the attic room of a rambling building near the canal basin, we participate in theatre games, mock auditions, readings and discussions about performance, theatre and film.

For an audition piece, I sit at a desk in front of Graham, a director, and run through a monologue I've managed to memorize in only a few minutes: my mind is racing, razor sharp. Recalling an exercise from the Barrow Group, the company I trained with in New York, I decide to add a non-contextual action to the monologue, and so, as I speak, I untie my shoelaces, take off my shoes, then take off my socks, which I touch to my nose and smell, all the while continuing to speak. Then I reverse the actions and complete the monologue.

The director is taken aback by this performance. 'I wouldn't give you the part,' he says, 'but I'll never forget your audition.'

After my turn is up I go into the corridor outside the attic room by myself; I sit and feel an unbearable sadness descend.

Overcome, I begin to sob quietly to myself; then I manage to calm down and go back into the workshop.

Graham and I become friendly. It was his girlfriend, Rachel, who told me about the workshop, and we often spend hours in their house in a north-side suburb, talking about our plans for the future. My play *Those Powerful Machines* interests them both; there is a role in it that would suit Rachel perfectly, and Graham thinks it would make a terrific Fringe production for him to direct. We make tentative plans to mount it sometime in the future – tentative because Graham has to complete work on a feature film he is committed to. Still, I feel excited that my play has found a team that could finally bring it to the stage.

Through an actor friend who is also a musician, I start a regular music gig, playing Delta blues in a rough-and-ready pub on the quays; my confidence knows no bounds, my energy and enthusiasm are ceaseless.

It dawns on me now that I was rash in my actions over the summer. I suddenly decide I want to reverse and rectify it all.

The first thing I need to do is make up with Jennifer, but when I phone her she is wary of me and rebuffs me, firmly telling me I need to be in Dublin, seeking treatment for my illness.

'I'm not bipolar,' I assert, and explain about the hypoglycaemia.

'I think you're in denial,' she says.

'I just want to come back,' I plead.

'You had a good life!' she yells back.

It cannot be denied; I did have a good life with her in New York, and now it is gone.

In October I make an appointment with Dr Kirby. I tell him that I am convinced I have a coeliac problem that explains all my mood and energy changes, and that I want to go on a gluten-free diet to solve them. He knows an expert in this I should consult. I am determined now to break off any form of relationship with my father and sister, and convinced the diagnosis of bipolar disorder I received years before was incorrect. Dr Kirby stresses the importance of getting away from the negative influence of my father.

My college friend Seamus has recently bought a house in Rathdrum, a small village in Wicklow, the county where in happier times I went on long hikes in the beautiful mountains, by myself or with Donal.

I meet Seamus for a pint in my local in nearby Ballybrack. Despite the fact we haven't spoken in two years, despite the fact that we weren't much in contact in the years before I went to America, despite the fact we really don't know each other too well any more, I convince him to let me move into his house in Wicklow with him. I won't take no for an answer and just keep haranguing him until he agrees.

He is worried about having a housemate in his new house, would rather some time alone there first. 'You must remember to turn off the stove when you leave the house,' he says, more than once.

'Of course I'll turn off the fucking stove when I leave the house,' I retort. 'Look, I just need a place I can stay a while, a place I can write, okay? Is that too much to ask? You have a room free, after all. I can't write where I am right now. I'll be really clean and quiet. Okay?'

'Okay,' he agrees, reluctantly.

In my next consultation with Dr Kirby, I find he is pleased to hear that I am making arrangements to move to Seamus's house; he thinks that getting away from my father, who I now regard as being sick in some way, is the best thing for me.

He wishes me to see a specialist about my hypoglycaemia, but I don't have the money to pay for the consultation yet; I promise him that I will go eventually. When I leave him, I tell Dr Kirby I'll return in a few months to let him know how I'm getting on.

Over the course of a couple of days at the end of November, I use my father's car to bring my clothes, guitar, music and several hundred books to the little artisans' cottage in Rathdrum. I have become convinced that my sister and father will take my books if I don't remove them from the house.

Once I have moved in, I find I am in the house alone nearly every day of the week. Seamus has yet to find work in the locality, and continues to stay with his family in Dun Laoghaire. The city of New York absorbed and accepted my energy, was a match for it, fed it. Now, in this quiet village, my energy levels suddenly plummet and I sink quickly into deep melancholy. At first it manifests itself as a blankness. I had great notions of going on long walks down country lanes and then writing all day on my return. But now I cannot write a thing. I simply don't have the powers of concentration to do so.

There are no decent shops in the village, and I don't have a car, so my diet becomes one of beans on toast, frozen pizza or fish fingers, bought from the newsagent's. Typically, I sit in the house all day and watch repeats of sitcoms. My books lie in every corner of my room in piles, and on the landing and on the stairs, but I cannot concentrate enough to read them. I watch more TV, I buy more processed food, I sit around with a growing sense of unease: the dawning realization that I have, somewhere along the way, taken a disastrous turn in my life.

Taking the train from the village, I go to see Dr Kirby

again in mid-December, desperate, and tell him how I am now doing: how miserable and guilty I feel since breaking up with Jennifer and leaving my father's house. With my mood shifting ever downwards, I begin to speculate once more that maybe I am in fact bipolar; I wonder, too, if it is not too late to return to New York and be with Jennifer once again.

'That would be repeating and re-establishing the same old kind of dependency relationship that has been the story of your life,' says Dr Kirby. 'You are addicted to dependency-type relationships and, really, it is just like a heroin addict going through cold turkey. This is what you have to go through, even if you are miserable. In a few months you will feel better and be free for the first time in your life. The one thing you don't need now is a relationship of the old dependency type, whether in New York or here, and you must work hard at establishing yourself as a writer from now on.'

He believes that the one person who was positive for me was my mother, and he encourages me to write about her. If I can only get through Christmas and my birthday in January, he says, then I will feel better in the New Year.

As Christmas approaches I grow more depressed. Eventually, I phone Donal, the old family friend, and implore him to come down and visit me. He must hear something disturbing in my voice, or perhaps he has pressing concerns of his own. Either way, he demurs, and so I spend the Christmas period alone in the house, and on Christmas Day eat frozen pizza for lunch and fish fingers for dinner. No one phones me, and I do not phone anyone.

Finally, I accept that I am not doing well here, that the village's isolation is getting to me. Also, I accept that I am depressed. In a series of rapid manoeuvres I announce to my father, to whom I have not spoken in weeks, that I am moving back to his house, and with my last vestige of energy I do so over the course of a couple of days.

A few days later, early in the New Year, my thirty-fifth birthday passes by without comment or acknowledgement from anyone, and I am again in the box room of my father's house in the suburb by the sea. I am unemployed, I am without any activity or occupation or motivation to seek those out, and I am deeply, disastrously depressed.

Depression is a way of feeling, a way of thinking and a way of being. It is all-consuming, all-encompassing. It is a way of life, the only life, an anti-life. Within it there is no without it. It is numbness, at skin level, and at muscle level, and at cell level. It is also a cold fog that envelops the body from head to toe, freezing in its grip. It is also a physical pain felt throughout the body as well as a mental pain that throbs through the mind.

The environment hurts: sounds – particularly loud noises – hurt. Lights, sounds and movement make the ache worse.

It pulses through the body, each pulse worse than the last. It keeps pulsing, and it feels as if it can't get worse. Then the next pulse comes, and it is worse. The pain increases with each pulse, until it reaches what must be the climax; but then with the next pulse it gets worse again. So there is the waiting, lying there, tense, waiting in dread for each pulse, pulse, pulse, which only worsens the feeling. Endless. Relentless. Unmerciful. Indifferent. Brutal.

Thinking, always thinking. Brooding on past mistakes, so many, irreversible, irredeemable, unforgiveable. Considering endlessly the present situation, which is dire, with no possibility of escape or change or alternative. Looking at the future in dread because it is hopeless, pointless, unlikely to produce change either. Looking at the self and seeing it as inadequate in every way: physically, emotionally, mentally.

Thinking on all the failings and failures, the lack of achievement in life to date, the missed and lost opportunities, the sheer lack of any good fortune, good experiences, good things to look back upon: and the future just a continuation, ad infinitum, of the past.

Concluding over and over again that life has come to an end, it is indeed now over. There will be no life after this. Death becomes appealing, as an idea, a sensation, a new way of being, as this is no life. Life is unbearable, therefore death must be bearable; all that is left now is finding a way to achieve it.

I could take pill after pill, pack after pack, of Paracetamol, then lie back and wait to sleep and not wake.

Or fill the bath, lie in it, take a razor and cut deep into the flesh at the wrist, watch the bath fill with red as life goes and the nothingness takes over; relief again just to dwell on this.

Or go to the woods, far from others, with a rope, find a tree, bind the rope to a high branch, then around my neck, and drop down. A gag or crack of bone and then nothing.

Such thoughts are the closest to joyful or hopeful it is possible to have.

When to do it. How to do it. Where to do it. Do it when the house is empty so there is no chance of being discovered during the act, no chance of rescue. Do it somewhere far away, in a rural B&B or a remote forest.

Just do it, though, and soon.

The pain of guilt over all I have done to others in the past overrides any thought of how suicide will hurt others now. No one cares, no one wants to know, there is no love in the world, no place in the world, no acceptance in the world. It comes into consciousness like a cold wash of icy water that wakes you to your real life: everyone hates you. So go, now. Die.

There is a stiffness, a rigidity in the limbs and torso and head. The torso is hunched, bunched up. Movement is kept to the minimum, the barest essential: the shuffle from bed to toilet and back. Head kept rigid throughout. Limbs stiff and pained.

Mute, too, by preference. Unsociable, of course, avoiding people, avoiding contact with the world. Remaining indoors, in bed. Better to smoke out the window, leaning against the sill, than to step into the garden. Painful torture when the out-doors beckons: when cigarettes need to be bought. Agonizing expedition then, shuffle stiff-shouldered up the hill to the shop and then back. Seemingly insurmountable distance. Back then to bed, for days, until the next enforced expedition out.

My father is in his own routine, his own world, and I seldom enter it. He is mainly in the living room, watching TV. Then he goes out once a day for a long walk to the shops in the nearby village: the butcher's or the chemist's. It is only when he is out, and if I can muster the energy, that I go to the kitchen and eat some toast, without appetite, just to quell uncomfortable hunger pangs. When I go out I do not buy food, only cigarettes.

When my father is out I occasionally stand at the stairwell, tie the belt of my dressing gown around my throat, then tie the other end to the bollard at the top of the banister. It does not seem feasible: there is no clean drop, not enough space or distance, the steps are in the way, my limbs are in the way. But if I were to fold my legs, or allow the weight of my head to pull the noose tight as my body slumped over my buckled legs, then maybe, just maybe. I mime it out, the belt gagging me throughout. Then I hear my father's keys at the door at the foot of the stairs; he is returning from his walk. I untie the belt from the bollard and return to my room.

Return to the brooding, the pain, the stasis, the swampy, icy fog. Thinking always of dying. Thinking of how.

Thinking of the railway tracks.

The tracks run along the coast, hugging the clifftop, a fifteen-minute walk from my father's house. Passengers get beautiful views of Killiney bay and its beach, particularly on a fine day when blue skies and sea and the glistening rocks make the vista seem almost Mediterranean. On fine days once I swam that beach, walked it, viewed the bay, mounted steep steps up to the coast road that ran along the railway route, walked to Dalkey and back. Now such pleasures are beyond me. Now the bay is no longer beautiful, and the railway tracks represent something new: an offer of death.

There is a spot where the tracks emerge from a tunnel in the cliffs. Here, I visualize, is the perfect place to wait and then throw myself in front of an oncoming train. There won't be distance or time here for the driver to see me as he emerges from the tunnel, no time to stop before the train is on me. The driver will see me for a flashing second but be unable to do anything about it.

The perfect place to die, then, and the perfect death.

I really want to die, but I need the means to do so quickly and without pain. When I pull a plastic bag over my head and fix it around my throat with rubber bands, the sense of suffocation frightens me. Pills may render me immobile but leave me conscious a long time before I die. To cut my wrists, or my throat, will hurt, really hurt. I press a blade to my wrist, my throat, but then I hesitate, pull back; I am afraid of the pain that will endure until death, during the period of waiting while the lifeblood flows out of me. I need something quicker. What could be quicker?

The train.

So, the railway tracks. If I can only get myself up and out

of this room and to the railway tracks, stand outside the tunnel mouth until the train comes and then, without a moment's hesitation, jump, throw myself, drop or fall quickly on to the tracks under the wheels of the oncoming train, then, yes, it will all be finally over, in the fraction of a second it takes the wheels to sever me from this world.

But the railway tracks are insurmountably far away for me in my enervated state, so all I can do for now is visualize and imagine. Even getting to the bathroom is an effort, the half-mile to the newsagent's for cigarettes an exhausting ordeal. How to walk the mile to the base of the cliff with the railway track and scramble up to it? Impossible. So I lie and I think of the tracks as the depression pulses ever worse through me.

Then the pulses grow too much for me, the depression grows too much to bear, and I do go. I force myself up with effort, I put on clothes, I slowly descend the stairs and put on shoes and coat, and I go outside. I walk to the railway tracks.

On this walk I meet no one. My world is an empty one, an unpopulated one, a suburbia that has been emptied of people. I see nobody as I leave the estate and walk the roads. I cross through another estate devoid of people and go under a railway arch and on to the beach. My posture is hunched, my gait shuffling, it is painful to move and I progress agonizingly slowly towards my destination. The beach is stony, and the stones slip under my uncertain gait. Only the promise of what is to come and the knowledge that I won't have to walk back keeps me going: I only have to reach my destination, after all, and then, mercifully, I can truly rest.

I walk the length of the beach. There must be people here, it is a popular walking destination: but I do not see them. They do not see me either, hunched and setting out to die, or certainly do not notice me, nor guess my intentions.

I walk the beach, to the end, then go up the iron stairway at the cliffs. Here is the point outside the tunnel that is my destination. I clamber over the balustrade, go up a brush-covered, scrubby wasteground. Now I am by the side of the railway tracks. There are the sleepers, the black tracks, the small grey stones that the sleepers are bedded on. Weeds and some rocks on the tract of land by the tracks that leads to the edge of the cliffs which front the shore. The sea is behind me, grey today. I am unseen up here, unnoticed. I stand by the railway tracks as I wait for the train to come.

Finally, I hear it, deep in the tunnel, and then glimpse it, a speck of light in the darkness, a strip of livery, a flash of window, and then the wheels, the steel wheels spinning, coming towards me, the wheels that will crush me and liberate me from this world. I push myself to go close to the tracks. They are by my feet now. I am so close to the tracks that I do not need to jump, merely allow myself to fall or drop down and my body will be across them, my head across them, in the path of those wheels: a clean cut, then. All I want. I brace to fall.

Then the train rushes out of the tunnel. The driver sees me and gives a warning blast of his klaxon. It is too late for him to stop before reaching me, because the train is there, on me, beside me, thundering. I shake from head to toe with it now it has reached me. Now is the time to drop, to fall, to die. The sound is deafening; I see the shocked driver so close now, his eyes, his expression. He is a witness to what I have come to do: he knows.

There is a moment, just one moment, when it is possible to get my body under those wheels.

And then the moment is gone.

I am standing by the railway tracks watching as the train hurtles by me. I am whipped and buffeted by its wind, and the noise the train makes hurts my ears and head and body. Passengers see me now, look dumbstruck to see someone so close.

I remain a moment by the railway tracks, in silence now. Failed. I have failed to put myself under the wheels.

Even more slowly than before, because I have used up so much of my energy getting here, I return to the estate, the house, the box room, the bed. There to begin the cycle all over again: running through all the ways to die in my mind, and reaching the conclusion that the train is the only way, and coming to the realization that I must leave now, this bed, this room, this house, and go to the beach, the coast, the cliffs, ascend the stairs, the hill, the clifftop, and stand once more, wait for the train, stand by the railway tracks.

Over and over again I go and wait for the train by the railway tracks and fail to throw myself under the speeding train.

What stops me?

Only the fear of failure: that there will be a moment when I realize this is the end, my method has worked and life is ending for me, whether it be by blood loss or suffocation or impact, followed, as I see it, by immediate waking, a waking to a new reality. A reality where I have survived the suicide attempt but it has maimed me in some way, left me with brain damage, or permanent organ failure, or the loss of a limb or limbs, and still agonizingly alive and depressed. Locked, in other words, in a hell of both mind and body in which I will lack the physical means to attempt suicide again and succeed, to liberate myself from depression.

I continue to plan, to practise, to walk to the railway tracks when I am able to, and feel that train rush by me and fill me with both fear and a sense of failure. But I still have that bigger fear of the bigger failure.

And so, I continue to live.

12. The Outsider

Late January 2004: I eventually find the energy to return to my GP for a consultation. He is glad to see I have gained a little weight and to hear that my concentration and sleep are improving, but he is concerned at my low mood.

February passes in a cloud and, by early March, with no improvement, I return to my GP. Dr Kirby is away, and I am feeling a sense of helplessness without his advice. By now my depression is truly paralytic. I brood over all the time that is being lost, that will be lost, and I feel I can do nothing about it. My GP is very concerned for me. In an effort to break the impasse, reaching for all possibilities, we now discuss the option of starting a trial of an antidepressant. I explain that while I am not bipolar – Dr Kirby has assured me that this diagnosis is incorrect – I know I have got high on antidepressants in the past, and this makes me wary of taking them. We consult in detail, don't rush into a decision, cognisant of the risks involved; but the fact is my mood is not, has not been, lifting. In my condition, my desperation, I am willing to try anything to feel better. So we make a measured decision to try a trial period of an antidepressant; I will start taking half the dosage normally given to an adult male.

Later in March I return to my GP for the follow-up; there has been a reduction in the anxiety I've been feeling but no major improvement in mood. Nor, however, have there been any negative side-effects; I have not become manic or elated.

In April Dr Kirby returns and I have a consultation with him. I tell him of my depression over Christmas and of doing the one thing he told me not to do under any circumstances: moving back in with my father.

'I just spend my days ruminating,' I tell him. 'I just lie in bed thinking about what a failure I am and how I let myself down, and I keep wondering why I came back to Ireland from America.'

He assesses me and concludes that there has been no benefit in taking the antidepressants, and so I will no longer take them. Instead he encourages me to seek work in a non-challenging environment so I can afford to move out of my father's house.

'Your one task is to achieve separation,' Dr Kirby says. 'You must get a job, any kind of a job, that will give you enough money to get a flat. Then you can start looking for a better job and start the slow, painful task of building yourself up. The very first step is to get up at eight o'clock every morning, go for a walk, and then make a list of the actions you have to do for the day in looking for a job.'

But it is impossible; months pass, and I still don't have the motivation to do anything, I continue to do nothing to improve my situation. It becomes apparent to me now that I simply no longer want to live. I don't even have the energy to plan for suicide any longer; but when I go to sleep at night I do not want to wake in the morning.

In early July desperation takes hold of me once more. I consult with my GP, and it is decided to reintroduce the very low dose of antidepressant I was on earlier in the year.

By the end of July there is still no improvement. Considering that I have been taking the antidepressant for several weeks without going high or getting elated, the dose is now doubled, to its normal adult level. Again, it is utter desperation that makes me do this; I see no alternative.

When I return to my GP in August, things have improved; now I am able to tell him that there is movement in my life, I am making changes, considering work again, training, options, getting out at last. I think, perhaps, I have found a medication that works for me.

In the city centre I meet Anto, an acquaintance from the performance workshop. He is also eager for change in his life, and we hatch a plan to look for a house-share, along with his friend David. I know neither of them well, but it seems like a way to get out of my father's house. I will pay rent through social welfare benefits until I get a job.

We move into a house in Stoneybatter, a red-brick cottage in a row of similar cottages. I have a small but quiet room upstairs.

Shortly thereafter, I get a job in a bar in a cinema, and then quickly leave it for a better job as a clerk in a video store. The video store has two outlets, one in the city centre and one in a nearby suburb. I work there nights, in one or other of the branches, depending on the roster requirements. I have mornings free and try to write again, for the first time in a year. But I find it hard to sit and focus for any length of time. Better to sit talking late into the night with David and Anto about plans to mount a play, in the cottage in Stoney-batter, smoking hash.

Things are speeding up. I feel my life is going well now, that I am well. The railway tracks are far behind me. All is well – except I am experiencing a terrible anxiety.

In October I go to consult with Dr Kirby once more, and complain to him of my sense of feeling life is speeding up, is slightly out of control. He tells me to come off the antidepressant, by reducing it first by a quarter, then to half, then discontinuing it entirely; and I am to ask my GP to prescribe me a sedative to deal with my anxiety.

My GP, when I see him, is concerned that I am not making much progress under Dr Kirby. Dr Kirby, meanwhile, is barely communicating with my GP, not seeking his opinion, merely availing of him as a conduit to issue prescription medications.

Despite gradually coming off the antidepressants and starting with the sedatives, things continue to speed up; I get confused, distracted, befuddled easily. At a party at the house in Stoneybatter I become overwhelmed by the number of guests.

Things keep speeding up, I feel I am reeling, life becoming something hard to grasp, slippery, out of my control.

Turning up at the city-centre outlet of the video store, I discover that I am rostered to be in the suburban branch. I have to get out there immediately, they are short-staffed, the manager is there alone and won't be able to deal with the evening rush without me. I set off for the other branch, gripped by anxiety: the manager at the suburban branch is an ill-tempered bully. I need to take a sedative, one would definitely help, but I don't have one on me. I make a detour, stop at a pharmacy and explain my situation to the pharmacist, that I am in consultation with a psychiatrist, I am having a panic attack, and that my GP prescribes me medication for anxiety. Although I have no prescription on me, he agrees to dispense an emergency dose of the sedative I am taking. Then he urges me, after I take it, to sit and rest a while as it takes effect. I do so. Now I am an hour late for my shift.

I finally feel calm enough to go to work. When I arrive at the video store the manager is in a rage.

I try to explain what happened, that I made a simple

mistake, reading the roster wrong, that I have health issues and needed to go to the pharmacy, but he shouts at me to get out and not come back.

Things are definitely speeding up.

Anto thinks that David and I are talking about him behind his back. He is paranoid, suspicious, jumpy. Great sensitivity is needed around Anto to convince him that we are not, in fact, talking about him. David and I make a point of never talking about him when he is not present.

Then I break the no-talking rule with David, because of my lost silver ring, and Anto's new girlfriend.

The ring is a plain band, a gift from a friend when we stayed in an ashram in the south of Spain many years ago. Although I've long since lost touch with that friend, the ring connects me to my love of Spain, to the spiritual, to a commitment to live more consciously. I have grown attached to it over the years and find wearing it grounds and settles me. Now it is lost and I think Anto's girlfriend has taken it from the bathroom by mistake; I mention this theory to David. We are in the living room, smoking hash. David looks alarmed that I am talking about Anto, but he says he'll ask him about the ring.

I am in the living room when all this blows up in my face. Anto is enraged: not only have I been speaking about him, but I have apparently accused his girlfriend of stealing from me. He won't believe me when I tell him that I'm sure she took it in all innocence.

'I just want my ring back,' I implore. 'Can't you just ask her for it?'

But his rage will not abate and then he snaps: he grabs a glass from the table beside him and fires it at my head. It smashes against the wall behind me, shattering and sending glass fragments all over the floor. My knees go from under me and, trembling, I fall to the ground.

'Please don't hurt me,' I cry, and I begin to sob uncontrollably. David and Anto look down at me in disgust, on my knees on the floor before them, hands up, begging for mercy, and blubbering.

Things now really speed up.

I find it hard to think logically, clearly, rationally. David returns my ring to me, silently, sheepishly, but something has been broken for me in that household in Stoneybatter and I feel it is no longer home. I am now terrified of Anto, of his potential for violence, and I am humiliated and ashamed by my hysteria in front of him and David.

With a sense of failure and resignation, I borrow my father's car in order to move my things back to his house in the suburb by the sea.

But I find it stifling to be in.

So now, instead, I am out a lot, feeling energy surge through me. Out all day, walking, walking, walking, and sometimes finding myself late in the city centre, resting until dawn in a twenty-four-hour internet café.

Out, seeing patterns in the world, patterns no one else can see, that only I can comprehend.

There is, for example, a pattern to the traffic-light sequence in Dun Laoghaire that only I can appreciate and understand. By pressing the buttons of the pedestrian crossing at the People's Park, I can control the traffic across all of Dun Laoghaire. I press the pedestrian button on one side of the road, cross over and press the one on the other side. There is a logic behind this that I alone can grasp. I return then and press the first button, an essential part of the process. I repeat the pattern. The lights go red: I have done this. It makes me feel elated to know that I have made this happen, that the traffic stops for me.

I do this for hours, all afternoon, until evening sets in and the daylight fades. Then I go on walking.

'You were seen,' my father tells me one day when I return to the house. 'You were seen in Dun Laoghaire.'

I do not know what he is talking about.

I stay up all night cooking strange concoctions with whatever I can find in the kitchen: potatoes, vegetables, all the Indian spices I can find. When my father comes downstairs, comes into the kitchen in the middle of the night and sees the yellow mess I have made, I tell him: 'I'm cooking ayurvedic food.' He replies angrily, but his reply is incoherent to me. I am rational, logical, sensible: I see patterns and meaning in the world. But he is not, does not. I conclude he is showing the early signs of dementia; his confusion at my normal behaviour only proves this.

I go to his brother's workplace in the city centre and explain my fears. Then I phone my father's GP with the same concerns; they don't believe me, which frustrates me further. I can see my father is incoherently rambling, cannot understand why everyone else denies it.

I walk around Temple Bar all day, barefoot, like a penitent or a pilgrim; there is a reason for this, a spiritual reason only I can grasp or articulate. There is a reason I must walk around the Friends' Meeting House building a certain number of times so that all will be made well, restored, put to rights. In the cinema next door I wordlessly implore a Chinese waitress to love me. I feel connected to her, a profound spiritual link she must feel also.

Going to my sister's garden flat in Dun Laoghaire, I bang on the door until she comes. When she sees me, she tries hurriedly to close the door, but I jam my shoulder against it and try to force my way in. She is terrified; now I don't even know what it is I want any more. Eventually, she manages to get the door closed, and I skulk away, obsessing over my father.

I go and knock on people's doors, ring their doorbells. Inside these houses, someone wants me to talk to them, I have the answers they need; inside, there is something for me. My father, out on his daily walk, sees me.

'Stop that at once, come away from there!' he shouts at me. He has his walking stick and waves it at me, ushers me back to his house.

I am at the door to the house, my father has bolted it from the inside, and I am banging, banging, banging to get in. So he phones the Guards and I am brought to Shankill Garda station and they take a statement from me and ask me to sign it. I take the pen they proffer and scrawl all over the sheet of paper they have put before me. To me this is all just a lark.

My friend Jer, the film director, is working in Portugal when I phone him on his mobile and accuse him of starting to make my screenplay *The Perch* into a film without my knowledge; it takes a lot of persuading to calm me down. In the end I feel certain that *The Perch* is on the verge of being made at last.

I never sleep, I'm up all night, creeping and skulking about the house, cooking ayurvedic meals, watching late-night TV, poking around my father's things in the living room, burying my belongings in the garden for safe-keeping.

I get into an argument with my father over his books, the collection that lines the shelves in the living room. I want them, I want all of them, up in my room, now.

'I'll have them in the end,' I tell him gleefully. 'When gone, I'll have them. So I might as well have them now.'

He ignores this, ignores me, stares at the TV. I want, need him to notice me and listen to me. I go to his armchair, lean over him and poke him on the chest.

'Listen to me,' I say.

He continues to ignore me.

I poke again, harder now, but get no response; his gaze does not waver from the TV to me.

'Listen to me,' I say again, and I poke and poke, the same spot just below his shoulder, harder and harder, until it is almost a punch I am delivering, trying to get him to look at me.

Finally, he can take no more and, sighing loudly, pulls himself out of his armchair and goes upstairs. 'You're just a madman,' he says to me as he leaves the room.

Occasionally I encounter people I know on my wanderings and try to spend time talking to them, but these encounters only emphasize to me my alienation. The acquaintances I meet all react in the same way: they look at me in incomprehension, disbelief.

I meet my ex-girlfriend Serena in a hotel for a drink and show her my mother's birth certificate, which I have pilfered from my father's files. The birth cert says my mother's middle name was Julia, which I think is significant because John Lennon's mother's name was Julia. I feel a strong connection to John Lennon and I think this is important.

I board an intercity train in Connolly station and travel to Drogheda, stay there a night in a hostel. There is no reason for this journey: I am merely impelled to go, so I go. The next day I walk around Drogheda town centre and end up in a shopping centre. I make a scene and two security guards escort me out of the building, eject me on to the plaza outside. They wait at the entranceway for me to leave the area, ensure that I do not re-enter.

In my pocket I have two sets of black fold-up Allen keys, intended for bike repair. But I carry them to use as knuckle-dusters. Now I pull the Allen keys out of my pocket and brandish one in each fist, the spikes sticking out between my fingers, brandish them at the security guards. One of them talks into his two-way radio, and immediately, it seems, a Garda car pulls up. I am in the plaza, waving my knuckle-dusters around, swaggering, threatening the security guards, when the gardaí arrive. They quickly subdue me and I am brought to the station.

The gardaí take all my belongings off me, including my treasured laptop, and they put me alone in a cell.

During the night I am unable to rest or settle. I stand at the door, a steel bulwark with a small peephole, drop my trousers and piss under the gap at its base so my urine flows into the corridor. This gets me noticed. Quite suddenly the room fills with gardaí, big men, who surround me. They beat me severely for what I have done, angry, chastising. But my mind has sped up so much now that I do not know whether the beating actually takes place outside my mind also, in the world, or merely within my mind. I do not know if it is real or imagined.

They let me go the next day. In my eagerness to be gone I leave all my belongings behind. I go outside, wander around the back of the Garda station and find a row of bicycles leaning against a wall. I take one and begin to cycle on the back roads towards Dublin, fifty kilometres away. At some stage I abandon the bike and start to walk, full of energy, despite having not slept, walking through country lanes and minor roads towards the city. Hours and hours of walking.

In the city centre, near the quays, down a laneway, I meet a gang of homeless men and tell them, with great excitement,

about my adventures in Drogheda. They stare at me a ⟍
trying to figure me out. Then they ask me do I have any mo.

'There's a little,' I tell the gang. 'I have a couple of hundr҇
in the Credit Union out in Dalkey. I can't really touch it,
though – they don't allow you to withdraw it unless you close
the account, you know?'

'But you can get it?' one of the gang presses.

'If I close the account.'

They wait while I work it out in my head.

'Yeah,' I tell them. 'I can get it.'

So we set out for the Dart station: I will bring them to
Dalkey and get them the money, which some instinct has
caused me to leave untouched all this time, despite my own
need.

'I think I might need ID to close my account,' I tell them.
They begin to grumble. 'And they might make me wait, they
really want you to just leave the money there, you know, in
case you need a loan, they don't encourage you to withdraw
or whatever.'

I babble away, the men jostling me as we walk. Then they
stop and confront me: they have lost patience, they want
what I have now, whatever I have. They tap my pockets, feel
them for change: I have nothing. They suddenly don't seem
so friendly any more, they don't seem so interested in my
adventures. I realize they never were, that I should not be
there with them: so I run. They do not bother to follow me
and I am alone once more.

I walk from the city centre to my father's house in the
suburb by the sea, another seventeen kilometres, but still
don't feel tired.

Back in my father's house I think that he has taken one of
my pens. I am sure I see it in the drawer of the cabinet in his
room where I have gone, uninvited, poking around.

He is furious that I am in his room, shouts at me to get out, and I shout back my accusations of theft. We come to blows. In this struggle I hold him tight to me to restrain his flailing fists, and we fall in this bear hug on to his bed: he kicks out as I stand up and hits my jaw, breaking a tooth.

He manages to force me out of his room, on to the landing, and slams the door shut. I stand outside his bedroom door and scream at him, sobbing, vile accusations and recriminations, all the pent-up resentments and anger of my youth spat out and thrown at him.

'I should never have fed you!' he shouts back.

I go downstairs, distraught and sobbing now, and leave the house. I get on my bike and cycle out into the night, erratically, weave through the traffic, out of control, narrowly avoid being hit by the cars that honk their horns at me and crash into the kerb of the roundabout at Glenageary. When I come to, groggy, a short time later, I can feel pain in my side, like I have broken a couple of ribs. Undeterred, I get up, ignore the discomfort, cycle back home.

Another day: there is a moment of clarity where I call into my GP and talk to him about all the stress I am feeling, mention how I was smoking too much hash and drinking too much at the house in Stoneybatter. He is extremely concerned, and immediately makes some phone calls. He talks to Cluain Mhuire, an out-patient mental health service, and makes an appointment for the following day; I assure him I will go.

The next day, I call in to my GP again. I intend to leave his office, get into a taxi and go straight to Cluain Mhuire.

But I don't go; instead, I return to my father's house.

At night, I don't sleep any more, I just wait impatiently in the box room for daylight.

*

I stand at the top of Stephen's Green, where the horse-drawn carriages wait in rows for customers. It is a glorious November afternoon, the sun shining, the air crisp, the sky blue. Only I know the reality, however: in Temple Bar there is a club, and in this club there are trafficked women, sex workers being held against their will. They must be saved, and only I can save them. I need weapons to do this. I need knives to defend myself against the traffickers, the slavers, knives to kill them. With a knife in each hand, I will enter the club and kill everyone who gets in my way and I will rescue all who need to be rescued.

And with this thought I feel a surge of energy go through me, a light filling me from head to toe and bringing with it utter clarity, complete understanding of the universe. I need to get that pair of knives, one in each fist, and I need to walk down Grafton Street in this sunshine and I need to kill them all. Kill everyone. This is what the universe needs. It will give me a place in the world, it will make sense of everything.

The horses stand on the road by the kerb of Stephen's Green, hitched to their carriages, all their drivers waiting for their next fare. Traffic and pedestrians pass. A light breeze blows, the sun shines down, the buildings look bright and clean. It is a pleasant afternoon.

Almost as quickly as the surge of energy came, it is gone. I walk away from what would have been carnage, I leave the city centre, I go home, and I do not sleep.

It is just another day.

13. Rough Sleeper

Late November. Jer phones me and confirms that he is going to make the film out of my screenplay *The Perch* at last. He wants me to play the lead character; it will be a guerrilla movie, shot not using conventional cameras but with clandestine ones. Scenes will be captured on CCTV and mobile-phone cameras surreptitiously, from a distance if necessary, all to be edited later into a coherent movie. I will not know when I am being filmed, so am to stay in character all the time, be the part, be in the movie constantly. Straight away after receiving this phone call I start acting in this movie.

At night now people come down out of the attic and into my bedroom, the box room at the top of the stairs in my father's house. They stand laughing, grinning horribly, at the foot of my bed, and they pull out my toenails. Jer listens patiently as I phone him and tell him my vivid memories of these people the following days; I go to bed in fear of them, awaiting their return.

There are rows of snipers positioned on the roofs of buildings. They are waiting for a signal and then they will start shooting, kill everyone below them on the streets. It will be a massacre; no one will stand a chance against them. Nobody else knows about these snipers; everyone goes about their business oblivious to the threat. But I live in fear of the snipers, and now I realize I have to leave Dublin before the slaughter begins. It is an overwhelming feeling, this fear I have; it distresses me that everyone will die and I cannot help them.

The radio speaks to me when I have it on. It speaks to me and me alone. There are coded messages only I can understand.

When the fear of the snipers gets to be too much, I buy a ticket for the ferry-bus in the terminal in Dun Laoghaire, and travel to London. A few nights after getting there, having spent some agitated nights in a cheap and cheerless B&B, walking exhausted up some Underground steps towards the light, I collapse, sink to the ground and pass out. It seems I sleep, but there is a physical sensation I experience during this, a dizzy, fuzzy feeling in the head; I go through some sort of passage, sleeping and waking at once.

When I come to, commuters are stepping over me, indifferent to my condition. Getting up, tapping myself down, I discover my wallet is gone. I am now homeless and penniless in London.

Now, I live in a waking dream world. There is the world around me, which I am sure does exist, but there is the rich world of my mind also, which exists to an equally vivid and valid degree. In that latter world, I am a private investigator investigating a complicated case. At times now, anxious and scared, I phone the security firm I worked for in New York, clearly able to recall the number despite the passing of time, despite my confusion, and getting through to the answering service, I shout urgent, desperate messages: 'Send help, there's an agent down!'

There are concentration camps dotted all around the perimeter of the city. Only I am aware of them. Standing on the platform of train and Underground stations, I stare for long periods at the carriages, full of people. Sadness overwhelms me; do they not know their fate? They are being sent to the gas chambers, to their doom. But there they sit, chatting and reading, oblivious to what lies ahead of them. Only

I can smell the fetid stench coming off the trains, see the decay of the carriages, their disintegrating fabric communicating death and genocide. The very windows are smeared with blood, and I can smell that blood vividly from where I stand, sobbing, retching at the stench.

At times, I see friends or recognize people from my past. They are all acting in the movie that Jer is making. So it is that I find myself being driven by some police officers in the back of their patrol car. Where they are taking me to, or why, I do not know, but I am quite unperturbed; I drive with them quite happily. They picked me up in the café of a local park, a bright, cheerful spot where I had been sobbing uncontrollably, overcome by sadness brought on by the sight of people strolling in the picture-perfect park, sitting in the café and enjoying their tea; things that were lost to me.

This feels better, being driven in the patrol car.

Beside me in the back seat sits Miriam, a girl I went out with in Dublin years before, now playing the role of a police officer; she must have been cast in the movie, too. Excited to be seeing her again after so much time, I am unable to stay in character, to act the scene, but speak to her as Miriam, and even hold her hand as I do so. She is patient with me, and kind, as I speak of our past time together, when we were lovers.

In a grocer's, counting out the change I have begged from passers-by all day so I can buy a can of beer, I see my old friend Pritch, goatee and all, standing behind the counter, now wearing make-up and a turban so as to play the part of an Asian shopkeeper. This time, despite my delight at seeing him, I stay in character and wait my turn in the queue to pay. The scene goes on, uninterrupted. He takes my payment, I thank him like I would any shopkeeper, and he does not acknowledge me either. But I know it is Pritch.

Because the area is familiar to me, I gravitate to Trafalgar

Square most days; this is where the National Gallery and Portrait Gallery are, places I went to with my family when younger, when travelling as a tourist, and where I worked years ago, in the café in the crypt of St-Martin-in-the-Fields, off on one side of the square.

On Trafalgar Square, too, down a series of steps, I discover a hostel for rough sleepers. Inside it is chaotic, overcrowded, the bathroom floor awash with water seeping from the toilets and the sinks as crowds of homeless men attempt to wash; there are no showers. There are not enough beds either, so I mainly sleep in one of the armchairs, and in the mornings chatter to anyone who will listen. One old man becomes the nearest thing to a friend at this time, but most of the men are surly, withdrawn, intimidating.

Above this hostel is a large concrete yard, backing on to the rear wall of St-Martin-in-the-Fields, and this yard is the site of a market, approached from a laneway, where stall-holders sell souvenirs and trinkets to tourists by day. At night, the stall-holders pack away all their goods, clear up the area, and this market yard becomes an overflow space for those rough sleepers who are turned away from the hostel in the basement when it is full. I spend many nights in this market, sleeping under the stalls, huddling in cardboard.

A time now of walking the streets all day until night, and then finding a hostel to stay in. Much time is spent on the street, aimless or begging, and many times the police detain me, and I am taken to a cell for the night, fed, and brought to court the next morning to be charged and face the magistrate. Then I am released with a court date. The reasons for these arrests are never clear to me. I suspect I must be breaking some ancient vagrancy, or loitering, or begging statutes unknown to me, and feel affronted by the injustice of getting arrested for being homeless.

But I do shoplift, for food, and other necessities. But sometimes I shoplift to fulfil a deeper need: a need to connect to my former self through having in my possession an object that reminds me of it.

So it is that I find myself in a religious bookshop, on a college campus, fingering a small and neatly bound Bible under the watchful gaze of a clerk who is evidently part of a religious order, dressed in a soutane. A Bible, because at times in the past I have sought the consolation of religion in my life, and this is one of those times; it answers a need for comfort, to read words speaking to the spirit when I am preoccupied with feeding the flesh alone.

Now I read:

> What sayest thou of thyself?
> He said, I *am* the voice of one crying in the wilderness,
> Make straight the way of the Lord.

Yes, I think: maybe I am that voice, crying out a message of truth in this urban wilderness I have found myself in. It sounds like the truth, it sounds like a message for me, it comforts.

Glancing up, I see the clerk is occupied with another customer; I pocket the Bible and dash out of the store.

Crossing the quad of the college, I become aware of the soutane-clad shop clerk close behind me. Breaking into a sprint, he accelerates and pursues me at the same pace. We run across the cobbled courtyard between colonnaded buildings, the college offices and dorms, and suddenly I begin to laugh out loud, overcome by the absurdity and ridiculousness of it all. Sinking to the ground, laughing, I expect this member of a religious order pursuing me to see the funny side, too, be compassionate and merciful and Christian about it all, laugh it off with me. Instead, he grabs the Bible I proffer out of my upheld hand, gives me an angry thump on the head, then storms off back to his shop in fury.

Off Piccadilly Circus, I wander around a large music store. There is an upper floor where musical instruments are on display and I ask a clerk if I can try out one of the guitars. He is suspicious of me, and stands close by me as I run through the Neil Young, Bob Dylan and Delta blues songs I can remember. As I keep playing, getting better at picking out the blues, the clerk seems to become reassured that I am, after all, a legitimate customer, and grows bored standing there watching, so goes and leaves me alone a moment. Without a thought, without hesitating, I leave the shop with the guitar. Then I start running.

Now I have a guitar, and I can play and sing and I will be able to survive being homeless in London: I can busk to make money, I will be the Irish homeless guy who plays Delta blues so well; I'll make a fortune. Giddy with the prospect, I stop at a kiosk and order a hot dog. When it comes to pay I find I don't have the means; logic has evaded me; I should have busked first, to make some money for the food. Now I explain to the vendor that my credit is good, that I will come back and pay when I have made enough money busking, that my prospects for doing so are excellent, indicating the shiny new guitar I left leaning against the side of the kiosk, as if to demonstrate my creditworthiness. But he is impatient with all this pleading, quickly grows angry and starts shouting at me, and I grow angry, too, at his obtuseness, shout back insulting him, until we are both screaming at each other, passers-by glancing at us uneasily.

Then he comes out from behind the counter and confronts me. We circle around the kiosk a few times, he threatening, me continuing to throw out insults. Eventually, he grows tired of this and returns to his business, attends to a waiting customer; I go back to retrieve my guitar. Of course, it is no longer where I left it.

Now it is back to begging once more.

I shoplift razors and shaving cream, go to the public toilets on Trafalgar Square and shave. It is another way of keeping a connection with who I was before, keep myself looking well, as I used to like to do. Then I lose the razors and quickly become dishevelled once again.

Often I sit on the steps of St-Martin-in-the-Fields and beg, mainly for cigarettes. At times I find myself wanting to go into the church, not so much to pray as to find respite from the city, or to find a priest who will listen to me. But every time I enter St-Martin-in-the-Fields a hulking security guard violently ejects me back on to the street; he is huge, a monster of a man, towers over me, and he can grab me at the chest with a thump and push me out easily. I am doing no harm, but when he observes me this security guard just sees a derelict, someone who dirties and desecrates this sacred place and puts off the respectful tourists, and he will simply not tolerate my presence there.

There is a statue of Oscar Wilde opposite the hotel at Charing Cross station. It gives me the idea to sit there and write an essay about Wilde, all that I now see and understand about his life, his tragic end; I can empathize with him, comprehend him, enter into his frame of mind in his final days better than anyone else. It is imperative I write down all my thoughts and theories about him.

But when I acquire a notebook and pen and try to write, my attempts quickly flounder; sitting out on the street on the memorial, which is shaped like a bench, I find it hard to get all my rushing ideas down on paper, after all. Easier to just go on talking about the idea for the essay to anyone who will listen to me on the streets.

It is a harsh winter, and I spend the days walking outdoors, exposed to the bitter air. The skin on my knuckles cracks from the cold, creating deep grooves that expose bright red flesh, ooze blood, pick up dirt; the bleeding washes out the dirt, and then they blacken again.

Now I get the notion, late in the evening, to practise t'ai chi, another remnant of my former life, in a quiet corner near the Embankment. Taking off my boots and socks, now barefoot, I begin to run through the various postures that make up the form of t'ai chi I studied. When I complete the entire cycle, I feel calm, and walk off, slightly dazed, wandering into the streets of London, still barefoot, thinking nothing of abandoning my boots. When I come back to get them, they are gone. This momentarily pains me; they had the softest leather I have ever worn and were a memento of New York, where I bought them. Later, in a hostel, I am given a pair of plastic flip-flops so as to not remain barefoot. Now I tramp around in the cold wearing them, my feet exposed to the elements.

A long queue into the hostel at Trafalgar Square, late at night; the usual crowd of rough sleepers are there, waiting to be admitted, and I join them. When I get to the steel doors, however, I am turned away. They do not give me a reason why. Rebuffed, I go back upstairs to the street, then down the laneway, intending to sleep in the market yard. My plan is to follow my usual routine, to take some cardboard from the piles found lying around the yard and make myself a bed under an empty market stall.

Before I can enter, I hear a raucous shout from inside the darkened yard: 'He's back!'

Dark figures squeeze out then through the gate, fast, one after another, until a dozen surround me in the shadows of the laneway outside the market: hard men, rough sleepers, headed by a gnarled and swarthy Scot who has always terrified me. They begin to punch me. They punch and kick and grab my hair to keep me still to take the beating, while, unobserved by any passers-by, they punch some more, hard, in this dark corner of Trafalgar Square. A blow hits my nose and blood erupts over my face. More blows, more kicks. They will not stop, and I wonder how I can survive.

Then a firm hand grips me by the neck and in the melee I hear a voice quite close to my ear clearly say: 'Keep your head down.'

It is the old man I often chatted to in the hostel, my only friend there, and now he is helping me. Doing what he says, I keep my head tucked down low, and the punches begin to lose their efficacy. Then I burrow even lower and see an opening in the mob around me. I break through, away from the gang, away from the laneway, and into the West End traffic that has to brake and swerve around me as I sprint across the road.

Running until breathless, I go as far as I can until I feel it is safe to slow down, then stagger into a late-night burger place and go straight into the toilets. There I see myself in the mirror: blood smeared across my face, my hands, all over my clothes. My ears whistle, my head is numb from the beating. The shock of how close I came to being beaten to death surges through me: they would not have stopped until I was lifeless before them. This, I decide, shall be the last night I dare go near the market.

Now it is harder and harder to secure a bed in a hostel; frequently I am turned away. It is always unclear why, but it is as if they know me already, and are wary of me, sick of me.

Now it is all rough sleeping, in doorways, on benches, anywhere. It does not feel safe to be in hostels anyway, near the other rough sleepers I am now afraid of.

When possible I try and go indoors for a while to warm myself. I sit in the National Gallery, it is free to enter, or in the lobby of the South Bank Centre, any large public place that I can loiter a while without being noticed or moved on. But usually, after a while, something in my demeanour or appearance or behaviour marks me out, and I am ejected, find myself back on the streets once more.

Walking. Walking all day. Walking until exhausted then trying to sit somewhere to shelter from the cold for a while. A train station, the Underground, a museum. A fast-food joint where the owner takes pity on me and gives me a meal without my asking. Sitting indoors as long as possible before being moved on. Then walking again. My only comfort the cigarettes I constantly bum off passers-by and can never get enough of. Then more walking. Until night, then finding some cardboard, a doorway, a place to sleep. Trying to stay out of sight, for safety. Not always succeeding.

Waking one night in a doorway to the sound of spattering liquid: looking up to see three well-dressed yobs out for the night, drunk, seeking a quick laugh. They stand over me and cover me in their urine. Dawn that day finds me down at the steps by the Embankment, washing myself in the river.

Sometimes stopping out of sheer exhaustion, unable to walk any further. Any doorway. Any park. Any bench. Waking one freezing morning having been shaken. Harsh morning, a bench by the edge of a busy road, a man standing over me, still shaking my shoulder. He stands back when I wake.

'Sorry,' he says. 'I thought you were dead.'

Sometimes riding on the late-night buses that rattle through the city at all hours; it seems easy to board them by the middle doors and not buy a ticket, hurry upstairs, the drivers not noticing or caring. Go upstairs then, sit in the back row, lie down and fall asleep as the bus hurtles through the night-time streets. Waking before dawn to realize I am in the depot, in the silence, surrounded by empty buses.

There are hospitals I gravitate to: one in Whitechapel, another in Elephant and Castle. Some I simply loiter in. In others I ask for treatment, wait for hours in Out-patients.

In one hospital, near Westminster, I spend the best part of a week, as a psychiatric ward in-patient. Here I am medicated, sometimes forcibly, bits of sanity creeping into my consciousness, telling me: you're not well. But once I am discharged, and the medication runs out, I return, quite gladly, to my life as a rough sleeper, which feels like a type of freedom, and has its own excitement.

Awareness, acute, unexplained, and suddenly I see myself as I really am: not an actor in a movie, not a private investigator, but homeless and unwell and vulnerable in London. I use a pay-as-you-go internet booth to fire off a panicked email to Pritch, who I believe to be travelling in Asia, but due to be back in the UK soon to visit his brother in Guernsey.

PRITCH:
I AM IN REAL TROUBLE. I AM IN LONDON AND I HAVE NO MONEY TO GET HOME AS I WAS ROBBED AND BEATEN UP.
CAN YOU GET A FRIEND TO MEET ME AT WATERLOO STATION INFORMATION CUSTOMER SERVICE OPPOSITE PLATFORM 6 ANY DAY THIS WEEK AT 7–8 AM (0800) AS I NEED

TO GO HOME FOR URGENT MEDICAL TREAT-
MENT.

YOU CAN CONTACT ME VIA THE METRO-
POLITAN POLICE IN LONDON, THE NHS
HOSPITAL IN WHITECHAPEL, OR A SOCIAL
WELFARE HOSTEL AT 121 WHITECHAPEL HIGH
STREET.

I NEED A LOAN OF £50 WHICH I WILL BE
ABLE TO PAY BACK.

OR MAYBE SERENA CAN ASK HER EX TO
MEET ME AT THE ARRIVALS LOUNGE OF AN
AER LINGUS CARRIER AIRPORT.

IN THE MEANTIME I WILL BE AT WATER-
LOO AT 7–8 AM UNTIL I GET A WORD.

HOPE YOU ARE WELL, WATCH YOUR BAGS,
ARNOLDO XXX

I send this message not only to Pritch but also to people
from the attic workshop I had attended in Dublin; to the
Edward Albee Foundation; to various theatre companies
and organizations in Dublin, London and New York; to
Cathy; to the head of the Irish Writers Union; to Jennifer; to
the editor of a magazine in the US that published a story of
mine; and many others.

Message sent, awareness dissipates as quickly as it came; I
do not go and wait for help in Waterloo station, or check for
messages in the places I suggested. Rather, I resume walking, and acting, and investigating my complicated case; I am
in a movie, I am a private detective.

Then, another sensible idea: if I could only spend a night
in a hotel and properly wash and have a good night's sleep,
then I would be in a position to figure out what to do, sort
myself out. There is a phone booth, and I phone my father in

Dublin, and amazingly, he accepts the charges. Quickly, I explain my plan to him: to get my sister to use her credit card to pay for a night's accommodation in a hotel for me over the phone. It has to be my sister, as my father does not have a credit card, to my knowledge; and my sister, I am sure, will want to help me.

'She doesn't want to know you,' is his response.

'Will you just ask?' I plead, frustrated at what I am sure is a lie. There is a momentary pause while I wait for him to decide, then he hangs up.

When in train stations, I often feel the urge to travel, and so I sneak past the guard at the barrier and board a train, any train, at random. On a train to Brighton, I am bright and bubbly and exuberant, eating some chips, offering them to the other passengers, who stare at me as I hop up and down the passageway, exclaiming: 'Do you want some crunchy munchy stuff?'

The train arrives in Brighton and I get off it, walk downhill from the station to the town centre, walk around all day: the beach, the pier. There are other rough sleepers around, and a hostel that will not admit me; at the end of the day I return to the station, manage to sneak back on to a train, and return to London.

Entering a building, bristling with energy, I state that I am a fire officer, come to carry out an inspection. Commotion ensues and the police are called. Searching me, they find items of toiletries they conclude are stolen; vaguely, I recall walking through a shop, pocketing razors and shaving foam. They arrest me for theft, and it is another police cell for the night, another court appearance, and then once more I am sent on my way, back into the city, walking, walking, walking, burning with energy.

Burning, burning, burning: the night passes, I am down by a canal, far from the city centre, an isolated, desolate spot.

There is a track leading up to the high street; I do not know how I got here, where I was going, where I am going. Now I follow the track up away from the canal-side walk, go up by a bridge, find myself on a high street among traffic and people once more. On the corner is an old-fashioned café, a real greasy spoon, offering tea, breakfast; I am hungry, as usual, but I have no money to pay for anything. When I go in and ask for food, explain my situation, the owner gives me a full English breakfast, no question of charging me.

Another phone booth, another impulse. Stacking the change I have accumulated begging beside the receiver, I'm beginning to shovel it in when the voice comes on telling me how much I owe; I am making a long-distance call to the apartment in Canal Street, the number of which I can recall vividly, as I have a punishing urge to talk to Jennifer.

The answering machine picks up, and when I hear Jennifer's voice recording I am wrenched by a sob. 'I have no shoes,' I cry into the machine; and it is true, I am still wearing the flip-flops, have been wearing them since losing my boots. Hearing the pips sounding to tell me I am about to be cut off, I shout, desperately: 'Please, Jennifer, will you marry me?'

Then the line goes dead.

Walking through Soho, I am hunched, shuffling, exhausted, strung out, but exuberant. In one clothes shop a woman, pretty, older than I, is putting the finishing touches to the window display, fixing some lacy garment to a mannequin. The street is crowded, bright, cheerful, shoppers and people out drinking and eating, commuters passing by; the Christmas rush is near. The woman, absorbed in her work, bends down to pick up some ribbon from the floor inside the store-front, and her blouse falls open loosely to reveal her cleavage, a glimpse of white bra.

Standing right at the window, I look down her blouse, my sexuality heightened and pulsating, pounding urgently through me, and when she notices me, glances up and sees me staring down at her, I grin back lewdly. She is startled, shocked, to be so abused, to have me look down her clothes; she grasps at her open neckline, is furious, but I am still grinning, feeling invincible and unmoveable there on the street. Clutching her blouse closed, she retreats from the window display and into the interior of the shop. Walking away, aroused, I am still grinning, feeling as if I have achieved some minor victory and full of my own importance.

Hungry. Always hungry. Not always able to beg enough to buy food in time to satisfy the endless, clawing hunger. Stopping by an overflowing bin to try to see if what seeped from it was edible. Leaning over, picking at a potato peel, I feel a blow to the ribs. Floored, winded, I look up to see a young man hurrying away. No reason for the assault, except that he was disgusted at the sight of a human being reduced to the condition of an animal.

Train stations not a bad place to rest. Lost in the crowds, unnoticed by Security for a while. Chatting to a young office worker who waits for her connection out of London. She asks about me, then says: 'Wait here.'

A few minutes later she returns with a bag: burger, fries and drink. I feel overcome by her kindness: I will get through another day.

Another train, travelling to I do not know where; I have got on solely to escape the cold and stay warm. When I get bored of going in the same direction, I will simply cross to the opposite platform and get a train coming in the opposite direction and return to London, avoid the ticket inspectors, go back on the street.

For now, though, warmth, sitting at a table in a train carriage.

There are others here, around the table, young people, with whom I chatter brightly. It is unclear, but they may be rough sleepers, too, or street drinkers; they are certainly not like the other commuters, and there is something knowing in the way we glance at each other, talk to each other.

There is a woman, my age, in tight black jeans and a tight black top. Pale, pretty and raven-haired, her breasts and thighs and backside bulge and strain against the restricting fabric of her clothes. She looks at me often and smiles, she seems to know something I am not privy to, and then somehow it is agreed that we will spend some time alone together. We leave the others at the table and I follow her down the rocking passageway to the toilet cubicle. Inside, shaking and rocking back and forth with the train's motion, I am consumed by utter lust for this woman, this stranger; it overwhelms me and leaves me breathless. She leans against the sink, smiling. 'You can look,' she says, still smiling, looking in my eyes, recognizing what is there, 'but you can't touch.'

My cock is going to explode, it pulses, its pressure and throbbing urges needing to be released; I stare at her in agony, in frustration.

But I do what she says.

I look.

I don't touch.

On Christmas Day, the lights are bright on Oxford Street, but all I think of is the sleet that begins to fall. I walk in a near-empty city, hour after hour. No hope of getting change; it looks like I will not eat this day. Then, behind King's Cross station, I find a shop open. When I enter, the heat is like a blessing.

Behind the counter a man nods to me. He is Muslim and we talk about the photographs on the covers of the Middle Eastern newspapers the shop sells. A picture of a young boy serving tea particularly strikes me: he seems so innocent and full of joy. The shopkeeper intends to close soon, but he listens to my story and lets me stay by the heater and really warm myself. Later he gives me food.

For him it is *zakat*, for me it is life itself.

Finally, he has to close the shop. He asks where I am going to go now, for the remainder of Christmas Day, for Christmas Night.

'Out there,' I tell him.

We stand outside in the cold as he pulls down the shutters and locks up. Then I turn to go.

'Wait,' he says to me, and goes back into the shop.

The cold seeps back into my bones again as I wait, watch the empty streets around me, think of the night ahead in a doorway. The door to the shop opens again and the shopkeeper returns. He thrusts something under my arm with a nod: a carton of cigarettes, twelve full packs. This makes me smile, the first genuine smile in months.

Something to get me through the night ahead, walking now until I find a doorway I feel is safe and sheltered enough to sleep in, another night on the streets of London in winter, another night freezing, lost.

PART III

14. The Return

Then I am on a train platform in Basingstoke; as usual, I have arrived here quite randomly, having boarded a train at Waterloo to stay warm. I have somehow acquired a football, and now I kick it back and forth along the platform until, inevitably, it falls off on to the tracks. As I jump down to retrieve it, a voice comes on the Tannoy ordering me to stay off the tracks, and I clamber quickly back on to the platform. The police arrive and quickly evaluate the situation. They detain me; another police cell beckons, another confrontation with a magistrate.

The officers are a man and a woman, quite young. They put me into their vehicle and we drive off. They are chatting to one another chirpily, glancing at me and smiling. But I can think of no reason for smiling as I picture the night ahead. I am too restless, too agitated, to spend a night in a cell, and I dread it.

But instead of driving me to the police cell to be charged and detained, they bring me to a hospital. They must recognize something in me: that I need help, not punishment. They see someone who is mad, not bad. There is a handover from police to hospital staff, everyone smiling broadly, and I am shown into a ground-floor office in the psychiatric wing of the hospital. Several doctors assess me in sequence, and to them all I deliver a rapid account of myself and my circumstances.

I feel my father knows where I am. He knows before it happens. This guy had a stroke. He thinks it's 1995. My phone was tapped, I had to get rid of it. I'm a writer. In '98 I had a diagnosis of manic depression, but I didn't tell the doctors I had been smoking cannabis and drinking a lot. I think that was the real cause. I've been in hospital three times. My mother died when I was nineteen. That affected me. I've got a trapped nerve in my back. I was in a hospital recently in London. They restrained me. They gave me drugs. The usual story: they discharged me, no money, no home. I'm due in court on 5 January. Theft, indecent exposure. The doctors in London were replacements in uniform. I don't want to go back to London without a gun. I was in the Territorial Army in Ireland for years. I want to arm myself and shoot people in the IRA. I want to get a rifle, I know how. Get a farmer to give me permission to hunt on his land then apply for a licence and just buy myself one in a hunting shop. The IRA are after me. I have names of people I want to shoot. My computer was stolen from me a few months ago. I'm not suicidal. Someone wants me dead, so I need to arm myself, but I don't have access to arms at the moment. One of my earliest memories is of my sister trying to kill me when I was two. She tied me to a Christmas tree and set it on fire. I'm a recovering alcoholic, and I smoke. I have a few broken ribs. I don't know this area. Somewhere near London. I haven't slept for five weeks, but I do get nightmares. My thoughts are racing, I do need to feel calmer. I do need to be in hospital to feel safe.

During all this, my mood swings from sad to angry, and I bang my fists on the table to get my point across. The doctors take note of the cuts on my hands, my cracked knuckles that bleed, the way I've shaved patches of hair from my head. Sometimes I laugh, or try to make a joke; other times the anger returns, particularly when I am being labelled manic depressive.

They take a family history, and decide I need to be in hospital. I agree to be admitted. They dispense medications I readily accept: two antipsychotics and something for anxiety.

After the admission procedure I am brought up to the ward. They show me my bedroom, a private one. It is small and cosy, and clean and warm. The nurse brings me then to the laundry room and I am allowed to pick out clean clothes for myself from a basket of freshly laundered clothing. Layer after layer of jeans and tracksuit bottoms and tops and T-shirts and shirts and sweaters. I pile them all on; some part of me is still preparing for the night ahead on the street, and I know from experience to have extras in case of damage, loss, or theft.

There is tea with biscuits, and more medications, and finally I manage to sleep in my room; but I sleep on the floor, not the bed. I am not ready for the bed; the hardness of the floor is more welcoming. During the night I suffer from nightmares that wake me, visions of night-time streets and beatings, arrests, confinements; or maybe they are memories. Leaving the room, I go and tell the nurses about the dreams and they make me more tea, which I sip gratefully until I settle down again.

The food served in the dining room is hearty, comforting: shepherd's pie, roast beef with Yorkshire pudding, toad in the hole, steak-and-kidney pie; and for dessert, sticky upside-down cake, Eton mess and garishly coloured ice-cream and jelly.

I spend a lot of time in the smoking room, rolling endless cigarettes and talking relentlessly to anyone who will listen to me. The nurse on duty is convinced I think I am Jesus, from all the religious references in my rambling discourse, but this insults me; I know I am closer to John, the one who Christ loved, and I would never presume to be Christ Himself.

Sometimes I become quite suddenly melancholic and retreat to my room. But as I settle, as the meds take effect, I begin to attend groups: creative writing, relaxation skills, art therapy, cooking. There are meetings with social workers and a patient advocate to see how I am feeling and getting on. A small payment is made to me on a regular basis in the form of what are called 'Samaritan Loans', enough for me to buy my own rolling tobacco every few days in the hospital shop.

When I run out of money I return to begging constantly for tobacco from the other patients. They don't appear to mind, but finally a nurse is forced to pull me aside.

'The others don't have much tobacco themselves, so you can't keep asking them for some.'

'But they don't mind. They always say yes.'

'That's because you force them to. You can be very insistent. You just shouldn't ask.'

There are hours now, twisting in agitation without a cigarette, until someone takes pity on me and gives me one; somehow, I limp along like this until the next 'Samaritan Loan'.

There are repercussions from my behaviour on the streets, legal matters to be resolved, court appearances and arraignments to be addressed, outstanding charges to be dealt with. The hospital appoints a local solicitor to address these issues for me, and a letter is written to the authorities explaining I am not fit to stand trial.

A patient becomes agitated and punches a wire-meshed window in the door leading to the stairwell. When I see the cracked window, evidence of someone else's violence, of a violent man, I become distressed and frightened: it is a reminder of the streets. It takes a while for the nurses to convince me it is safe to be in the ward.

There are times I am deemed well enough to leave the ward by myself for a while, though there is little in the grounds beyond a car-park. The main hospital building has a chapel, and I go there often to sit and think and, on occasion, to chat to the chaplain.

On a bench beside the car-park, a woman sits beside me and chats a while. She has been visiting someone, and gets my story from me.

'I wish I had some more money,' I tell her.

'What would you do if you had more money?' she asks.

'I'd buy a phone card and call my friends and tell them I'm all right.'

She considers me for a moment, thinking. Then she takes out £10 from her purse and gives it to me. But returning to the ward, I realize I don't know anyone's phone number; the numbers were lost, with everything else I lost in my time on the streets. So I buy some tobacco.

In early January they offer me a transfer to St John of God's back in Dublin, but I don't want to go; I feel safe in here in Parklands Hospital, don't want to go back to Ireland.

There is a room in one end of the ward that is apparently never used; no one ever goes there, perhaps because it is not permitted to smoke in it. It has a large-screen TV and a VHS player, and one VHS cassette; I put it in the player and run it. It is a compilation video of 'eighties pop music – Blondie, Spandau Ballet, Dexy's – and I play it over and over, sitting with my face a few inches from the screen, listening to music that is strangely comforting, a link to my adolescence, when I sat with my mother on the sofa and watched *Top of the Pops*.

From the car-park, I observe the highway just outside the hospital campus that leads to Basingstoke town centre. Eventually, carrying a slip of paper with the name and address and phone number of the hospital, in case I get lost, I walk along the highway meridian and into Basingstoke. There I find a mall, and in the mall, a public library. It is large, two levels, and brightly lit, and welcoming. There is internet access, and I sit at a computer and get online, and log into my email account; despite all the confusion, I am able to remember my password. Now I can connect with my friends, let them know that I am safe, ask for help.

JER: IN SITU A BIT AND SAFE. WE CAN TAKE THIS IN STAGES NOW. I AM IN A GOOD PSYCH HOSPITAL IN STH ENGLAND: PHONE NO TO FOLLOW ADDRESS COMPLICATED. I WILL CALL; PLEASE LET ME KNOW IF PRITCH AND CO ARE OK AS I AM DAMN WORRIED. AND ABOUT YOU ALL. WE WILL GET THIS TO WORK BUT PLEASE KEEP EVERY MEMBER OF MY FAMILY OUT OF THIS AS IT IS THEY WHO ARE FUCKING ME OVER.

Please phone me. In a hospital now at last with good care, but need help and advice, also worry about friends. I am near Southampton, England, not far from London. I am safe but lonely and really confused, and scared by what has been done to me.

After sending the email, including all the phone numbers of the hospital that I have scrawled on my scrap of paper, I log off and walk back to the hospital.

The next day, after creative-writing class, Jer phones me in the hospital. I am on an upswing, full of grandiose ideas, hard to talk to. But we do manage to talk of practical things, like how he can lend me some money, and my possible return to Ireland. It is a lengthy conversation, and good, and reassuring: when I hang up I feel less isolated and alone.

*

At dinner, everyone else is getting more shepherd's pie than me, and I take this as a slight, begin to shout at the kitchen staff, who stare back at me blankly, trying not to provoke me. The nurses come and manage to calm me down.

Food is an obsession: getting enough, wanting to always have some extra, not running out, never feeling hungry.

In my room, to make it more cheerful, more my own, I mark the walls with drawings in chalk; the nurses complain to me about this and ask me to rub them off, explaining other patients will have to use the room in future.

Early in the morning I feel hungry and, still convinced I suffer from hypoglycaemia, I storm into the nurses' office demanding food. They offer me a cup of tea that I decline, and suddenly I grow furious with them, go to the payphone in the corridor and dial 999 and request an ambulance, stating it is an emergency. Then I return to the nurses' office and threaten and curse them.

Later, I tell the doctor sheepishly: 'I was being melodramatic.'

It is a flash of self-awareness, an owning up. A small thing. I am aware, now, that the energy of mania did not really dictate my actions at that moment: I did. I had agency, I allowed it to take over. Admitting this to the doctor, I tell her I'm not yet ready for the outside world, and that I want to live in Southampton, a seaside town not too far from Basingstoke, when I do leave the hospital, and to go to university there, and that I am in fact a citizen of the UK and so entitled to receive benefits, housing, supports, grants.

On 5 January 2005, I wake up, stride into the nurses' office.

'It's my birthday,' I declare, 'and I want to wear a frock. But not in front of the doctor.'

*

In art therapy I use the patients and staff as models for drawings and make artworks that reference my experiences on
the streets. Some of these are collages, and I stick on bits of
cigarette rolling paper, and the foil from a cigarette pack, to
complement the images; I feel a certain confidence return as
I do these artworks.

Now I begin to think more about practicalities, like benefits, and housing entitlements, and having no ID or proof
of nationality. There is a patient advocate, Sam, who comes
into the hospital and helps me with all these things, but I
often grow irritable and frustrated in our meetings as I consider all the things I need to get resolved in my life.

'No one is fucking helping me,' I tell him, fuming, growing agitated, and I have to be reminded not to swear so much
on the ward.

Meeting with a consultant doctor, I tell her: 'I experienced a
big panic attack last week. I was meant to go on holiday to
Guernsey, and I was on my way to meet my friend Pritch in
Heathrow, but he didn't turn up because of the storm.' This
is the version of events I have put together to make sense of
why I was in the airport just after Christmas, and it has a
certain logic to it; Pritch does indeed spend a lot of time in
Guernsey each year, and was in Asia at the time of the tsunami. 'I have dreams where I am being chased. My friend
Pritch is in Hong Kong, he's safe, he will visit me. I have a
friend in Paris who is trying to help me.'

I begin to recognize that it might, in fact, be easier for me to
get by in Ireland than in the UK. I make enquiries to the
Irish embassy and their passport office in London with
regard to sorting out some ID for myself.

Meanwhile, the nurses explain to me that they have faxed

Uxbridge magistrates' court detailing my situation, informing them that I would not be fit to attend court the following week to face charges of theft of a defibrillator in Heathrow airport. This news calms me.

At a meeting with a doctor, I am now full of plans and ambitions, impatient: 'I want to go to Dublin to get some money. I have money in an account there, but I can't transfer it as I have no ID and I'm homeless, and my ID was lost. But I spoke to the Irish embassy and they are considering issuing me with a temporary passport. I want my benefits sorted immediately. And the other patients are intimidating.'

The doctor listens to my confused outburst patiently, then manages to persuade me that the weekend is not the best time to go to Ireland as I wouldn't be able to get much done, everything would be closed. Calmer now, I talk of other things: the skin on my hands is still dry and cracked so the doctor prescribes me some E45 cream. Placated by this attention, I go back on the ward.

'I'd like to do some volunteer work with the YMCA,' I tell the nurses, remembering how much I loved the Y in New York. They tell me that it is a good idea, but suggest I wait until I'm better. 'I want to learn another language, too,' I go on, full of plans now. 'I'm getting bored on the ward. And I want to move to Malta. I'm fascinated by their culture.'

Ideas for the future are rushing through my mind. Restless now, thinking of what is next, wanting to be out: something is changing in me.

'I don't like the smell of Paula,' I tell the nurses, referring to a patient I'm normally friendly with, 'and I want to eat my dinner in my room because of that.'

Smells bother me inordinately, so I spray myself with

225

some women's perfume I have found on the ward. I have become convinced I can smell blood off women, that I can smell when they are menstruating, and the smell affects me profoundly, makes me dizzy, nauseous. At other times I am convinced I can smell a woman's breast milk, if she is pregnant or breast-feeding for example; this, too, I find to be physically repugnant as an odour, an odour it seems only I can sense.

'If you are not happy to be in Paula's company, you should stay in your room,' the nurses tell me wearily.

Later, the sense of olfactory offence diminishes, and I go back to chatting and being friendly with Paula. X

At creative writing we end up talking about the theme of prejudice, and I state that I feel I have been the victim of prejudice and discrimination and misunderstanding because of what I am; I'm thinking of all the confrontations with the police and authorities, and how difficult it is for me to access housing from the local authority.

I complain of toothache, remnant of the fight with my father. They bring me to the dentist to check out my cracked tooth. I'm put on antibiotics for a gum infection and get a temporary filling, which helps. Meanwhile, I secure the services of a local solicitor to lodge an official complaint of poor medical treatment on my behalf against the hospital.

I have been experiencing a strange and uncanny sensation for months, an extreme drowsiness, a sudden onset of exhaustion, that makes me feel as though I am sleeping when in actual fact I am conscious and awake, though with blurred vision and a fear I'm having a stroke. These I refer to as my 'passages', and I'm convinced they are caused by undiagnosed concussion, which in turn was caused either by my bicycle crash or the time my father accidentally kicked me during our struggle. But no one in the hospital believes me when I tell them I have concussion, nor about the passages; to them, it's just another thing I rant about whenever I can get someone to listen.

There's a suggestion that I be referred to a night shelter in Basingstoke on discharge, but I refuse to go; I want to be properly housed somewhere, I feel I am entitled to this.

Contacting the magistrates' court in Uxbridge, I find out they did not receive the letter that was sent by fax explaining why I had not been able to attend court the previous week, and that a bench warrant for my arrest has been issued; this enrages me, and I storm into the nurses' office.

'I will present myself to the local police station for arrest,' I tell the nurses. 'I'd rather be in prison overnight than stay here.'

Also, I want physiotherapy for aches and pains, and to see a neurologist for my passages and concussion. I tell the nurses that I need psychoanalysis, not medication. The nurses in turn tell me to stop cursing.

'That's racist,' I retort. To me, using swear words is a typically Irish trait; trying to get me to stop is therefore racist, to my thinking.

I want treatment for my sore ribs, too, but my complaints are assumed to be the whingeing of a hypochondriac. Finally, after endless pestering, I get X-rayed: four ribs are shown to be fractured. There is little that can be done to treat them except wait for them to heal naturally. But I have some sense of righteousness that I have been proved correct, and that I do indeed, as I have long maintained, have broken ribs after all.

The doctor conducts an assessment of my mental state. It is mid-January.

'Can you tell me why you were admitted to hospital?' she asks.

'I was suffering from panic attacks,' I tell her. 'I was detained at a train station for acting strangely and brought to hospital by the police for acting dangerously on the platform.'

'What was your daily routine before your admission?' she goes on.

'I was homeless,' I reply. 'Mainly, I was riding around on buses and trying to get food. I came from Ireland to London for the weekend, but I was robbed and couldn't get back home. I was beaten up when I was on the streets. While I was in Ireland my father beat me up, too, and I've been suffering from head trauma and seizures. I've been disorientated.'

'Do you get on well with the other patients?'

'Yes, but at the moment I like privacy. Some of the patients on the ward frighten me and freak me out. But on the whole, I prefer talking to people because I get lonely.'

'What about the staff?'

'I don't feel I can talk to them.'

'What are your goals in life?' she asks.

This makes me reflect.

'I want a home,' I finally tell her. 'I want to be safe and happy. I'd also like a wife and children and go back to being a playwright.'

'What's stopping you from doing these things?'

'Don't have enough money. I don't have an address, or a phone, or internet access. And I'm very stressed and anxious.'

Near the end of January, walking around the hospital aimlessly, I come across a stack of health information leaflets, and pick through them idly. One is an NHS-issued leaflet about bipolar disorder, and I take it away, go and sit in my room, and read it.

Bipolar is a serious mental health condition characterised by extreme mood swings – manic highs to depressive lows.

The leaflet gives facts and figures about bipolar, and details treatments and prognosis. It talks about living with bipolar, and managing the condition. The plain matter-of-factness of the leaflet gets through to me; it cannot be ignored or denied. Into my consciousness the idea plants itself and is finally absorbed and accepted: what has happened to me, what is happening to me, is an effect of bipolar disorder. The diagnosis the doctors have applied to me is correct and appropriate.

Chastened now by this knowledge, I go and seek out a nurse and ask for some one-on-one time.

'I've been reading a leaflet on bipolar disorder,' I tell him when we are alone. 'I recognize now I was having a manic episode before my admission. I'm worried now that having this diagnosis will affect my life and make me unable to do things.'

It seems suddenly impossible to have any sort of normal life: a career, a relationship, creative pursuits. The nurse reassures me that there shouldn't be any significant restrictions on my lifestyle, but that I will have to be more careful about avoiding stressful situations, alcohol and illicit drugs.

The doctors sit me down, and I tell them that I feel ready to leave, that I have had enough of the hospital. Some part of me, stifled by the confinement of hospitalization, still clings to how I was before, to the pleasures of the high, and urges me to believe that the street is the place to be; I long for my freedom, the sheer exhilaration of it, the liberty and openness of the streets, the thrill of mania.

But the doctors talk me down, and I am now able to see, thanks to this period of rest, food, sleep and good care, that it is better to stay on in the hospital. Much as I want my freedom, to be out of the ward at last, I want even more to be no longer agitated, anxious and distressed: I want to be made well, and to understand and manage this condition that I now accept I have. I accept I need help; and I choose to stay on in the hospital.

They explain to me, too, that I need a mood stabilizer to manage my illness, and I start on one I haven't tried before, Valproate. Meanwhile, I am to be transferred to St John of God's as soon as a bed is available; there are many benefits to being back in Dublin, such as access to social welfare benefits and the support of family and friends.

My current financial problems still seem overwhelming and make me anxious and tense. The doctor recommends I attend the relaxation sessions, coping skills and cookery classes, as well as art sessions. Overall, he makes me understand that it is my mental health that is now the priority.

Walking to Basingstoke town centre, I again go to the library and now send an email to my friends:

Hi:

I am back from missing in action. Since I saw you last i have, well, been in a lot of bad places. i am not sure you would believe me if i told you most of it. Basically, I have had a bit of an old nervous breakdown. I am in an English hospital and I am getting a transfer this week back to Dublin, where I will be taken care of in St John of God's Hospital. I will take it easy from here on in. I should be back to Dublin in a week. It would be really nice if you could come visit me. All the best,

Arnold

Separately, I email Jer:

Hi Jer,

Thanks again for all your help. I am in a library and managed to send an email to all the people I needed to get in contact with. The transfer thing is being machinated, if that is a word, as we speak. I should be back in Dublin shortly. I will then concentrate on getting my head, mind, body and life together. Hope to see you real soon, you have been an amazing help to me and I would not have made it through without your help. Basically, you are a damn good friend and a pretty decent bloke.

Hope to see you soon, buddy, and thanks again,

Arnold

Finally, I am able to collect a money transfer, and I can afford to travel to London to be issued with a temporary passport; it will be possible now to travel back to Ireland.

I'm keen to get back to Dublin and begin to distance myself from the hospital. Now when I leave my room, for a drink of water, or food, I no longer talk to anyone, ignore the nurses when they say 'Hello' to me, increasingly try and eat in my own room, to isolate myself.

Thinking of my departure, I ask the art therapist what will happen to all my drawings, which I will be unable to bring with me; she tells me she will hold on to them for three years in case I ever want them back. This comforts me, to know they will be well taken care of.

I will need somewhere to stay in Dublin upon my final discharge from St John of God's Hospital, so I phone my father and ask can I move back to his house. He agrees. This is a relief, but I am doubtful he will keep his word.

The nurses confirm my travel details with me. This makes me take sudden umbrage: I feel they have been making plans about me behind my back, and have not kept me abreast of developments.

When I phone my father again, he tells me I am no longer welcome to stay in his house after my discharge from St John of God's. It is as I suspected. Trying to reason with him, I explain to him that I have been unwell, and that now I am well, so my behaviour will be better, and implore him to change his mind. But he refuses to discuss it further, and remains adamant that I cannot stay in his house.

'I'm sorry,' I say, trying to apologize for all I've done to him.

'Ach, anyone can say they're sorry,' he snaps back.

I will have no home to return to now in Dublin; all that is certain is that Jer will collect me at the airport and I will go to be admitted to St John of God's. What happens after that is uncertain.

At 11.30 a.m. on the morning of 28 January 2005, almost a month to the day since my admission, I am discharged from the hospital outside Basingstoke with a week's supply of medicine, put into a taxi and driven to the airport for my flight to Dublin.

15. The Fog

A friend of mine, a Venezuelan woman I know from the performance workshop, is sitting in the arrivals hall at Dublin airport. She has just arrived back from a trip home, and I sit with her, tell her my situation: 'Maria, I'm homeless.'

She is calm, comforting and, a devout Christian, begins to pray for me.

Jer arrives and the three of us leave in his car. But he has nowhere to bring me: he has no home in Dublin currently and is returning to Paris the next day. Maria is not in a position to accommodate me either. After dropping her off, Jer and I drive around the south side slightly at a loss, debating what to do; I am unwilling to phone my father again to ask to be let back into his house. Eventually, we revert to the original plan of getting me admitted to St John of God's.

I am assessed by the registrar on call. 'I had a nervous breakdown,' I tell him. 'I was psychotic, out of touch with reality. I kept passing out. It was very traumatic. The mania has passed now. I feel very anxious, I can't read a newspaper or watch TV, can't concentrate, I can't cope. I left everything in a mess when I went to England. I had been depressed for a year. I don't want to harm myself, it's more like I want to roll over and give up. I have conversations in my head, a kind of brooding. I was paranoid when I went to England, but I'm not any more, and I'm not having any seizures either. I was off meds since 2000, Dr Kirby took me off them. Now I take Valproate and an antipsychotic, they started me on those in England.'

The registrar now tells me that I am not, in fact, unwell enough to be hospitalized. He goes outside to the corridor to talk to Jer for a while; on his return he informs me that, as I have nowhere else to go, and as I have just been discharged from another facility, he will allow me to stay one night in the hospital.

The hospital staff refer me to a social worker, to assist me in finding housing, and they make an appointment for me to see a housing officer in Dun Laoghaire. They inform me, too, that my father has taken out a barring order against me and that he will enforce it if necessary.

The pressure now builds for me to leave the hospital and seek emergency accommodation in a hostel for the homeless in Dun Laoghaire; but I baulk at this idea, recalling the London hostels. In a panic, I decide to phone Serena, who visited me so often in St John of God's when I was here before, and who I last saw, briefly, in the winter, when I was manic. When I get through to her I explain the situation, and appeal to her to put me up; ever considerate and kind, she agrees.

In Serena's house, in County Wicklow, I sleep on a fold-out bed in a vestibule between the front door and the living room, which is awkward for both of us, and I wonder if it is tenable. Desperate now, but rational and calm, on an impulse I phone my father again, and he listens to what I have to say.

'They want to put me in a hostel,' I tell him. 'I have nowhere to go. Please let me come home.'

Despite all that has happened, all that I have done to him, he only takes a moment to consider his reply, then says: 'Of course. *Mi casa es tu casa.*'

Putting down the phone, I immediately pack what few belongings I have into a plastic bag, leave a note for Serena, go and catch a bus, and return to live in my father's house in the small estate in the suburb not far from the sea in south County Dublin.

A few weeks later I make my way, in a shuffling, slow walk, from my father's house to the beach; a thick fog rolls off the sea at Killiney bay. My gait is stiff, I am huddled over, shoulders tight, as I walk, and I slide and stumble over the stones by the edge of the water. The sound of the waves hitting the shore is muffled by the fog. Only the sound of the seagulls overhead and far-off, occasional foghorns punctuate the eerie silence.

A figure looms out of the mist ahead of me, and as we approach each other I recognize him: it is Doyle, from my primary school, who I used to spend a lot of time with as a child. We have not seen each other in years. Now he greets me, asks me what I am up to. It is impossible to meet his eye – I am too ashamed of the breakdown, the hospitalization, ashamed, too, about living at home with my father, unemployed, with few prospects beyond being a permanent mental patient.

'Are you all right?' he finally asks, puzzled. He can tell that, at some level, I am sick, I think. At this question I glance up, shake my head.

'Not really,' I admit.

There is nothing more to be said after that; I'm not going to tell him all that ails and worries me, and he can think of nothing more to add either. We part, walk in different directions, disappear into the fog.

My brain is in a fog of its own. It is not functioning properly. The synapses, I feel, are no longer firing and connecting. It doesn't even feel like depression; it just feels like nothing, nothingness, an absence of all feeling, agency, motivation.

During the days I do nothing, and nothing occurs; it is a

true doldrums. There is lying in bed, there is smoking, there is a forced-out shuffling walk to the beach every day, trips to the shop for more cigarettes. There is sometimes television late at night, when my father has gone to bed. He and I seldom interact, although once a week he will cook a meal of lamb chops for dinner and expect me to join him. At these meals he sits opposite me but positions his chair at an angle of forty-five degrees so his gaze is away from me. We sit, we eat, we do not talk. When my sister calls to the house I do not meet her or talk to her either. Isolation seems easiest.

Friends do sometimes reach out to me. Jer calls when he is in Dublin, sometimes with his Parisian flatmate Barti, an aspirant film producer. The two of them accompany me to the beach; they slow their pace to match my shuffling gait. We walk up and down the strand and they talk about their projects and activities, probe me about my own aspirations.

'Jer says you wrote a really good screenplay,' says Barti.

'I don't know,' is all I can manage to reply to this. It is actually agony to walk up and down this beach, the stones sliding under my feet constantly: it takes too much energy.

'I'd like to read it,' Barti goes on. To this, I don't reply at all; it is too painful to be reminded of my past hopes; it is a life I can never return to now, because of my illness. All gone, lost now, never to return: I am certain of this.

'I'll give it to you,' Jer says. After that we don't talk at all, just make our way slowly up and down the beach, and then back to the house, where they leave me, promising to call again soon.

I go for consultations with a psychiatrist at Cluain Mhuire, the out-patients' clinic near Blackrock. In these sessions the doctors find it hard to motivate me to do anything to change my life. I have been given a referral to attend a programme to help in recovery from serious mental illness, held in Burton Hall, a large house on the edge of an industrial estate a half-hour bus ride from my father's house. I tell the doctor I am too anxious to do anything and don't have the bus fare to get to Burton Hall, even though, with disability allowance, I actually do have a bit of money; I am just being negative and passive about everything. The doctor regards me as having a dependent personality, encourages me to try to help myself more, be more self-reliant, to put some structure to my day. But I cannot motivate myself to do anything, have lost interest in all my activities and pursuits and feel that it is all hopeless.

But then, something stirs, a vague spark of motivation; I phone Burton Hall at last and agree to attend the programme there.

Then there is a day I want to give up again. It all seems too much; thinking of all that I have lost, I just want to sleep and never wake. Phoning my pharmacy, I tell them, 'I think I may have taken too many of my Valproate tablets today. Would that kill me?'

They ask how many I have taken, and I give some random number and they assure me it wouldn't kill me.

'How many would kill me?' I ask now, brazenly.

This, they refuse to answer and, concerned, they urge me to phone my doctor.

But I have decided now: I will take an overdose and sleep, never wake. The programme in Burton Hall is a few weeks away yet, and I just feel exhausted, too exhausted to go on, overwhelmed by all I've been through and by the thought of all I will have to go through to get well again and have a normal life once more; I do not think I will ever be happy again. I want to sleep, and go on sleeping, and never have to face another day again, never have to struggle or make any effort.

But the meds are running out, there isn't enough, and any-way, I don't know how much is enough; it's annoying they wouldn't tell me over the phone. I go to another pharmacy with my current prescription.

'Would all fifty-six tablets in the prescription kill me if I took them all at once?' I ask the pharmacist. 'Or how many would I have to take?'

She looks me over; I am agitated now, rocking from foot to foot. She tells me she has to go and phone my doctor at Cluain Mhuire. When she returns, she refuses to give me the medications.

At my next out-patients' appointment in Cluain Mhuire, the doctor I see informs me that my meds will from now on be dispensed on a weekly, not a monthly, basis.

Jer visits me in late spring and, as usual, we walk on Killiney beach. Barti is with us also. He has by now read my script *The Perch*, and suggests we rekindle the project, with Jer direct-ing. Hunched over into myself, I don't take in any of this, don't register any enthusiasm, but agree passively that they can do what they like with the script.

Barti and Jer set up a production company so they can apply for funding to film my screenplay, and begin to seek out an executive producer for the project. Still thinking it is all hopeless and I will never return to creative life, I take lit-tle active interest in this process; but a flicker of desire, to be back in that world, is ignited somewhere in me.

The programme at Burton Hall starts in mid-summer. Now I have structure to my week, for the day at Burton Hall runs from 9 a.m. to 4 p.m. The group I'm put in consists mainly of teenagers. They have, variously, experienced psychosis and depression and issues relating to eating disorders, and some have substance-abuse problems. One eighteen-year-old calls me 'middle-aged'; I feel he could be right. I'm only thirty-six, but I do indeed feel old and weary among these youths.

This is not group therapy, and we're not encouraged to discuss our diagnoses or medications, nor talk about anything personal. We have an urge to talk about all that ails us, however, but anything we say, if it is of a personal nature, is deemed 'inappropriate'. Instead, there are presentations on mental health issues and care, relaxation sessions, various types of occupational therapy, and job skills workshops such as basic computer training, word-processing and CV preparation.

We're asked to complete a computerized questionnaire to find out what kind of career would suit us. The questions are mainly multiple choice, and I fill in the questionnaire dutifully and submit my answers for the computer algorithm to figure out what job I should be pursuing. After a moment the answer comes back: 'Writer'. This I feel to be bitterly ironic, an act of sarcasm on the computer's part; for I haven't written anything apart from the nonsense of madness in my notebooks for years now, and don't know if I will ever be able to write anything seriously ever again.

When the doctors ask me, I tell them I'm okay, but when they press me further I rate my mood at three out of ten. They refer me to a group therapy session that uses cognitive behavioural therapy methodology, emphasizing action over thinking. It will start in the autumn.

There are social outings to the local hotel, where, strangely, we are allowed to drink alcohol, if we wish. We sit around and try to make small talk with the care workers who have accompanied us; but I have nothing to say, no news, no interest in anything. One by one, the other participants all drift off to the patio outside to smoke. I am left alone with a care worker, looking out at the group of young people outside smoking and chattering away. The silence grows oppressive between us where we sit inside at our table.

'This is ridiculous,' she says at last, which only makes me feel worse, admonished.

We go on trips to a local pitch-and-putt course, all piling into a minivan, and we go bowling, and to parks, just to walk around. It is all vaguely humiliating, but I keep going doggedly to the programme, as I want to get better, and I want to do the CBT session when it begins.

Standing, bored, on the pitch-and-putt course, feeling isolated and adrift, I remember how recently I was happy: living in New York with Jennifer, swimming in the ocean at Amagansett beach in summer, skiing or hiking upstate in winter. It was a good life. Despair grips me as I consider all that is lost, irretrievable, and how I now live: in my father's house, attending this ridiculous and degrading 'rehabilitation' programme. Turning away from the others, I begin to cry, hoping the others do not see. Then I pull myself together and go back to playing the game.

Feeling has broken in, which is a change.

But the fog quickly returns, and I continue to move without engagement or enthusiasm through my days.

During one of the interminable breaks between sessions at Burton Hall, a young woman sits beside me. We are sitting outside on a balustrade overlooking the grounds. I have not seen or at least not noticed this woman before; she seems to have just arrived.

'Can I have a cigarette?' she asks me.

'I don't have any more,' I tell her, lying; I just don't want to give her one, in case I run out later on.

'I can finish the one you're smoking,' she suggests, referring to the stub I am still inhaling from. There is only an inch remaining.

For no reason, selfishly and spitefully I reply: 'This is my cigarette. I'm going to finish it.'

She gets up, visibly agitated by this, and goes into the building.

A few moments later, discarding what is left of my stub, I go inside, too, for my next session.

But it has been delayed, postponed because there is a commotion, an incident; the young woman, distressed and unable to calm herself because no one gave her a cigarette, has punched her fist through the glass window of an interior doorway. Now blood covers the door and is splashed across the carpet; the care workers are huddled together. The woman needs urgent treatment, the blood must be cleaned up, sessions are suspended. The woman herself is in shock at the pain she has caused herself.

'Right, let's get this cleaned up for a start,' says the leader of my group after the woman has been taken to hospital; nothing is going to be happening with sessions for a while.

Going outside for a smoke again, I think: I did this. To her. I light the cigarette I could have given her and so have avoided all this, the cigarette that would have calmed her and prevented her from getting so upset that she self-harmed.

Guilt and shame descend; again I feel something; then the fog descends once more.

Careers coaching consists mainly of encouraging participants to consider pursuing taking roles in the service industries.

'Cleaning is good,' they intone. 'You can get a good wage working as a cleaner.'

It's obvious that the care workers don't think we are

capable of much beyond menial labour because we have mental illnesses. They make me wonder whether they are, in fact, correct in this assumption.

When it comes time for us to do a month's work placement, I choose to do an administrative role in a theatre and arts centre, one I haven't worked in before. They put me to work sorting out a large cache of archival materials. The task is not demanding, I am left on my own to do it and find it pleasant enough, and the staff are friendly and supportive; certainly, the job is better than cleaning, or being in my bed all day feeling bored. It is a first tentative step back into the world of work after a long absence.

But walking home from the Dart station after a day working in the theatre, approaching my father's housing estate, coming down the steep hill just outside it, I find myself brooding: I will never be able to change my situation, get back on track with my career, earn enough money and gain enough confidence and independence to move out of my father's house, leave his orbit. Never dispense with my need for him, my need for his acknowledgement, love and validation. We have barely been speaking since my return, and I have found no way to broach all that has happened, nor to say sorry in a way he could ever hear, believe and accept. His forgiveness seems impossible to receive.

When I come into the estate and round the corner and face the house, I notice that the curtains are drawn upstairs in my father's room, which is unusual, as there is still daylight. As I let myself in, I hear the radio playing in his bedroom upstairs; normally, he only has the radio on at night when he is going to sleep or sleeping. Usually at this time he would be making his dinner or watching the evening news. Why has he gone to bed so early, closed the curtains, put on the radio as if it were night?

Going upstairs, I see the door to his bedroom is closed; I go to it, knock gently and ask:

'Dad? Are you there?'

There is no reply to my enquiry, just the sound of the radio playing on. Feeling numb, lethargic and foggy as usual, I tentatively open the door and look in.

My father is lying on the floor between the bed and the window. He is still, and his left hand is clutched, like a claw, to his chest. A moment passes and then I realize he is dead. There is nothing but stillness in the room. The radio bothers me and I turn it off and sit on his bed a moment, contemplating his body. Then I go downstairs and phone the emergency services.

'You better get someone to come,' I tell the operator. 'It's my father. He's upstairs. I think he's dead.'

In the kitchen I light a cigarette and use a jam jar lid as an ashtray; normally, I wouldn't smoke indoors, as my father wouldn't approve, but now he is no longer here to object. So I smoke. Still I feel an absence of any trace of feeling. Just a dullness, a void, that endless fog of the mind. The ambulance arrives, and the medical team go upstairs.

'Is he dead?' I ask when they return, although I know the answer already; they confirm officially with me that he is. Now the police are called, examine the scene of death; they ask me do I have anyone I wish to call. My uncle, my father's brother, comes to mind; he lives locally, but I have not spoken to him since I offended him with my claim that my father was senile; I have not apologized to him for my appalling behaviour, too ashamed to face him. Now, I phone him with the news that my father has died. He tells me he will come shortly.

Next I have to phone my sister. We have not been speaking much recently either. She is currently on a placement working abroad, and I reach her on her mobile phone.

243

'You better come home,' I say, not wanting to tell her our father is dead over the phone in case it distresses her, thinking it best to tell her in person. 'It's Dad.'

But she senses something in my voice and asks: 'Is he dead?'

When I reluctantly confirm that he is, she tells me she will come home immediately.

My uncle arrives and sits with me while I smoke and drink some of my father's brandy; we talk little, and I feel dazed. There is little to be said either, as my father's body is carried out of the house in a thick plastic body-bag shortly after. Eventually, everyone leaves – the police detectives, the ambulance crew, my uncle – and I am left alone in the silent house.

The next day I phone Burton Hall and St John of God's and inform them of my father's death; I will have to absent myself from sessions for a while. Then I walk to the local hospital, where my father's body lies in the mortuary, to identify him formally. It is the first time I have clearly seen his face in death, and it shocks me; I turn away quickly at the sight.

'It's him,' I confirm to the official, and then I leave.

My sister returns from overseas and proceeds to arrange the funeral; I take a passive role throughout.

The funeral itself barely registers with me. There are family and friends, many of whom I have not seen in years, but I do not talk to them in any meaningful way; I am still too ashamed of my recent history. After the burial, when the mourners are inside the pub near the cemetery having their drinks and sandwiches, I stand alone outside in the car-park and smoke cigarette after cigarette, lost in my thoughts, my non-thoughts. Nothing, really, is going through my mind.

*

My sister calls to the house and tells me that she would like to live there, too.

'But I'm not sure that I can,' she says hesitantly.

'Why not?' I ask.

'Because I'm afraid of you,' she admits.

After a moment, by way of reply, I lean forward and gently hug her. 'There's no need to be afraid of me,' I assure her; and it is agreed.

The vocational programme comes to an end, and nothing replaces it. Still without drive or motivation to do anything for myself, I spend most of my time sleeping or dozing in bed. There is a tentative rapprochement between my sister and me and we now occasionally cook and eat a meal together, meals during which we talk a little, despite my insularity and wariness and unease and shame over all that has passed between us, all that I am and have done.

I'm too tired and unmotivated and uncaring to do house-work, or to wash myself. Consequently, my room, the box room at the top of the stairs, grows rancid with my body odour. Snoozing in bed, I hear my sister shout up at me, not unkindly, from the foot of the stairwell: 'Arnold! I love you dearly, but you stink! For pity's sake, have a wash!'

This gets through to me; I am ashamed. And so, for the first time in what seems like months, I have a bath and freshen the room.

Jer still meets me and tries to draw me out. He wants to bring me to a script-development workshop in Germany in the New Year. To me, it all seems pointless – I can never return to that world. But his enthusiasm and passion for the project cannot be diminished, and so he persuades me to write a letter to the workshop organizers as part of our application.

'*The Perch* is a very personal screenplay, which, as you will see, crosses some boundaries and breaks some rules,' I write. 'It will not be to everyone's taste. Still, despite its broken chronology and waywardness, I believe there is a strong story and good, emotionally developed characters.'

It is the first coherent piece of writing I have managed to complete in almost two years.

In a clinical assessment, I tell the doctor how I feel I have ruined my life, lost a good job and relationship, that my future looks bleak, that I am not a worthwhile person, that I'd prefer it if I were dead. We discuss the possibility of putting me on an antidepressant. I'm still afraid to do this, because the antidepressants have made me go high in the past, but the doctor assures me I will be supervised closely while on it, so I agree to do so for a trial period.

I spend Christmas in Jer's family home with him, his girlfriend and his parents; his mother is particularly patient and kind to me. For my part, I am mainly silent, morose, withdrawn.

As the year ends, I can't help but wonder if the fog will ever lift.

16. Healing

Early in 2006, Jer and I receive a letter from the Irish Film Board turning down our application for development financing for *The Perch*. But the rejection is couched in a supportive way that encourages us and motivates us to pursue the project further. Shortly after, we get confirmation that we have been accepted into the script-development workshop in Potsdam, a programme that will match us with a professional script editor.

These outside validations, though tentative, have an effect on me, and I feel something stirring. Motivation. Ambition. The need to be creative once more. They plant a seed of a thought: that things could be different. Hope.

Some work still needs to be done on the script before we travel to Germany, and I find I am motivated to do so. I set up a work area in the spare bedroom, clearing my desk, putting out my laptop and printer, getting paper and pens and drafts ready.

My sister wants a workspace, too, so I put up a desk for her in the living room, which she appreciates. She notices that my mood can still dip low at times; on these occasions she makes me food and leaves me be, confident that time and a little peace and care will heal me. Because day by day, even hour by hour, there is a struggle to be fought against despair, which hovers nearby and always threatens to overcome me; but I push against it, the film project now motivating me, giving me purpose and something to work towards.

I meet Jer in Paris. He brings me out to a local brasserie

and we eat and drink well, in celebratory mood. The next day we fly to Berlin then take the train to Potsdam.

The workshop is held in a modern hotel. There are seminars, screenings and group sessions with our script editor and the other participants. It is the first time in quite a while I have been put into a social situation with my peers, and I find this challenging, but manageable, and gradually enjoyable. I have to discuss and defend my creative work, and this is also a challenge: to be articulate when I still feel clumsy and stuck. Another difficulty is that, while *The Perch* contains many autobiographical elements, I am still profoundly ashamed of my diagnosis and history, do not want to be known as suffering from a mental illness; consequently, I keep all this to myself, even when sharing the knowledge would help the discussion.

Standing in my bedroom in the hotel getting dressed in the morning, I catch sight of myself in a full-length mirror. At home there is no such mirror, so I have not had a view of myself totally naked in a considerable time; and I am shocked and dismayed by what I see. My stomach is bulging and bloated, huge and heavy; the leanness I had in New York, the muscularity following the summer's swimming in the ocean off Montauk, is long gone. This, to me, seems an inevitable, inescapable part of being counted among the mentally ill.

Back in Ireland, I'm again given a place in the cognitive behavioural therapy group. Whereas before, I didn't see the point in doing anything to help myself feel better, now, because of Potsdam, I've seen that things can be different and I look forward to joining the group. There is still in me a reluctance to believe in a happy future for myself, but I do at least now feel like going on, and I have a curiosity about what going on might actually entail.

The sessions are held once a week in St John of God's, and I drive there in what had been my father's car, the red Ford Fiesta. We sit in a large circle and the facilitators engage us in exercises and discussions that make us challenge and question our negative thinking, our assumptions about depression, our response to our moods. The idea is that we must act, do something, modify our behaviour, in such a way as to be proactive against our depressive tendencies and, consequently, to change them. Instead of waiting to feel better before taking action, we must do something, regardless of mood or motivation.

Summer, which we are now entering, is traditionally the season when I sink into deep depression and, again, my mood dips. But I persevere with the group, participating as best I can. The others understand and validate what I am going through, and this helps; there is no judgement here, only support, acceptance of someone going through a hard time.

There are many questionnaires to fill out, goals to set and reflections to write. I am still brooding on all that has been lost, still feeling depressed, and initially my questionnaires and worksheets are filled with negative thinking:

I'm an idiot.
The future is hopeless.
I've made a mess of my life.
I'm absolutely screwed.

During breaks, the majority of us go and stand outside in the gardens of St John of God's and smoke. There we swap battle stories, and talk of more personal issues that we may be reluctant to air to the entire group. Such conversations help me feel I am not alone with my problems and give me a way to talk about them with my psychiatrist at Cluain Mhuire.

We're taught to counter negative thinking, and to challenge it. This is new to me, used as I am to letting my thoughts spiral into despair. Now I counter the thought 'I left my job and the good life I had in New York' with the counter-thought 'It wasn't my fault; I wasn't well.'

Goals are set: 'Call a friend and arrange to meet.' 'Go out and have a coffee and read the paper.' Small goals; achievable.

One day I write: 'Send out job application.' But this I still find hard to do. How to explain the large gaps in my CV?

Also challenging is that there are a lot of days to fill between the sessions, days when my low mood takes over.

On one occasion, Jer, visiting Dublin, is not able to meet me due to other commitments. My mood-assessment sheet consequently becomes a litany of paranoid complaint:

> He doesn't like me any more.
> He doesn't want to be friends any more.
> There's something wrong with me.
> Nobody likes me.
> I have no friends.
> Very bleak future.

When I get nowhere with a job application, I write:

> I'll never get a job.
> There's something wrong with me.
> I won't have enough money.
> Future uncertain.

Writing these lists helps identify the thinking that causes my low mood; then the work begins to challenge that thinking:

> I have some very good friends.
> My friends like me.
> I have held on to jobs before.

I am good at keeping in touch with people who live
  abroad.
I am good at initiating contact with people.
I am taking medication.
I am okay.
I'm checking job ads.

Optimism: so simple a thing, and yet so profound. By degrees, in faltering, tiny steps, my life is changing for the better.

I force myself out of the house, take the Dart to Dun Laoghaire, where a new bookshop has recently opened. There I buy a copy of a newspaper, the *Guardian*, or the *Observer*, or the *Irish Times*, and go and sit in the café that is located upstairs. Once settled with a coffee, I read, for the first time in what seems like years. It has been so long since I have been able to concentrate. Now, finally, I can read a newspaper, short articles at first, then longer features.

One day at home I feel bored, really bored, and become aware of a strong impulse to alleviate that boredom, instead of giving into it passively. It occurs to me to read something other than newspaper articles. I pick up one of the unread books lying around my room and begin to read, finish it, then pick up another. A few days go by in this reading and I feel more energized, feel motivated to make this day different from the same day last week, when I just lay in bed.

There is a stack of unused book tokens in my room, Christmas and birthday presents accumulated over the years when I was too unwell to use them. Now, the next time I am in Dun Laoghaire, I browse around the shelves in the bookshop and buy a pile of books that I have read about in the newspapers. The following week is spent reading novels, with breaks for smoking, eating and group therapy. A part of me that I had thought lost for ever has returned: I am a reader once again.

Now, filling in my 'activity-tracking schedule' at group, there is something new:

1 p.m.–2 p.m.: Having lunch, reading
2 p.m.–3 p.m.: Reading
3 p.m.–4 p.m.: Reading
4 p.m.–5 p.m.: Reading
5 p.m.–6 p.m.: Visiting friend
6 p.m.–7 p.m.: Group
7 p.m.–8 p.m.: Group
8 p.m.–9 p.m.: Group

That is Monday, and it becomes a typical Monday. On the Tuesday, I read ten hours, broken only by eating and a trip to Dun Laoghaire. Wednesday, seven hours reading; Thursday, five.

Weeks go by, reading, going to the bookstore to replenish my stock, then retreating, exhausted, back to my room to read some more. But now, too, there are more frequent social meetings with friends, and sorties further afield, into the city centre, to other bookshops.

It occurs to me, faintly at first, that I'd like to work again in a bookstore; that I could actually do so if allowed the chance, that I am ready.

This is a change in thinking: planning for the future. This is healing.

Now, guardedly, with this new buoyancy in my thinking, I note in an activity-monitoring form that I am eating well, helping with housework more, maintaining personal hygiene, going out to the pub and meeting friends, listening to music, even going to the cinema. My sister and I are getting on well now. We get into the habit of having Sunday meals with wine, taking turns to prepare them. These meals become increasingly elaborate occasions, and cooking reconnects me with yet another part of myself that had been for too long neglected.

My friend Michael Paul visits from Rome and is delighted to see my progress. I promise him that when I have the money I will visit him in Rome: more motivation to find a job, more planning for a future.

Then, entering the bookshop in Dun Laoghaire, I see a notice in the window:

> Experienced booksellers wanted.
> Apply within.

Simple, clear, enticing: for I am a bookseller, have been one in Spring Street bookstore in New York, John Adrian bookstore in London, Fred Hanna and Dubray in Dublin. But I dismiss it out of hand: I am not ready for work, I've still not finished the CBT course, I don't have the confidence to face the public, I have too long a gap in my CV, that long period with no work, and anyway, the last jobs I had were illegally held ones in New York, for which I have no references and which I left in bad circumstances.

Still, I can't help thinking of the staff discount I would get if I did work in the bookstore.

In the next group therapy session it dawns on me that now is the time to really put the CBT techniques I've been learning into practice. I need to force myself to act, regardless of my mood, regardless of what my thoughts are telling me; the motivation and benefits will come later.

The notice is still in the bookstore the next time I visit.

At home that night in my workspace in the spare room I write up a CV and an application letter, obfuscating the gap in employment by listing all the training courses I have been doing.

A few days after handing in the application I am called for interview. I am nervous, worried that I'll have to reveal my mental illness and hospitalizations, two things that still fill me with shame. But in the interview all they want to know is do I like books, do I know about books, what my interests are, and can I deliver good customer service. The next day the manager phones and offers me a job as a senior bookseller.

It is a challenge, after all these years out of the workforce, to return. But it is a pleasant place to work, the staff and management are friendly and chatty, I'm surrounded by books all day and by people who are interested in books; it's a good job for me.

More grounds for optimism and excitement: my screenplay *The Perch* receives development funding from the Irish Film Board. Now I have some extra income, and I can give my sister some money towards the household expenses, which she has so far been covering by herself. The funding affirms my faith in the script, and in my writing.

Jer and I subsequently spend a week working on the script. We consider actors, meet co-producers and casting agents, put together all the pieces that are needed to apply for production finance. It seems impossible to fund a feature film, but the energy going into the project feeds into other things I do, and so for the first time in years I feel able to undertake new creative work.

Consequently, on a Tuesday evening after my shift has finished at the bookshop, I go into the city centre and, despite feeling shame at all that has transpired since last attending, I attend the performance workshop that I dropped out of years before.

Nervous, vulnerable, ashamed, I go in and reconnect with all the actors, directors, and writers there, and reacquaint myself with Graham and Rachel, who took such an interest in my writing before. Settling in, feeling welcomed, I reassert and reaffirm myself as a writer.

17. The Opening

It is not always easy in the bookshop: there are bad days, when I am curt or aloof with customers. Sometimes I am pulled aside and admonished, and I am too ashamed to explain that I am in a low mood. I just struggle through and hope the next day will be better.

Often, now, it is.

At the performance workshop I am not a 'patient', or a 'mentally ill person', or a 'service user', or 'bipolar', or even a 'bookseller'; there, I am only a writer, respected and validated as such.

The CBT group is finished. I continue to attend out-patient psychiatric services at Cluain Mhuire, for supervision and observation and assessment, and prescription of meds. I'm still on Valproate, the mood stabilizer, and Olanzapine, an antipsychotic. The Olanzapine makes me drowsy in the morning, what's called a 'hangover effect'; looking at the list of side-effects, I see 'sleepiness' and 'extreme tiredness'. This makes me worry that I will never be able to write well again, as the morning has always been when I write.

Early in the new year, 2008, Graham comes to my house and we fill in an online application to submit my first play to the Dublin Fringe Festival. I continue to go to work and attend the performance workshop as we wait for a decision. In the spring we get word we have been accepted into the Fringe: *Those Powerful Machines* is finally going to be produced, directed by Graham and starring Rachel.

As usual, in the months leading up to the anniversary of my mother's death in August, I get depressed. But this depression never gets as bad as it used to. I continue to go to work, and to the performance workshop, and prepare for the Fringe.

At the workshop I get talking to Paul, a playwright only slightly older than myself but with a vast amount of experience. He recognizes in me a seriousness of intent and a love of theatre and we quickly become good friends. During the process of getting *Those Powerful Machines* on stage, he becomes a mentor to me, guiding me through every stage of production and helping me deal with the stresses and strains of it all, even while he oversees his own Fringe production.

There are casting auditions, there are marketing materials to be produced, there is fundraising to arrange, as well as workshops organized by the festival for the participants. I am gradually improving, doing better in the world, but I still have negative thoughts and feelings, and my diary is the depository where I write them all down.

05.07.08

Went to Fringe writing workshop today. Paul there also, I do like him. Really tired. Printed out TPM revisions. Every day is so slow. The tiredness is fucking me up big-time. Maybe this is the old Summer D? That won't go till after August? What if I just go: fuck, I can't stand this? But: I need to sit with the discomfort a little longer. I am not in a good place on any level right now: I am just getting by. This is not the time to make any big decisions.

06.07.08

Shitty fucking day. This is the old d really: seasonal.

14.07.08

When did writing become about money? When did I think I should write to make money? As opposed to writing how I wanted, as I wanted?

18.07.08

Felt like utter shit today. Another work day. And I didn't sleep much last night. Not elated though; just feel like shit.

I want to be an 'Artist'

And travel a bit

And work out my shit (impossible?)

25.07.08

Everyone gets on my nerves. I'm the old Arnold, the 91–95 AF, the cranky, obnoxious, fuck. Back in the old litany that filled so many diaries: I feel like shit.

Need to rest. Need to talk to friends, but not in pubs, in crowds with stranger + acquaintances, not in town. Need a few days off work. Need to walk, sit in the garden. Xst. Fuck. The early-August-approach D. I am completely helpless. Going to do nada. Try to rest. And walk. Get some fresh air. Okay, I know what the matter with me is. But what to do about it?

26.07.08

Felt like shit, tense + angry all day. And the fucking noise and irritation of people. How I long to be alone.

30.07.08

Went for a swim. Managed about 250m + was puffed. Bol-lox. Felt good though.

Work in the bookshop is tolerable, but occasionally a customer or manager will complain to me about my demeanour, service, performance. Managers come and go; they are generally younger than me, though one, Greg, is about my age. This makes me self-conscious about where I am in my life.

31.07.08

I made some query to Greg about a book about depression . . . which made him go on a little rant about how such books are all rubbish anyway or whatever, and then say 'Of course you know the way to get over/ cure (can't recall now) depression? Just cheer up.' I turned away livid, and in utter disgust, which made him say 'Turn up that frown! Smile.' What an utter, utter, total fucking asshole. That is a level below my father's to be honest. I am relieved now I told no-one about being D; but Jesus what a hostile environment to admit to having a mental health problem.

I am still D. The days off helped, but being back to work + all, the tiredness gets me down . . . Need to really do anything positive now – can't really walk . . . the weather was awful . . . prob too tired to swim in the eve . . . too tired to eat tonight so had 2 slices of toast.

1.08.08

I always get D the August Bank Holiday Weekend (M's anniversary. Fuck. It. Is. 1988–2008. Twenty fucking years! I have now been on the Earth longer with her dead than with her alive. How fucking bizarre.

I went for a walk. I think it helped. What really helped was getting away from all the noise. I should go into a box and not come out until this D 'lifts'.

02.08.08

Poxy day, really. I just felt such inner rage. I don't think I can write at all anymore to be honest. Could I get by w/out med?

I mean, here I am D as ever before on med. So what is the point? It will lift with the end of Summer; but the meds will still be there stopping me from writing anything good, right?

03.08.08

Really losing my mind. The days not so bad though . . . The thoughts only crash at night. I need to get out more and I can't as I have no energy to go anywhere in the evening.

04.08.08 Monday Bank Holiday

Anniversary of M's death: 20 years.

Work boring and then very busy. My attitude to customers now has gone through the floor.

During the auditions for the part of Roddy, the last role to be cast, I make detailed notes on each of the ten or twelve actors we see. In the end, we cast a dynamic and powerful young actor who comes to the workshop, Thomas, who I feel is perfect for the role and has an incredible presence on stage. With the cast now in place, I feel more confident the play will work.

Rehearsals are held in the Focus Theatre's building, and I feel honoured to be working on such hallowed ground. I attend one rehearsal a week, after which Graham drives me on his motorbike, which I cling to in terror, to a nearby bar for our script meetings. He gives me all his notes from the day, and I go home and work on the rewrites, making the script tighter, sharper, quicker, better. It is an exciting process, but I'm nervous about it all, anxious about failure, about the potential humiliation of bad reviews, poor houses, bored audiences. Paul listens to all my worries and doubts patiently and assures me that the play is stage-worthy and good, giving me more confidence.

But it's hard to get up in the morning, due to the hangover effect of the meds, and I still suffer from anxiety and disordered sleep.

11.08.08

Dr Greene totally pissed me off today. I wanted to make a appt this week to talk about sleep prob. He said next appt would be Oct and could I hold off till then. Finally I said 'Do you want to wait until I lose my job or am hospitalised before you do something to help me?' His response was to tell me to stop being 'abusive' stop 'threatening' him etc. Finally he agreed to give me a week sleeping tablets. He said I could write to 'my consultant' to ask for a different doctor. He said he didn't want to prescribe sleeping tablets long term.

I told the guy I get Summer D and he ignored that; and ignored me when I said I'd be better in a few months.

Went to reh tonight. Fun being at reh. Worked out some script changes with G. Got to keep some stuff, lost other stuff. Nothing major. I really worry it is going to be a disaster. Not critically but in terms of people coming to it. Felt fucking awful today. Wish to fuck I could cheer up.

12.08.08

Swam. Felt very good.

24.08.08

Actually made a big effort with sister this evening. Cooked nice dinner (bass and asparagus), showed her how to burn CDs.

R is smashing in rehearsals.

Can tomorrow be better?

How?

How to avoid conflict and stress. The world won't change. But I'm hardly a Zen master who can ignore every ignorant asshole who quite literally comes at me. So it strikes me: I need to feel better about myself, do something.

But how can I do anything when I am so tired?

A Sunday newspaper interviews me about the play. I'm afraid that my mental illness will be discovered and revealed, that I will have to admit to my diagnosis and my history of hospitalizations. During the interview, in a city-centre hotel, the interviewer senses I am being evasive; although I tell her about the play, and the production process, and a little of my background, I am ambiguous about everything else and she can tell I am holding back.

26.08.08

Today: interview.

'This is a personal profile . . . you know that if you don't talk more it will be a very short piece . . . are you happy with that?'

'Who's going to be there opening night . . . anyone special in your life right now?' Oh God, fucking awful.

Fuck so fucking humiliating.

'Have you had to overcome any challenges in your life?' She had an agenda she knew and when I didn't give her what she wanted and expected . . . she put the screws on.

'I'm a shy person,' I tell the journalist, and then go on:

If I had a different personality, I'd probably be doing something more public, like acting. Most writers are private people, and writing can be a very solitary occupation, as you have to be able to work on your own for hours on end. I like to be challenged at the theatre, and I want the audience to laugh, to think, and be uncomfortable at times. The actors are great and it's slightly flattering and humbling seeing the play coming to life.

Referring to my parents, I say:

Not having them there is hard, but you have to go on and do it in their memory anyway. I think my father would have been very proud of the playwriting and my mother would have been very proud of my short stories, because she wrote some herself, although she never showed them to anyone.

Our venue for the two-week run of the production is the New Theatre, a beautiful, small theatre space at the back of a radical bookstore in Temple Bar. When I walk in and see the set built there for the first time I get a shot of sheer joy: it is splendid to see a physical manifestation of my imagination. The night before the first preview, however, I leave the technical rehearsal full of worries. Anxiety has gripped me again, the fear of failure; I am certain everything is going to be a disaster, and it's all my fault, as I haven't written a good enough script. I phone Paul and tell him my worries; he talks me down.

04.09.08

I am going to be in such a state at the opening. There is no way I am sitting through the performance. What will I wear? Maybe I should get my head shaved or something. Actually that's quite a good idea.

But that's a true sign of craziness, right?

I am so sensitive to noise it is horrible: everything I feel physically.

263

05.09.08

First run-through. Phoned P and he perked me up. Was able to talk to G in a non-hysterical way. Had a few pints with John.

08.09.08

1st preview. (following on from dress reh).

: S did a heroic job.

: Donal there.

: J good phone support.

: John there but I was too fazed to talk to him.

: had some good connected talk with G + feel better about that.

Tomorrow: going to be fucking hell in a hotplate. Fuck. Got haircut. My old style.

On the opening night I work with Thomas on stage before the curtain goes up and make changes to his final monologue in the third act, the climactic outburst of the play. He, a true professional, rises to the occasion splendidly, learning the new version of the monologue with only minutes to spare.

Once the curtain goes up, I leave the theatre: I am too nervous to watch the performance. Instead I go to a Japanese restaurant and eat a light dinner, then to the Irish Film Institute and have a pint; then I return to the theatre, pace around the bookshop out front while I wait for the play to end.

Listening to the final words of the performance from outside, I step into the auditorium just in time to get the blackout on the final act and to see the curtain call. The audience reaction is rapturous and raucous. Standing at the back of the auditorium, I feel the power of an audience's enthusiasm, feel a sort of joy I have not experienced before.

Immediately, the thought darts through my mind: 'I have to do this again.'

All the stresses and anxieties over the production have been worth it, for the sheer electricity of this, and the feeling of validation. In this moment, after years of being without direction, hope, desire or ambition, having given up on the possibility of having a happy life and a fulfilling future, I know that I want something positive and rewarding and enriching for myself, that the past is now behind me, that I have a role in life, a sense of direction, a future, a vocation to build towards once more.

Now, I am a playwright.

Now, I do not feel like someone who will always be labelled mentally ill. Now, I just feel like a writer, because I am a writer, and I will go on writing.

In my diary that night I write a simple entry:

09.09.08 Opening night.

Felt better.

18. Vigilance and Hope

We never made it as far as Pórtugos.

Pórtugos, where it is said that the town fountain flows with naturally carbonated water. I had been anticipating and imagining this water for years, since reading about it in a magazine – wondering what it would taste like, what it would feel like against the tongue. It was one of the things that had brought me to this part of southern Spain: to taste the water from that fountain.

My girlfriend Tessa and I had planned to hike for five days along the GR-7 route through Andalucía, as far as Pórtugos. But on the third day, Tessa's old ankle injury flared up and we could go no further. Frustrated we could not go on, I became increasingly exasperated and irritable until finally we were arguing under the burning sun on a mountainside in the Parque Natural de Sierra Nevada.

The next town was Lanjarón, on the edge of the Alpujarras, and we got a room in a pensión with a view overlooking the Valle de Lecrín. Later, over dinner, already regretting my outburst on the mountainside earlier, I managed to make up with Tessa.

Lanjarón is a spa town, and the following day Tessa and I discovered the spa, the Balneario. That afternoon we booked ourselves in, donned the dressing gowns and togs and flip-flops they issued us with, and began our treatments:

the steam bath, mineral-water jacuzzi, mineral-water circular shower, and the relaxing massage.

I took a break and went out on to the landing. Set into a marble plinth were two fountains: the Fuente San Vicente and the Fuente Capilla. I filled my beaker with the water from each in turn and drank both.

Out of the Fuente Capilla flowed agua naturalmente carbonatada: the finest water I had ever tasted.

My recovery didn't happen on the opening night of *Those Powerful Machines*. That was a significant breakthrough – in my perception of myself and of my potential. But my recovery took place in increments over a number of years leading up to and following that year of 2008.

Looking back at that time, I see that, while I was experiencing a lot of difficult emotions, I was also living a very full life. The illness, while still present, was not stopping me. After *Those Powerful Machines*, I continued working in the bookshop, going to the performance workshop, making Sunday dinner with my sister. I travelled, swam, saw friends, went to yoga, hiked. In 2009, my second play, *Shafted*, was produced. *The Perch* never got further than development stage, but I continued to write screenplays and made several zero-budget short films with the participants of the workshop. My third play, *Griswold*, was produced in 2012.

All through this period I continued with psychiatric outpatient services through the public health system, and I continued to take the mood stabilizer Valproate and the antipsychotic Olanzapine. The latter continued to be problematic: it caused weight gain, it made me drowsy in the morning and, most pressingly, I felt it affected my creativity. As it seemed to be doing its job, I was loath to change it, and in fact assumed that it would never be possible to do so – that the fog of morning was the price I had to pay to remain well.

During this period, my father's house was sold and I moved closer to the city centre. This meant I was placed with a new psychiatrist, who was willing to listen to my concerns and talk them through with me. I began to attend sessions with a helpful psychotherapist, too, but I felt I was holding back from her, and there were no significant breakthroughs. When she left her practice on maternity leave, I didn't immediately pursue a replacement therapist.

It was in the summer of 2013 that I first met Tessa, a woman who captured my heart and my imagination completely, and who brought love, light and happiness into my life every day.

At Tessa's urging, I began volunteering in the Irish Writers Centre in Dublin. I was initially dubious about volunteering, but it was another of those moments where I decided it would be better to do something than to do nothing. The centre subsequently employed me and I have worked there ever since. Now I had a structure to my week, stimulating work I looked forward to in a place where I could meet interesting people. Working there boosted my self-esteem and self-confidence and drew me out as a person, distancing myself ever further from the unwell person I had been and so speeding my recovery.

I wanted to be able to go for runs and hikes with Tessa, but was too physically unhealthy to do so. So I quit smoking for good, and took up running. Slowly, I rebuilt my physical fitness, until we were indeed able to go for runs and hikes together.

This breakthrough in my physical health made me take stock. I had to ask myself: 'What am I doing for my mental health?'

The fact was I needed to do more than just take my pills. So now I started attending therapy again, with a new therapist. Not holding back this time, I explored every aspect of my life with him, forcing myself to be vulnerable and open in our sessions, and this led to significant progress and the occasional breakthrough. Not only did we talk about the effects of my mother's death and my father's moods but we also considered my ongoing anxiety and sleep issues. Most significantly, I now began to challenge my tendency to pathologize every difficult emotion I experienced as a sign or symptom of mental illness. This meant I was able to feel less like a person with bipolar disorder and more like a person experiencing the ordinary vicissitudes of life.

My new psychiatrist listened to my concerns about the side-effects of the antipsychotic medication I was taking and, consequently, I came off the Olanzapine and replaced it with a different antipsychotic, Aripiprazole. The effect of this change was profound: I lost weight and, even more importantly, the drowsiness and fog dissipated. Now I felt more alert and energetic in the mornings; I was able to spend that time writing again, and I found I was able to write as passionately, fluidly and meaningfully as before. Above all, I felt more connected to what I was doing, more alive. An essential part of me had been restored.

Around this time, Tessa was volunteering in Peru. While visiting her, I was inspired to explore the life of another Irishman who had spent time there: Roger Casement, the humanitarian and rebel executed in 1916 for his part in the Easter Rising. This led to my next play, *McKenna's Fort*, about Casement's life. Paul, my friend from the performance workshop, directed the play, and another close friend, Michael, played Casement. *McKenna's Fort* debuted in the New Theatre at Easter 2016, the centenary year of the Rising; it sold out many nights, and was attended by President Michael D. Higgins and Sabina Higgins. It was subsequently revived in the Teachers' Club as part of the 13th International Dublin Gay Theatre Festival, where it won the Oscar Wilde Award for Best New Writing. The success of this play, and the pleasure I felt in researching and writing it, made me feel my creativity was now truly restored.

My recovery has not been all continuous improvement, free from setbacks. It has had its ups and downs, difficulties and challenges. It has included periods of doubt, worry and even bouts of depression.

Recovery has not eliminated my character flaws: I can still lose my temper, be irritable, fractious, impatient, intolerant, complaining, pessimistic, bored, petty and show poor judgement. But what my recovery has meant is that, over time, I have felt better in myself and, above all, stable in mood: now I can make plans for the future, confident that they won't be derailed by illness.

So it is that weeks, then months, then years go by, and slowly, but gradually, and definitively, the brain, the body and the mind repair.

Feeling excited does not lead to uncontrollable exuberance, euphoria, nor to mania: it is just excitement. Feeling sad does not lead to self-excoriating despair, melancholy, nor to suicidal depression; it is just sadness.

My recovery did not happen by itself; time alone was not enough. It required effort, action, agency and the help of others. It was only when I stopped waiting, passively, and took active steps to help myself that recovery really took place.

The late Michael Paul Gallagher SJ, my very close friend, left a wonderful legacy of writing and spiritual reflections. In his final book, he wrote:

Each day has its lights and shadows, its pendulum from yes to no. But the 'no' is always weaker, provoked by some lack of energy or vision. The 'yes' music returns, not as joyful acceptance, but as quiet readiness – unalone.

Recovery feels like this.

Many of the people who knew me when I was unwell are still friends, but many have not remained so, and some professional relationships have also been lost. With the notable exception of my sister, to whom I remain close, my family are out of touch with me. I am still ashamed of my behaviour while ill and would find it difficult to approach everyone I affronted and explain myself, offer apology, seek rapprochement; consequently, many relationships have been lost for good.

A few years ago, I ran into Tom Murphy on the closing night of a play in a theatre in Dublin. I decided to go and apologize to him for my disturbing behaviour in Annaghmakerrig years before. Approaching him where he sat perched on a stool near the bar, I nervously explained who I was, how we were acquainted, and what I had done that I wished to apologize for.

'I'm sorry,' I said to him. 'I was a bit mad at the time.'

He took a moment to consider me, then replied.

'Weren't we all?' he said.

In my current therapy I have been dealing with my feelings for my father and, where once there was anger, now there is just sadness. I regret that in his last years he only saw me when I was profoundly unwell, and that he did not live to see me recover. He never got to see any of my plays performed, something which might have been grounds for a connection between us, rapprochement even. Perhaps he would even have been proud of me. I will never know.

In therapy I began to look at things more from his point of view, and this led me to accepting how difficult he must have found my illness to cope with. He was afraid of the illness and regarded my diagnosis as being nothing less than a death sentence. It was this fear that coloured his relationship with me in these years, along, of course, with my volatile behaviour.

The emotional dependency I felt for him lingered for a while after his death, but as I became more forgiving of him, less judgemental, less embittered and angry, I finally grew more independent emotionally. I do feel he let me down when I was unwell, but I no longer feel resentment over this, as I understand the reasons behind it better; nor do I feel anger at his treatment of me in my youth. I have put it away.

On a day-to-day basis, I do not see myself as a person with a mental illness. I still experience anxiety, but I am far from alone in this. Likewise, I have difficulties sleeping – and so do many of my fellow citizens. They do not pathologize this as mental illness; nor should I. These things, in other words, may be related to my bipolar disorder, but they are also common human experiences that I share with others.

At times I am happy; at times I am sad and I suffer. I have good times, and not so good times. This is life, not illness.

While I am optimistic and excited about the future, my history of mental illness means that I occasionally worry that I will not always be as well as I am now. The worry is not there all the time, and as long as I do what needs to be done to manage my condition I should not have a relapse. But at times of sadness, I'll be concerned it will slip into depression; at times of exuberance, I worry it is euphoria.

But the fact remains that I have had no manic episodes since the ones recounted here. Nor have I experienced any periods of suicidal or catatonic depression. And I've learned that for me, recovery and wellness depend on five elements: therapy, medication, exercise, meaningful work (creative, as well as occupational) and a loving relationship and relationships with friends and family.

All these are essential for me to live a normal life, devoid of madness, a life that leads to contentment: happiness even.

Now it is winter, which used to be my favourite season, because of its distance from summer, when I used to get depressed. But I don't experience such depression any more, and I look forward to summer as a time when I can swim in the sea – in Monkstown, where my sister lives, or Cork, where Tessa comes from, or Kerry; Banna strand remains a favourite, because of childhood visits and its associations with Roger Casement. But winter brings its own beauty, and I love the quality of the air as I walk in the nearby park now, and how it makes us all huddle in the pubs in the dark evenings, chatting and staying warm.

In reflecting on my decade of madness, I have often felt amazed that such things could be part of my past. The behaviour was mine, it was me, and I take responsibility for it; but at the same time I know that it was caused by the illness, so I feel a certain distance from it all. Mainly, I feel in awe of the fact that I am well; that I am living a full, rewarding, enriching life, out in the world, with work, friendships, a loving relationship with my girlfriend and a close relationship with my sister, as well as a creative life.

The alternative, the thought of which still fills me with fear, was all too close.

I am awestruck by my wellness, by my recovery; and I am grateful.

October 2017

In our hostal in Nerja there is a rooftop terrace, a kitchen open to the sunshine where we prepare our own meals, and a view of a cobbled laneway. We leave our room, wander the tourist-thronged streets; later we sit in the church of Parroquia El Salvador and Tessa says a prayer and lights a candle before we return to the crush of people outside, the blistering sun.

We go to the beach and swim in the Mediterranean, still warm in autumn; it is blissful.

Coming out of the water, I join Tessa on the beach. She hugs and kisses me.

'You're so smiley!' she says.

It is true; I am smiling.

I am happy.

Acknowledgements

I would like to acknowledge and thank all those who have given me support and encouragement as I wrote this book, and in many other ways.

Thanks, with much love and gratitude, to my sister, for all her support and encouragement through the writing of this book, and more. To my friends Paul Kennedy, Michael Bates and Jeremiah Cullinane for all their support through the writing, and in life. To Dave Lordan for inspiration, support and encouragement. To the Flying South Community for giving me the courage to first tell my story in public. To Anthony Glavin, Martina Devlin, Rob Doyle, Lia Mills, Brendan MacEvilly, Susan Tomaselli and Paul Fanning (no relation), for kind words along the way. To Darran McCann of the Seamus Heaney Centre at Queen's University Belfast, and to the life writing class of the MA in creative writing at Queen's. To Sarah Bannan, Raphael Montague, Gerry Mansfield, Gráinne Flynn and Martin Phelan, for advice and assistance. To the Arts Council for its timely and generous backing, and to Marcella Bannon and Jennifer Lawless. To Laura Jane Cassidy for reading and advising on an early version of a section of this work. To Stephen Kane, my friend and former landlord, in whose house I wrote this book – after my lease had expired. To Valerie Bistany and Bernadette Greenan of the Irish Writers Centre, Dublin, for superlative practical support and for giving me time off at a crucial stage in the writing of this book. To Orla Martin,

Pádraig Burke, Kate Cunningham and all the staff, interns and the board at the Irish Writers Centre for kindness and support along the way.

To all the team at Penguin Ireland for their help and support. Special thanks to Brendan Barrington, for superlative editorial work and for all his encouragement in the writing of this book from its earliest stages.

Finally, and especially, my everlasting gratitude to Tessa for all her support, encouragement and love.